Nigel Jones is a historian, biographer and broadcaster. Formerly the Assistant Editor of *History Today* and *BBC History* magazines, he now writes full time and leads battlefield tours of the Western Front. His film about the excavation of Wilfred Owen's dugout on the Somme, *Journey to Hell*, directed by Catrine Clay, was shown on BBC2's *Ancestors* series in March 2004. He is currently writing a short biography of Owen, and a study of the Edwardian era.

WWI

AC701

£4 —

THE WAR WALK

A Journey Along the Western Front

NIGEL JONES

Foreword by Sir Alistair Horne

CASSELL

Cassell Military Paperbacks

Cassell
Wellington House, 125 Strand
London WC2R 0BB

First published in 1983
by Robert Hale Limited
This Cassell Military Paperbacks edition 2004

British Library Cataloguing-in-Publication Data.
A catalogue record for this book is available
from the British Library.

ISBN 0 304 36683 8

Printed and bound in Great Britain by
Cox & Wyman Ltd, Reading, Berkshire

www.orionbooks.co.uk

In memory of my father
Frank Hazell Jones
whose bad eyesight kept him out of the trenches
and of his brother
Rifleman Ernest David Jones
who had good eyes
but lost his life . . .

Contents

CONTENTS

Illustrations

Plates

ILLUSTRATIONS

The 'Casemate Panard'
Trench dug-out today
British troops with captured grenades
André Coilliot

Section 3
Vimy Ridge Memorial
Vimy Ridge trench
Somme trench
British troops milking cow
A Lewis gun crew
British troops crossing the Somme at Brie
The bridge at Brie today
Battle of Tardenois
German dead
Padre with wounded
Douaumont Ossuary
Ernest Jones in the year of his death
Grave of Ernest Jones
Sgt.-Maj. Leslie Ibbetson
Will Holmes
A Verdun veteran

Maps

*Contemporary war photographs reproduced by courtesy of the Imperial
War Museum, London; modern photographs by courtesy of J. F. Valet*

Foreword

by Alistair Horne

Anyone who has visited the battlefields of the US Civil War can testify how superbly preserved and 'presented' are such legacies of the national heritage as Fredericksburg, Antietam, Manassas, Bull Run, the 'Seven Days Battle' and Gettysburg. Through them the casual tourist and the serious student of history alike can acquire a remarkably clear view of the course of that great conflict, as well as its wider significance. The same cannot be said, alas, of the great battlegrounds of the Western Front where the issue of the First World War was decided. Yet there are many better reasons why their memory should be perpetuated; the universal consequences of 1914–18 were historically far greater than that of the American Civil War; so too were the tragic sacrifices imposed in terms of human life; and, chronologically, it all took place half as long ago. Why the scars and memories of the Western Front have been so extensively obliterated is largely owing to geography and economics. Whereas the vastness of the United States affords plenty of space in which to create National parks protective of their history, battles such as the Somme took place on some of France's most fertile farmland, which her economy demanded had to be returned to the plough as soon after the Armistice of 1918 as was humanly possible.

There are a few well-known national shrines that are maintained, sacrosanct. There is Ypres, of grim memory to the British Army, where still the Last Post is sounded every evening at 8 p.m.; there is the great Canadian memorial at Vimy Ridge, where a few yards of 'permanent' trench are to be seen, though the sandbags are only concrete replicas; there are the ubiquitous cemeteries and occasional monument on the Somme; and there is Verdun. The battlefield I myself know most intimately, Verdun is also the best preserved and the one area where it is possible to follow the course of its terrible ten-month-long battle with the clarity one finds in the United States. This is partly a result of the unique and atrocious character of the ten-month-long battle (which Nigel Jones explains well) and partly because Verdun still represents, to France, the most poignant of all her battle honours. Apart from the afore-mentioned relics, however, the 'serious student' has to poke and ferret around, often at risk to himself from unexploded shells, crumbling masonry and hidden dugout shafts.

Perhaps nobody has ever done this more assiduously than Nigel Jones. With a father who served on the British First Army Staff at Arras, and an uncle killed—aged 18—near Ypres in 1915, he had powerful sentimental motives for performing what he aptly describes as a 'Calvary'. This involved walking on foot virtually the whole of the Western Front, starting in Belgian Flanders and ending on the 1918 American battle-front of the Argonne—and, finally, at the famous Armistice clearing in the Forest of Compiègne, followed by well-deserved resuscitation in the Champagne cellars of Moet & Chandon. In the course of his 'Calvary', Mr Jones's sore feet taught him the realities of the First War more immediately than any history book could. In one vivid passage, for instance, he describes how, after walking along the course of the German front as it stood on the eve of the great Ludendorff offensive of March 1918, he re-learned what the Allied soldier had to learn, painfully, then: '. . . that the static frozen nightmare of the trenches had cracked at last like the shell of some monstrous egg, and armies were sent spilling across the landscape like yolk'.

Such first-hand experiences make this book a most valuable companion to anyone wanting to explore the Western Front—or even to do so from the depths of a comfortable armchair at home. To render the whole more comprehensible, he has skilfully blended his peregrinations with a succinct sketch of the main events of the War, supported by an interesting range of 'then-and-now' photographs. There is also useful information on how to go, what to read, and what to take. Sadly, many of the permanent memorials of the Western Front, such as the Lutyens monument at Thiepval, are already crumbling and in drawing attention to them Nigel Jones has performed a useful service. But what is most appealing about this highly personal—yet dispassionate—book is the discovery of, and involvement in, the tragic and heroic saga of the First World War by somebody born more than three decades after it was all over.

A.H.

Acknowledgements

By far the most pleasant part of researching and writing this book was the unstinting help offered to me and the enthusiasm shown by so many different people—most of them total strangers. To see how so very many were willing to put themselves to real time and trouble aiding a green questioner, gave a great boost to my jaded faith in human nature.

First, chronologically, I must thank Mr Alistair Horne, whose magnificent book on the Battle of Verdun *The Price of Glory*, inspired me at the beginning with the idea of walking and writing about the Front. Mr Horne also effected an introduction to the Imperial War Museum, so invaluable an aid to anyone thinking of writing on the Great War, and I must extend a collective 'thank you' to the staff of that institution, especially the librarians and the keepers of the photographic collections who made many valuable suggestions and opened up several fruitful avenues, some of which—alas—I had no time to explore.

I must also thank Miss Rose Coombs, late Special Collections Officer at the Museum and acknowledged authority on the Western Front, who spared some of her time to talk with me and answer my questions.

My next debt is to Mr John Giles, Chairman of the Western Front Association, and possibly the only rival to Miss Coombs in Western Front expertise. Mr Giles took a sympathetic interest in my project in the early stages and made several helpful observations. Mr Bill Hogg, another WFA member, offered me the distilled experience of his fifteen years of walking the Front, and Mr Peter Scott, Editor of the Association's journal *Stand To!*, printed my appeal for information.

On the literary front, Mr Hunter Davies, author of *A Walk Along the Wall*, *A Walk Around the Lakes* and *A Walk Along the Tracks*, kindly let me 'steal' his idea for my book, and also gave me early encouragement when the idea was only budding in my mind. At about the same time, a chance encounter with Mr Norman Longmate—author of many books on the Second World War—pointed me in the direction of my present publishers. To both, my thanks.

Miss M. Allen, of the Royal British Legion, put me onto useful addresses,

ACKNOWLEDGEMENTS

and the editor of *The Legion*, Mrs Debbie Eales printed my appeal for information from veterans which brought in many replies.

I must thank Mr Peter Liddle for sending me information about his enormous Personal Experience Archive of the War at Sunderland Polytechnic, and Mr Alexander Barrie, author of *War Underground* for answering my queries about the fighting beneath the front.

Major Tonie and Mrs Valmai Holt, organizers of tours to the battlefields, also kindly put me in touch with some veterans.

Mr Antony Rose, of the Commonwealth War Graves Commission, tracked down information on the location of the grave of my uncle near Ypres and answered other queries with great patience.

The authorities at the Royal Hospital, Chelsea, offered me facilities to interview four of the Great War veterans who are residents of that admirable institution.

My colleagues at the Press Association, Mr Roy Heron and Mr Tony Mills gave many generous and helpful hints to a raw writer from their extensive knowledge of authorship and publishing respectively—and of the subject itself.

I have left my deepest debts to the last; this book is written for, and owes its existence to, the survivors of the Great War, with whom I conversed or corresponded. All of them were kind and invaluably helpful to someone who could have no conception of the depth of their experience: C. W. Ashton, Reginald Beale, Wilfred Blaber, Val Field, Joe Foster, 'Mac' Francis, Archie Gale, Antoine Godde, Harry Greig, Jim Haddock, A. W. Hancox, Will Holmes, my late father Frank Jones, Ernst Jünger, Arthur Lamb, Hector MacDonald, Geoffrey Muir, Charles Quinnell, Walter Smith, William Smith, L. C. Stewart, Herbert Sulzbach, Sidney Thacker, the late Montague Tutt and Edward Worrell.

Mrs H. M. Ibbetson was kind enough to allow me to read and quote the unpublished diaries of her relative, Leslie Ibbetson, of the Australian Imperial Forces, who was killed in action on September 29, 1918.

Mrs Kathleen Sargent allowed me to use the recollections of her late father, John Larrad.

Mrs Adela Margaret Hill let me see the letters of her brother, and Mrs Mary Dups those of her family.

Mr J. Luxon, Mr R. W. Hawkins, Mr A. Ralphs, Mr E. J. Williams, Mr George Briggs, Mr Donald Price, Mr James Mack, the late Mr Claude Manning, Mr Bill Muir, and the late Mr A. Stuart Dolden all wrote or spoke to me about their war experiences, though it was not possible to use the material in the book.

Mrs Lucy Cooper, Mrs Violet Gibbons and Miss Jean Sleath all wrote offering material about their relatives who fought on the Western Front, and I offer them my thanks and apologies that it was not possible—principally for reasons of space—to use these contributions, although I truly appreciated the additional knowledge and understanding of life at the front they afforded me.

Mr Alan Clarke, Lt.-Col. N. J. Field and Mr T. W. Jones, though not themselves veterans, saw my appeals for information and sent me much helpful material, and Mrs Joan Stewart Collis provided me with a rare English language copy of Ernst Jünger's book *Storm of Steel*.

Penultimately, some personal debts of friendship—to Stephen Plaice for touring Arras, Vimy Ridge and the Somme with me and offering the fresh vision of a poet's eye; to my collaborator, Jean-François Valet, who shared my enthusiasm and who took such trouble to take, develop and print the modern photographs in the book. He was also my companion on many walks and provided me with accommodation in Arras and Verdun.

Stephen Crossley, my other collaborator, who, after also visiting the battle-fields with me, bravely took on the task of drawing my maps, though he had no previous cartographic experience. I hope the reader will feel, as I do, that he did a splendid job.

Miss Christine Mathé helped with the typing at an early stage and Mrs Angela Hubbard gave advice on graphics and layout.

Lastly, my supreme debt is to my wife Christine who patiently endured my frequent absences on the Western Front with equanimity, introduced me to her great-uncle, a veteran *poilu*, and bore the double burden of her first pregnancy and the final typing of an almost illegible manuscript at the same time. To her, goes my love and eternal gratitude.

The book itself, of course, is my own work and responsibility, and none of those I have mentioned are in any way to blame for its defects—though they are to be praised if it has any merits. If I have left anyone out of the list inadvertently, my apologies in advance.

Nigel Jones

Introduction to the 2004 Edition

Twenty years ago, to while away a long and tedious train journey, I picked up a book by the prolific author and journalist Hunter Davies. Its intriguing title was *A Walk Along the Wall*. Time was tight, the train was about to leave, there was no chance to browse—it was a case of buy and fly. Settling down in my seat, I discovered that the book was an appealing blend of history, travelogue and personal musing, based on the author's own meanderings from one end to the other of Hadrian's Wall. Not an ancient history buff myself, I found his light touch an accessible way of walking the old wall, and the book absorbed me utterly. By the end of the journey I had decided—with Mr Davies's permission—to shamelessly steal his idea (and his alliteration) and adapt it to my own purposes.

I had been brought up on the Great War. Where contemporaries of my generation had fathers who had served in the Second World War, or even later conflicts, almost uniquely among my peers I could boast a father who had been a veteran of the first of the twentieth century's great bloodlettings. Hardly was I out of rompers before my septuagenarian dad was whisking me over the Channel and taking me round the battlefields of the Western Front, that awful 400-mile-long wall of wire on which a generation had hung, suffered and died. I was shown the memorials and the cemeteries—including Talana Farm at Boesinghe, outside Ypres, where my father's younger brother, Ernest, dead aged just eighteen in July 1915, lay with his Rifle Brigade comrades under a headstone which read, fatalistically, 'Thy Will be done'.

This early exposure to the war was reinforced at every stage of my childhood. The 50th anniversary of the conflict had recently passed, marked by the just re-screened magnificent twenty-six part BBC series *The Great War*. Books such as the late Alan Clark's iconoclastic *The Donkeys* at one pole of the debate, and John Terraine's indulgent biography of Douglas Haig, *The Educated Soldier* at the other, had ignited a Great War of words which has crackled on sporadically ever since. The basic outlines of the debate are familiar: Clark's book represented a view that had been steadily gaining ground among both historians and the general public since the death of Haig and the publication of Lloyd George's *War Memoirs* at the end of the 1920s, reinforced by the spate of anti-war memoirs that had appeared around the same time, as if a dam had burst after a decade of shocked silence since the Armistice. Books like Robert Graves's *Goodbye to All That*; Erich Maria Remarque's *All Quiet on the Western Front*; Siegfried Sassoon's many volumes of memoirs and autobiography and the military critiques of Basil Liddell Hart had enshrined what may be called the 'mud and blood-bath' idea of the war in popular consciousness.

Broadly, this view held that the war had been a gigantic exercise in futility. Fought out over issues that could have been settled around the conference table, it had been a meaningless struggle for a few yards of blasted ground orchestrated by out-of-touch, pot-bellied, walrus-moustached generals from their comfortable chateaux miles behind the trench lines, where the flower of Europe's youth was sacrificed for nothing, or next to nothing. The war had left a disillusioned legacy of madness, mutilation and bitter depression for its embittered veterans, had solved nothing, and had merely postponed another and greater round of hostilities for twenty years.

The Second World War seemed simply to reinforce this jaundiced view of the First: reluctantly fought by Britain despite an overpowering tide of pacifist sentiment whose main component was memories of the Great War, this, of all wars, seemed a righteous struggle against manifest evil; a black and white war of clean-cut moralities against whose stern certainties the grey abominations of 1914—1918 stood out in even starker contrast. Such remained the prevailing trend in the Great War's historiography until John Terraine's work heralded a major revision among historians writing in the 1960s.

Terraine, followed by successive generations of scholars such as Brian Bond, Correlli Barnett, Richard Holmes and Gary Sheffield, were working against the grain of popular feeling with courage and energy. They succeeded in turning the tide—at least among serious historians. Broadly again, their contention was that the war had been a necessary and, above all, a successful struggle against rampant German militarism. That no peace settlement—as pleaded for by the likes of the war poets Siegfried Sassoon and Wilfred Owen—had been possible during the war, faced with the unwillingness of Germany to reach a compromise that would make them regurgitate the territory that they had triumphantly swallowed up in 1914. Above all, the overwhelming argument of these revisionist historians was that the British army had learned and profited from the awful stalemate offensives of Loos, the Somme and Third Ypres (Passchendaele). Utilising the fearful new technology and tactics of war-winning weapons like the tank, or the creeping barrage, a tough and experienced army had struggled up the steep incline of its 'learning curve'—which became the overused touchstone term among the revisionists.

So it was that by the turn of the twentieth century that had encompassed the cataclysm, a new orthodoxy had been established among historians of the Great War. Among the public, however, it had to contend with a powerful countercurrent, a strong swell of pacifism reinforced by the ubiquitous presence on GCSE curricula of the war poets, with their message of pity, suffering and the futility of all war. Some of the modern military historians like to point out that the attitudes epitomised by the war poets were not typical of other junior officers, still less of the 'other ranks'. But this too is misleading. In fact, as the cultural historian Paul Fussell has pointed out in his epochal study *The Great War and Modern Memory*, no war has ever been more literary.

The subalterns, the junior officer class, from which the war poets were overwhelmingly drawn, may not all have gone to war with A. E. Housman's *Shropshire Lad*, with its classical allusions and bathetic mourning for doomed youth, packed in their knapsacks, but they were schooled in its attitudes and steeped in its imagery just the same. The letters of the 'Argonauts', the group of gilded young men recruited into Churchill's private army, the Royal Naval Division, and shipped off to die at Gallipoli, are replete with references to the Trojan wars and the fact that they had been fought near by. It has been calculated that some sixty-four published poets perished on the Western Front alone, not to mention the countless amateurs who died with them.

The picture of the war that we receive is not as cut and dried as it seems at first sight. Clearly, even the war poets were made of sterner stuff than their latter-day admirers sometimes appreciate. Two of the greatest—and most pacifist—of them, Sassoon and Owen, won the Military Cross, and you did not win this medal—only one grade down from the Victoria Cross—for nothing. In fact, as well as being poets of pity who mourned the passing of a doomed generation of beautiful young boys, Sassoon and Owen, by bitter paradox, were fierce, highly trained and enthusiastic killers. Sassoon delighted in personally raiding the Boche trenches with his tunic pockets stuffed full of 'bombs', while Owen won his MC just weeks before his death—and after writing the poems on which his pacifist reputation rests—for capturing a German machine gun and turning it on the fleeing foe. 'I am the enemy you killed, my friend' indeed.

I was fortunate in that I was researching and writing *The War Walk* early in the 1980s when survivors from the conflict were still relatively thick on the ground. With the help of the Royal British Legion, and the newly-founded Western Front Association, I was able to locate and interview more than thirty old soldiers who had seen service on the Western Front. Their views on the war were as various and contradictory as any assorted group on any given issue: some mourned the spirit of patriotism and sacrifice in which they had enlisted and fought, and which they saw as lacking in a selfish, materialistic modern society. Some were still bitter at the futility of the loss of so many friends and resentful of the harsh military discipline that kept them at the task in hand. Some had clearly never recovered from their war experiences; others were almost boastful as they recounted them. And if there were none who shared the politics of pacifist protest with Owen and Sassoon, there were few gung-ho, 'gun the Hun' flag-wagging jingoists either. Of course, seven decades had misted memories and oral history is notoriously subjective and unreliable, but it remains tellingly invaluable for all that.

Two decades on, we are about to round the corner of another cusp of history: the moment when the very last of the old soldier survivors finally fades away and the Great War leaves the realms of living memory and becomes—even more than it is already—myth. What is perhaps surprising is that this cataclysmic event is not losing its power to move and horrify us— rather the reverse. Just as the war and the Western Front engages some of our finest contemporary imaginative writers such as Sebastian Faulks, Pat Barker, Adam Thorpe and Geoff Dyer, producing bestsellers like *Birdsong* and the *Regeneration* trilogy, so too does it grip the minds of young people to whom it must seem impossibly distant. I have had the pleasure of conducting school groups around the still haunted landscapes of the Somme, and have witnessed the quasi-mystical force with which these sixth formers have responded to the landscape, and the cemeteries, empathising with young people no older than themselves who came here to die. As long as we still ask our young people to do that, the Great War will not—and should not—be forgotten. For here on the Western Front, to quote Sassoon, 'was the world's worst wound'—one which, even now, has hardly healed.

Nigel Jones

Chronology of Events

1914

June 28—Assassination of Archduke Franz Ferdinand of Austria in
Sarajevo.

August 4—Great Britain declares war on Germany.

September 5–7—Battle of the Marne. Race to the Sea.

October 26–27—Battle of the Yser. Trench lines form.

October 30–November 12—First Battle of Ypres.

Christmas truce—Fraternization between front line troops.

1915

March 10–12—Battle of Neuve-Chapelle.

April 22—Germans use poison gas at second Battle of Ypres.

May 9—Battle of Aubers Ridge.

May 15–25—Battle of Festubert.

September 25–26—Battle of Loos.

December 19—Haig succeeds French as British C in C.

1916

February 21—Battle of Verdun begins.

July 1—Battle of Somme begins.

November 19—Battle of Somme ends.

December 6—Lloyd George replaces Asquith as Prime Minister.

Battle of Verdun ends.

1917

February–March—Strategic German withdrawal to Hindenburg
Line.

March 16—Russian Revolution. Tsar abdicates.

April 4—United States enters war.

April 9—Battle of Arras and Vimy Ridge.

April 16—Nivelle offensive on the Aisne.

April–August—French armies mutiny. Nivelle replaced by Pétain.

June 7—Battle of Messines.

July 21—Third Battle of Ypres (Passchendaele) begins.

November 10—Battle of Passchendaele ends.

November 13—Clemenceau becomes French Premier.

November 20—Tank battle at Cambrai.

1918

March 21—First Ludendorff offensive ('Michael') at St Quentin.

April 14—Second Ludendorff offensive—Battle of the Lys ('Georgette').

Foch becomes supreme Allied C in C.

May 27—Third Ludendorff offensive on Aisne ('Blücher').

June 9—Fourth Ludendorff offensive ('Gneisenau').

July 15—Fifth and final Ludendorff attack at Reims ('Friedensturm').

July 18—French counter-attack at Villers Cotterets.

August 8—British counter-attack at Villers Brettoneux.

September 13—Americans take St Mihiel salient.

September 26—Americans attack in Argonne.

October—Hindenburg Line breached.

November 11—Armistice.

Part One
How the Front was Formed

1. The Powder Trains

Archduke Franz Ferdinand has been murdered with his wife, the Duchess of Hohenburg, by two Serbs at Sarajevo. What follows from this is not clear. You feel that a stone has begun to roll downhill and that dreadful things may be in store for Europe.

Herbert Sulzbach, 'Diary', June 28, 1914

June 28, 1914 marked the end of an era that will never return.

Herbert Sulzbach to the author, November 6, 1981

The shots fired by Gavrilo Princip, with fatal effect for the Archduke Franz Ferdinand of Austria-Hungary and his wife Sophie in Sarajevo on June 28, 1914, lit the sparks of two powder trains which were already primed and piled. The fuse took several weeks to splutter into detonation, watched with a sort of fascinated horror by the peoples of Europe who could not believe that the long years of peace were over.

The twin powder trains were the two rival alliances which knitted the greatest powers in the continent together in a deadly web of rivalry, hostility and hatred. Middle Europe was dominated, indeed largely composed of the two autocratic empires of Germany and Austria-Hungary, allied with Italy as the Central Powers, a loose understanding which Italy would betray when it came to the crunch in 1914. Her place was to be taken by Turkey and Bulgaria.

Flanking them to west and east were the Entente Powers: an unnatural alliance of convenience between France—still sore from her humiliating defeat by Prussia in 1870, and itching for *Revanche* and the return of the lost provinces of Alsace-Lorraine, annexed by a victorious Bismarck—and the most rigid reactionary autocracy in the world, Tsarist Russia, which, despite her dynastic ties with Germany, remained suspicious of the driving Teutons and resentful of the domination of Slav cousins by the ramshackle Austrian Empire.

1

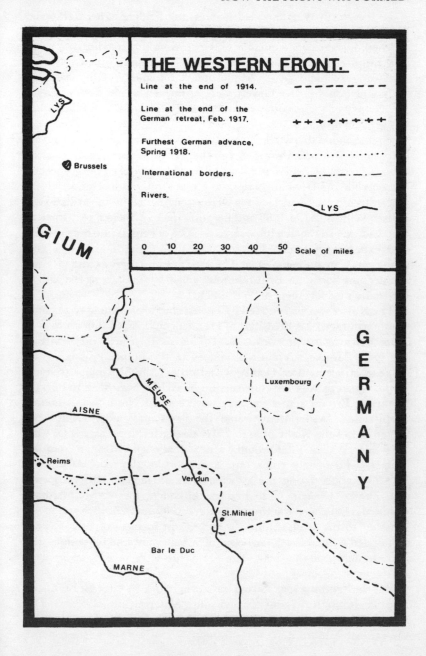

THE WESTERN FRONT.

Line at the end of 1914.

Line at the end of the German retreat, Feb. 1917.

Furthest German advance, Spring 1918.

International borders.

Rivers.

LYS

0 10 20 30 40 50   Scale of miles

To the North-West brooded Britain, still holding to her traditional policy of aloofness from European conflicts but, as the new century dawned, increasingly conscious of the growing threat to her commerce and Empire from the industrial might of Germany which was even beginning to challenge her unquestioned domination of the seas. The fears and hopes of the Powers were enshrined in a series of treaties which pledged them, with various degrees of firmness, to aid each other in the event of war.

To compound this witches' cauldron, a spirit of exaggerated chauvinistic patriotism was abroad in Europe, taking a particularly virulent form in Germany, where pseudo-philosophers preached the gospel of a Herrenvolk and Germany's right to a place in the sun of Imperialism. The extreme militarist factions were strengthened by the accession of Kaiser Wilhelm II in 1888 and his subsequent dismissal of Bismarck, who had turned the tiny impoverished state of Prussia into the dynamic and expansive German Empire. The new Kaiser's arrogance and ambitions were unbounded, and he used any and every excuse to beard the sleeping lion of the British Empire which he saw barring the path to Germany's achievement of 'Weltmacht'.

The Kaiser was surrounded by a court coterie of fawning sycophants who encouraged his delusions of grandeur and egged him on to ever more extravagant provocations. Taking as their text the words of the great Moltke, architect of victory in the Franco-Prussian War, 'War is an element of God's eternal order', the first major triumph of the warlords was the construction of a High Seas Fleet to directly challenge Britain across the grey waters of the North Sea. Admirals Tirpitz and Müller inaugurated the fleets and undertook the enlargement of the Kiel Canal in 1911, the better to prepare it for war. The Boer War of 1900 brought a new challenge to Britain from the Kaiser, who openly came out in support of the rebel Afrikaners. In 1904, appreciating the growing German menace, Britain joined the *Entente Cordiale* with France, although the Kaiser, nothing daunted, challenged the French Empire in Morocco in 1905 and sent a gunboat to the same country in the Agadir incident of 1911. Britain responded by building a new class of fast and powerful battleships, the Dreadnoughts, in the 1900s. The war clouds were looming up for all to see.

But the lightning that started the storm struck on a distant European frontier, in the Austrian-occupied south Slav province of Bosnia. The small states of the Balkans had only recently shaken off the dead hand of the Turkish Empire, and the resulting power vacuum made the region a cockpit into which the competing Russian Romanov and Austrian Habsburg empires were not slow to move.

The strongest Balkan state, Serbia, had emerged victorious from the Balkan Wars of 1912 and 1913. Enlarged to twice her former size, she turned her eyes to the north where her sister Slavs were still under Austrian hegemony in Bosnia.

A sinister Serb secret society, rejoicing in the name 'Unity or Death', held powerful positions in Belgrade, the Serb capital. The members of the society, better known as the 'Black Hand', had taken an oath to unite all the south Slavs in the Balkans under Serb leadership. To achieve their dream of a greater Yugoslavia, they were prepared to die themselves and to plunge their country, and perhaps the world, into war.

Whether they knew it consciously or not—and the evidence is contradictory—these pan-Serbs were acting as the long arm of Tsarist Russian imperialism, grasping as ever towards the age-old goal of access to the warm waters of the Mediterranean.

In turn, the Black Hand had their own catspaw, a tiny society of young South Slav fanatics, most of them hardly out of school, who called themselves Young Bosnia. These student nationalists were burning to free their land from the yoke of Austria, and their ideals coincided with the ambition of the mysterious leader of the Black Hand, Colonel Dragutin Dimitrevic, known as 'Apis', head of Serbian military intelligence.

The ingredients for the explosion were now in place; all that was missing was an opportunity, and Austria was soon to provide a golden one. The heir to the Austrian Emperor, old Franz-Joseph, was, thanks to the suicide of the Emperor's son Rudolf at Mayerling, the Archduke Franz Ferdinand. The Archduke was by all accounts an exceedingly unpleasant man. Brutal, cruel, a blind and bigoted autocrat, whose only redeeming quality was a devotion to his wife Sophie. She was a Czech aristocrat whom he had married for love, in the teeth of opposition from his Habsburg family. Embittered by the humiliating treatment his wife was accorded by the Vienna court, the Archduke was brimming with hatred and a desire to exert his own authority.

In June 1914 he decided to attend the Austrian army manoeuvres in the recently annexed province of Bosnia. On June 28, he found himself in the Bosnian capital, Sarajevo. June 28 was Vidovan, the sacred day of the Serbs, the anniversary of their defeat by the Turks in 1389 at Kosovo and the beginning of 400 years of Turkish domination.

The Archduke's presence on Serbian soil on such a date was a

5

flagrant provocation which could only rub Serbian sensibilities on the raw. It is a measure of the Archduke's arrogance that he could have chosen to make such an inauspicious visit. But, despite the auguries and several warnings, security in Sarajevo for the visit was lax to the point of non-existence.

Even the schoolboy conspirators of Young Bosnia, thoughtfully equipped by 'Apis' with guns, bombs and poison capsules, could not fail. The first sign of trouble was a bomb hurled by one of them, Cabrinovic, at the Royal car. The device wounded twenty people, but the Archduke decided to continue his visit regardless. Providence did not give him another chance. He commanded his chauffeur to make a detour to visit the wounded, the hapless driver lost his way and the automobile came to a halt directly opposite another plotter, Gavrilo Princip. Princip did not hesitate. He drew his pistol and fired at the royal pair. The first shot struck Archduchess Sophie, the second hit the Archduke himself, severing the jugular vein under his tight military collar. By noon both were dead.

The cataclysmic event had occurred, but, like the immediate silence after the shock of an earthquake, the world went on for a while as if nothing had happened. The British fleet went ahead with a state visit to their German rivals, the diplomatic courtesies continued as usual. Beneath the calm though, a bush fire was running through Europe, consuming the old world like so much dead brushwood.

The Austrians were the first to react. Despite the Archduke's un-popularity, the warmongers in Vienna, personified by the Army Commander, General Conrad von Hotzendorf, were not going to let the chance slip of crushing the upstart Serbs once and for all. The deaths in Sarajevo had to be avenged. The Kaiser approved the projected Austrian action and then left on his yacht for a Baltic cruise. The war that he had so long desired had come to fruition with its chief architect away and incommunicado.

On July 23 the Austrians sent an ultimatum to Serbia, demanding the arrest of the man behind the murders, the suppression of anti-Austrian propaganda, and the entry of Austrian officials to supervise the repression.

The Serbs meekly bowed to all the demands save the last, which would have meant virtual abdication of sovereignty to the Austrians. Austria curtly dismissed the Serbian reply as unsatisfactory and, a month after the murders, declared war on Serbia on July 28. Austria's war machine moved into action with an immediate bombardment of Belgrade. Russia had already mobilized her forces in the regions close to

Austria, and the cautious diplomats found themselves swept aside by inflexible military plans that could not be halted. The stone had indeed begun to roll downhill, and it pulled a whole civilization into the abyss as it fell.

All the great powers began to execute their long-laid mobilization schemes, which depended on precisely-calculated railway timetables, and any delay or backstepping would have thrown the military machines into chaos. Two days after the Austrian declaration of war, Tsar Nicholas II signed the order for a general Russian mobilization. The next day, Germany, too, mobilized in support of Austria, and, on August 1, declared war against Russia.

Even at this late stage the diplomats were hoping against hope to preserve peace. The British Foreign Secretary, Sir Edward Grey, said that Britain would stay out of the European conflict if Germany refrained from invading France. But since an integral part of the German war plan was to knock out France before turning to deal with Russia, thus avoiding the nightmare of a war on two fronts, non-intervention in France was, from the point of view of the German military, a non-option.

Back from the Baltic, the Kaiser, snatching at the straw of peace, was curtly told by the German army commander, Moltke, that eleven thousand trains packed with conscript troops were already steaming towards the Franco-Belgian frontiers. There was no way, he told the disconsolate Supreme Warlord, of avoiding the inevitable.

Wilhelm, reluctantly recognizing where his bombastic sabre-rattling had led, dutifully approved the invasion of France and Belgium on August 3. As the German armies marched into Belgium, Britain invoked the treaty of 1839 which had set up the Belgian state and guaranteed its permanent neutrality. It had been signed by Prussia as well as Britain, but the Imperial Chancellor, Theobald von Bethman-Hollweg now contemptuously dismissed it in the Reichstag as 'a scrap of paper'. As the long columns of German troops wound into Belgium, Britain despatched at ultimatum demanding their withdrawal, but once again it was too late: events had moved too far, too fast, and at midnight on August 4, Britain was at war with Germany.

In every capital of Europe a kind of mania seized the population. "Everyone or nearly everyone was intensely patriotic," said my father, recalling those days. Gentle, life-loving poets like Rilke, Peguy and Rupert Brooke were caught up in the prevailing mood and wrote verses hailing the coming of the War God to crush the long corruption of peace, and purify a complacent generation.

7

In London, huge crowds besieged the recruiting offices. In Berlin, conscripts en route to the barracks had sprigs of flowers stuck over their clothes as though already corpses. In Munich, a scruffy bohemian artist named Adolf Hitler gleefully laughed out loud in the midst of a huge crowd as the war was announced.

Only a few small voices were raised against the current. In Paris, the veteran socialist leader Jean Jaurès pleaded for peace and then went to have a peach in schnapps at a favourite café, the Chope Croissant. As he raised the drink to his lips, a nationalist fanatic, his head turned by the prevailing patriotic frenzy, shot him through the open window. The French government braced itself for a workers' uprising, but it never came. The workers were already on their way to answer the call-up. The children of *La Patrie* were answering the ancient call. The German socialists were equally co-operative with the mood of the hour. Meekly, with the sole exception of Karl Liebknecht, they voted en bloc for the war credits demanded by the government. The Kaiser exulted: 'I see no more parties—only Germans'.

In the ruling circles of London, the mood was less ecstatic: on the evening of the first day of war, Sir Edward Grey looked sadly out of the Foreign Office windows as a lamplighter went on his rounds. Sir Edward uttered a strangely prophetic sentence, for he himself went blind in later years: 'The lamps are going out all over Europe', he said, 'we shall not see them lighted again in our lifetimes'.

2. The Haymaker

But that two-handed engine at the door,
Stands ready to smite once,
And smite no more.

John Milton, 'Lycidas'

The mighty two-handed engine which stood at the doors of Belgium and Luxembourg at the beginning of August 1914 was the fruit of long and careful planning for *der Tag* of war which the militarists who ruled Germany always knew must come sooner or later.

Above all it was the work of one man: Graf Alfred von Schlieffen, Chief of the Imperial German General Staff from 1891 to 1905. Schlieffen succeeded the great Moltke, architect of victory in the Franco-Prussian War. Dismayed by France's rapid recovery from that conflict, Schlieffen realized that a second and final round must be fought. He had no doubt that the hereditary Gallic enemy was the main threat, and discounted as negligible the danger that Russia would invade Germany through the back door of Prussia in the East while she was locked in struggle in the West.

Schlieffen evolved a plan, which bore his name, to deliver a smashing, savage and fatal blow to France, by launching a huge mass of men in a great wheeling ring through the flatlands of Belgium and round Paris, scooping up the French capital in its path. This gigantic right wing sweep has often been compared to an enormous flail, scything across France and scattering resistance like so much chaff. I prefer the image of a boxer's right hook, a swift strike which Schlieffen calculated would knock France out in a lightning six-week campaign. This huge hay-maker of a punch would be delivered, in Schlieffen's original conception, by an immense avalanche of 53 divisions—three-quarters of the German army—while a skeleton force of only ten divisions stood on guard against a possible Russian invasion from the East.

By sweeping down like a wolf from Belgium on the fold of France, Schlieffen would by-pass the French fortifications and the main body of the French army. The latter, he correctly anticipated, would launch a frontal attack to liberate the lost provinces of Alsace-Lorraine which would be defended by a weak German left wing.

Schlieffen embodied his plan in its final form in a memorandum of December 1905 which he bequeathed to his successor, Helmut von Moltke, nephew of the great commander of 1870. But in retirement, Schlieffen could not resist tinkering further with the scheme. He became obsessed by Hannibal's tactics in the great Carthaginian victory at Cannae when the Carthaginians triumphed by enveloping the Romans simultaneously from either flank. In a study of this ancient battle published in 1912, the year of his death, Schlieffen advocated that a similar double envelopment be employed against France. He suggested that his right-wing wheel should complete its circle— pivoting round Paris, until the armies facing East would catch the French in the plains of Champagne and squash them against the frontier forts where the German left lay in wait. Boxed in from front and rear, France would not only be knocked out: she would be annihilated.

Schlieffen had complete confidence in his scheme, saying: 'In the iron hand of a ruthless and determined commander-in-chief, my master plan cannot fail'. His great fear was not of defeat but that his successors would meddle with his precise calculations and upset the delicate balance on which success depended. He strove to stiffen their resolve in colourful language—emphasizing the importance of the sweep through Belgium he said: 'Let the last man on the right brush the Channel with his sleeve'. Even on his deathbed, facing eternity, his life's work was still uppermost in the old man's mind. 'It must come to a war,' he croaked. 'Above all, keep the right wing strong'.

Perhaps death was kind to Schlieffen in removing him two years before his plan was taken from the perfection of the drawing board to be tested in the grim forge of war. But all might have gone well, had not Schlieffen's successor as commander-in-chief been the 'younger' Moltke, in reality a sick man in his late sixties. Moltke was anything but a chip off the old block: cautious, civilized, afflicted with an admirable but fatal lack of ruthlessness, and prostrated by an imaginative sympathy with the suffering of his soldiers. His caution made him fearful that France would break through his weak left. While sticking to the outlines of the Schlieffen Plan, he disobeyed the old man's dying injunction and withdrew men from the right to strengthen the left. He was also worried that Russia would invade Prussia behind his back and sacrificed part of his western forces to shore up the eastern defences.

When war broke, Moltke's dispositions had left him with a still-mighty force in the west numbering 1,485,000 men. The huge host was drawn up in eight armies, the greatest armed force in history.

Furthest north, on the extreme right, was the First Army with 320,000 men, the strongest of all, commanded by General Alexander von Kluck, a fierce old fire-eater of 68 who liked to compare himself to Attila the Hun. Kluck's role was to be the fist of Schlieffen's swinging punch. He was to batter his way through the Belgian frontier fortress of Liège, seize the capital Brussels and press on into France, finally having the supreme honour of taking Paris itself. Kluck was to be supported on his left by another strong army, the Second, commanded by another elderly Prussian, General von Bülow, with 260,000 men. Next came the Saxon, von Hausen, with 180,000 in the Third Army.

The centre and left wings were largely commanded by royalty, epitomizing the archaic autocracy of German society. Duke Albrecht of Württemberg commanded the Fourth Army (also 180,000). The Fifth (200,000) which was assigned the never-to-be-achieved objective of taking the famous French fortress of Verdun, was in the hands of the Kaiser's eldest son and heir, Crown Prince Wilhelm, soon to be christened 'Little Willy' by British cartoonists. Below him, guarding the annexed provinces of Alsace-Lorraine, where the main French attack was expected, was the 220,000 strong Sixth Army of Crown Prince Rupprecht of Bavaria, who quite fortuitously was to prove an excellent field commander. The German extreme left was brought up on the Swiss frontier by the Seventh Army under von Heeringen (125,000).

Facing this formidable array was the Belgian army, under their King, Albert, mustering in their fields and fortresses something above 117,000 men. The British Expeditionary Force (BEF), commanded by Sir John French, which was hastily disembarking in the Channel ports, totalled a relatively tiny 111,000, although deficiency in numbers was somewhat made up for by sheer professionalism, especially in shooting power. Below them lay five French armies. From north to south, these were Lanrezac's Fifth Army (254,000), Langle de Cary's Fourth (193,000), Ruffley's Third (168,000), de Castelnau's Second (200,000) and Dubail's First (256,000). It will be noticed that the greatest French strength lay on their right, facing the relatively weak German left in Alsace-Lorraine. This was in line with the French Plan of Attack known as Plan XVII, which projected a lunge to liberate the lost provinces. This strategy was to prove almost fatally costly and mis-guided.

It is not surprising that the French were eager to launch into the attack: their military thinking had been dominated since 1871 by the doctrine of the offensive *à outrance*. The leading apostle of the furious frontal attack was Colonel Grandmaison, a staff officer who raised the theory of infantry assault, carrying all before it by a bayonet charge, to the level of a mystic cult. It took a river of French blood, over 300,000 lives, for the theory to be disproved on the battlefield. One of the dead was Grandmaison himself, falling at the head of his regiment. These so-called Battles of the Frontiers were to prove the wisdom of Germany's contrasting tactics of outflanking an opponent. Nineteenth-century Napoleonic *élan* was no answer to blood and iron.

As the French shattered themselves in fruitless attacks against the 'Blue Line' of the Vosges, momentous events were taking place to the north. They were to prove the superiority of metal over muscle. Remorselessly, like a heavy hammer being brought down on a series of nuts, the huge guns manufactured by Herr Krupp reduced the Belgian forts to piecemeal surrender. By the middle of August the bastion of Liège had fallen, and Kluck's columns were pressing towards Brussels. His failure to capture Antwerp immediately, and the consequent detachment of two corps to invest the port, was no more than an irritating hitch to the relentless momentum of the advance. The Schlieffen plan was unfolding exactly according to schedule, like an enormous clockwork juggernaut.

Only one intact force blocked the path: the BEF, who attacked Kluck on August 21. The first shots that the British fired in anger came near Malplaquet, scene of a bloody Pyrrhic victory by Marlborough. The Germans brushed the tiny BEF aside like an annoying gnat, and the irresistible advance went on.

On August 23, Bülow's Second Army cannoned into Lanrezac's Fifth, on the Sambre-Meuse river line near Namur. Despite heroic counter-attacks by two of the panicky Lanrezac's subordinates, who were later to become famous—Generals Mangin (nicknamed 'the butcher') and Franchet d'Esperey (known as 'desperate Frankie' to the British)—Lanrezac proved cautious to the point of timidity and ordered a general retreat. The BEF, hampered in their liaison with Lanrezac by language problems, found themselves out on a limb near the mining town of Mons. For the loss of some 1,600 men, General Smith-Dorrien's Second Corps held up Kluck for a day and covered the retreat of Haig's First Corps. The Germans, not even realizing that the

British were in the field, were pulled up short as the withering rifle fire of the British caused heavy casualties. But having inflicted the bloody nose, the British continued to retreat on the next day, the 24th.

This first fighting at Mons acquired the force of a myth at home: it was rumoured, and swiftly asserted as fact, that an angel had appeared to guide the BEF. The check to his onward march infuriated the Kaiser—he called the BEF 'a contemptible little army', a badge which they were proud to adopt as their own. A new, hysterical note of hatred had intruded into the war. The armies had set off fully confident that they would be 'home before the leaves fall' as the Kaiser told his troops, or at least by Christmas, as the British believed. But already there were growing signs that the war would not be so clear-cut. The Germans were aghast to find themselves opposed not only by soldiers, but by sharpshooters in mufti, or *francs-tireurs*, who sniped them as they tramped wearily through the Belgian villages.

Their reprisals were swift and savage: civilians were rounded up and shot in their hundreds, Dinant was sacked, and the ancient library of Louvain University was deliberately burned. In return, these examples of Teutonic 'frightfulness' spawned fantastic tales of atrocity in the Allied Press. Gruesome stories of crucified prisoners, maimed children, violated nuns, and priests hung upside down as living clappers in church bells, were printed and widely believed. The age of the big lie and propaganda was born in a welter of viciousness spinning into a vortex of mutual hatreds.

In the meantime, the German wheel continued to revolve. It rolled across the Belgian border into France. But even as victory seemed within his grasp, Moltke made the first of a series of blunders which was to cost Germany—and the world—dear. The Russians had mobilized more quickly than expected, and had had the temerity to cross into East Prussia and inflict two small but wounding reverses on the Germans at Stalluponen and Gumbinnen. The elderly German commander in the east, von Prittwitz, was as inept as his name suggests. He panicked, and pleaded with Moltke for permission to evacuate East Prussia—a withdrawal from the ancestral homeland would have been an unheard-of humiliation for the Germans. Moltke had to act; he recalled General von Hindenburg from retirement and sent him to replace Prittwitz. As his deputy, he despatched the hero of the fall of Liège, General Erich Ludendorff. The partnership of these two men was to be the main factor behind Germany's success for the next three years. But in assuring victory in the east, Moltke damaged his chances of securing it in the west, for with Hindenburg and Ludendorff he sent two corps from

Kluck's army, and a third was shorn off to besiege Maubeuge, a Belgian town still obstinately holding out. The effect of this shearing was to break one of the fingers in Kluck's fist—Moltke was pulling his punch even as the blow was dealt.

On August 25, only two days after Mons, Smith-Dorrien decided to stand and fight again at Le Cateau: the story of Mons was repeated, though on a bloodier scale.

Once again the Germans attacked in tightly-bunched waves, and once more they were met with rifle fire so intense that they thought the British were equipped with machine guns. At nightfall Smith-Dorrien fell back, having lost 8,000 men and 38 guns. On the 29th, Lanrezac too, spurred on by the French commander-in-chief, the stolid and imperturbable General Joseph Joffre, stood and fought Bülow, checking him at Guise, near St. Quentin—but it was only enough to stem, not halt the onslaught, and Lanrezac was replaced by the fire-eating Franchet d'Esperey.

By September 1, Kluck was across the Oise, the last river barrier before Paris. His forward units were a bare 30 miles from the capital. On September 2, the French government abandoned the city, leaving its defence in the hands of its military Governor, General Gallieni. The decisive moment of twentieth-century history had arrived.

3. The U-Turn

We have lost the war. It will go on a long time, but it is already lost.

Crown Prince Wilhelm, September 7, 1914

I have the feeling that I may be called to account for all these ghastly disasters.

General Count von Moltke, September 7, 1914

If General von Kluck had not turned away from his designated line of march and swerved south-east instead of enveloping Paris from the north and west as had been the original intention, the world today would be a very different place. Paris would probably have fallen without a fight, and the demoralized French would most likely have surrendered. A chastened and humiliated BEF would have fled to the Channel ports with its tail between its legs. Russia would still have been decisively smashed at Tannenberg and the Masurian Lakes. Germany would have drawn heavy indemnities and in due course withdrawn, immeasurably strengthened . . . Hitler and Lenin and Stalin would never have been heard of, and the Second World War would never have been fought. If . . . but then, he did turn, and on that decision heavy consequences were to hang.

But one must not lay too much guilt on poor Kluck, a fighting general who had been spectacularly successful. For one thing, the order to turn came from Moltke, isolated at Supreme Headquarters far away in Luxembourg. Floundering in a fog of conflicting reports from east and west, many of which were hours out of date even as he received them, Moltke was in a state of despair and fear bordering on total breakdown. He was disturbed that for all the apparent victories of the march, few prisoners had been taken and little enemy equipment had been captured. It seemed clear that the French and British had been defeated but not destroyed, and were in fact falling back in good order, inflicting costly checks on the Germans as they retired.

Moltke was still worried by the situation in East Prussia where the dynamic duo of Ludendorff and Hindenburg had not yet pulled off their crushing victories. Furthermore, the speed and distance of the westward march had revealed two flaws in Germany's meticulous planning: communications were poor, and the further the armies advanced the longer became the lines of supply which had to be guarded and maintained. Finally, the troops were tired—they had been marching and fighting non-stop for a month in the broiling heat of high summer, and the soles of their boots were now wafer thin. Kluck's army in particular, which had travelled farthest and fastest, was in a state of near-exhaustion.

In the dying days of August, Moltke, alarmed anew by a gap opening up between Kluck and Bülow, issued a directive ordering them to turn their armies south-east, inside Paris, and drive the French away from their capital. It took some days before news of this vital shift of axis filtered through to the French, still bracing themselves for a direct assault on Paris. When aviators observed the massed columns of Kluck streaming to the south-east the lively mind of Governor Gallieni grasped his chance. As his officers exclaimed 'they present us their flank!' Gallieni resolved to strike. On September 4, Joffre was apprised of the changed situation, and after hours of silent brooding in the garden of his HQ at Bar-sur-Aube, he authorized an attack.

The spearhead of the advance was a newly-formed French army, the Sixth, under General Maunory. Sir John French was prevailed upon to lend the BEF for the attack. On the 5th, the scattered series of actions known as the Battle of the Marne began. Gallieni rushed troops up from Paris in taxis to join the assault.

The allies drove into the gap between Kluck and Bülow. Prompted by an officer despatched by Moltke, the two generals made a steady fighting withdrawal, in some places throwing back the French as they left. By the 10th, Kluck was back in Soissons on the Aisne, while Bülow retired to Reims.

It was hardly 'the miracle of the Marne' of subsequent myth, but it was enough. The seemingly invincible advance had ground to a halt. This fact alone immensely heartened the dispirited allies. For the Germans, the failure to take Paris doomed them to lose the war— eventually. But it was to take four years of mud, blood and barbarism before that fact became apparent.

There now opened a series of interlocking engagements known as the 'Race to the Sea', with each side trying to outflank the other, which ended with them both deadlocked on a continuous front of 400 miles stretching from the Channel to the Alps. The Western Front was born.

Both the British and the Germans turned their attention to the Channel ports in their first attempt to seek an end to the stalemate. Winston Churchill, the First Lord of the Admiralty sent the Royal Naval Division, which included Rupert Brooke, to stiffen the Belgian garrison holding Antwerp. It was in vain—Antwerp fell.

Meanwhile Moltke had suffered the consequences of the Marne and had been replaced by Erich von Falkenhayn, a favourite of the Kaiser. The new commander felt there was a chance of breaking through Flanders to the Channel ports, and he ordered the Duke of Württemberg to move forward, taking Ostend. The remnants of the Belgian army, with a few French and British, were heavily outnumbered by 160,000 to 50,000, but they barred the way forward. Clinging desperately to the last corner of their country which remained unoccupied, the Belgians stood on the line of the River Yser from Nieuport, on the coast, to Dixmude, north of Ypres. The advancing Germans bombarded both towns and set them on fire. By October 25 the Belgians, having stood up to incessant attacks from seventeen German divisions, were exhausted.

The Belgian GHQ turned to the French General Ferdinand Foch for help. A Gascon, he had underlined his reputation as a pugnacious fighter when, under heavy attack on the Marne, he sent Joffre the famous message: 'My centre is yielding, my right wing giving way: situation excellent. I attack tomorrow'.

Foch took one look at the parlous state of the Belgians and another at the surrounding flat polders of Flanders, before offering a sagacious piece of advice. His brilliantly simple suggestion was to open the lock gates on the Yser river and canals and flood the whole area. If men could not stop the Germans, then water would.

Belgian engineers immediately set to work damming the culverts along the embankment which carried the Nieuport-Dixmude railway, until the embankment became a water-tight dike. Then they jammed open the coastal lock gates at high tide, and breached those drainage channels which had survived the shellfire to allow the water to spread across the fields. The whole plain between Nieuport and Dixmude was deliberately handed back to its natural master, the sea, and transformed into a vast basin. The Belgians organized a new defence line along the railway dike, and orders were given to hold it at all costs.

On October 26 and 27, the water began to seep into the German lines. Desperately they floundered forward in another series of attacks.

They were combating not merely the Belgians, but a more insidious enemy that was to become the bane of the war: mud. Their attacks were beaten back by the French and Belgians as the whole front line area filled with water. Dead, wounded, guns and munitions were all swallowed up in the huge swamp. The Battle of Yser was over.

Part Two
Digging in

4. In Flanders Floods

Water is everywhere; in the air; on the ground; under the ground. It is a land of dampness. In this kingdom of water it rains three days out of four.

Le Goffic 'Dixmude'

I was lucky. My first visit to Flanders must have come on several of the one day out of four that it does not rain; the climate was crisp and the sun shone. For symbolic reasons my departure from England coincided with Remembrance Day—November 11. The ceremony at the Cenotaph never fails to prick my eyes with tears, even though I have no connection with either war—being born seven years after the Second, and a full forty years after the First.

I moved from Whitehall to Victoria, where so many of the troop trains departed at the start of the long journey to the trenches. The writers of that characteristic Great War song: 'Goodbyee, goodbyee, wipe the tear, baby dear from your eyee', composed their light-hearted ditty after observing the heart-rending farewells at the station barrier. The railways had a two-way traffic of course, but the grim hospital trains usually rolled into the terminus at dead of night, to avoid lowering civilian morale with an open display of the carnage.

I had intended to travel via Dunkirk, i.e. to follow the route taken by the British, but found that a cheaper boat-train to Ostend was departing sooner and altered my travel plans accordingly so that I would start my journey from behind the lines in 'German' territory. Planning ahead is the enemy of spontaneity. Opening the Sunday papers as the train sped through Kent I read reviews of a clutch of new books about the First World War, presumably published to coincide with Remembrance Day. It struck me anew how much the war is—still—part of our lives.

Even a commonplace thing like a wristwatch is a legacy of the conflict. Before 1914, gentlemen wore pocket watches, but officers in the trenches found wristwatches more convenient for quick synchronization and the habit struck. The war also altered time in other ways— British Summer Time came about because of a campaign to 'Save daylight' so that farmers and factory workers could produce more efficiently. Our notorious licensing laws were an unwelcome product of the same stringency; it was thought that inebriated munitions workers would be a danger to themselves and others.

I looked up from the papers to see the train passing under the Folkestone undercliff, between the chalk cliffs and the sea. The troopships usually left from Folkestone and the Road of Remembrance down the cliffs which the soldiers tramped is today planted with rosemary. For the first time in my memory I clearly saw the Calais cliffs across the Channel and realized how close we are to Europe in a concrete sense. It seemed easier to understand that Britain could not stay out of a struggle taking place only a score of miles across the grey waters of the Channel.

The four-hour sea passage to Ostend passed without incident over a sea as calm as a millpond. Once in the Belgian port, the bad side of my improvised travel became clear: it was late at night, and I tried three hotels before a fourth—the Strand, which was the most expensive— accepted me. The cost was between three and four times what I had budgeted for, but then the room did have a bathroom, WC and colour TV on which I was able to pick up British channels.

But the hotel proprietress, Jacqueline Van Rysbergen, made up for the extra cost by her outgoing friendliness. After the other guests had finished their breakfast and left, I plied her with questions which she willingly answered, belying the dour image of her fellow-Flemings.

I started with Belgium's perennial national question: the linguistic barrier. The country on whose behalf Britain entered the Great War is essentially an artificial entity cobbled together by the great powers in 1839 for diplomatic convenience. They locked together the Flemish in the north, who speak a Dutch dialect, with the French-speaking Walloons in the south. They placed a family of German princelings, the Saxe-Coburgs, on the throne and called it a nation. The language question has always been a bugbear, pulling the two communities in opposite directions, with the royal family forming a thin varnish over the crack.

The conflict has been sharpest at times of high social tension. After the Great War the Flemish were accused by the French of collaboration, and the same charge was made after the Second, reinforced by a constitutional crisis over King Leopold III, whom the Walloons accused of over-hasty surrender in 1940. Although a referendum narrowly reinstated Leopold in 1950, the Walloons refused to accept him and he abdicated in favour of his son Baudouin, the present king. The language divide is reinforced by political and economic differences—the Walloons tend to be more socialist and secular—perhaps as a result of the heavy industrialization of their regions in the nineteenth century. The Flemish, traditionally farmers and fishermen, are more conservative and catholic.

Until recently the Flemish suffered an inferiority complex as the speakers of a minority tongue. They felt discriminated against, particularly in Brussels, the capital, which is a French-speaking island inside a Flemish enclave.

Things have changed, however, and the Flemish not only now form 60 per cent of the population, but have also developed light industry and tourism which has earned them new prosperity. The Walloons, in contrast, have seen the heavy industries of their region—steel and coal—drastically reduced by recession and foreign competition in the same way as the north of Britain. Belgium vies with the UK for the highest unemployment rate in the EEC.

The day of my arrival coincided with Belgian general elections, which as usual had produced no conclusive result but had seen a slight swing to the Right, which in Belgian terms meant toward the Flemish. Mrs Van Rysbergen blamed the unions for the fragile state of the Belgian and British economies by 'pricing themselves out of international markets'. She was bitterly opposed to Japanese imports and startled me by proudly proclaiming that her car was BL, saying with some logic: 'most of my customers are British. If BL goes bust, they won't come here so often'. She even pointed out that her TVs were Dutch and her hi-fi German/British. 'I won't let anything Asian over the doorstep', she said stoutly. It was touching to find someone with a vestige of faith left in British workmanship.

It turned out that Mrs Van Rysbergen was half-Polish, and had no love for the Germans. 'Some of them come in here as if they still occupy the place, but I just say "Yes, Adolf" and they soon shut up'. Her mother was the daughter of a Polish gynaecologist who had been shot by the Nazis. 'In 1939 the Germans requisitioned the hospital he ran, for their own wounded. He told them that he would treat their men, but he could not throw his patients onto the street. So they shot him. In the hall of his own hospital. My mother found his body when she came home from school.'

Mrs Van Rysbergen's parents met when her father was deported to Germany for forced labour. 'He was a mining engineer and they put him to work on a project to extract petrol from coal'. I complimented her on the fluency of her English and she said all Flemish were the same, though English visitors often made the fundamental mistake of addressing them in French—a sore point. 'If a Fleming likes you, you are their friend for life—but if you tread on their toes they are hostile.'

She said the French only lived for the day, but the Flemish 'kept an apple for tomorrow'.

On Flanders she declared that the whole landscape was still liable to sudden inundation from the sea, and showed me a white mark at the bottom of the bar which had been caused by the floods of February 1953, in which 1,800 people had been drowned along the Flanders coast. The same tide also wrought death and destruction along the coastline of East Anglia.

Asked about the Belgian royals, Mrs Van Rysbergen said that Queen Elizabeth, the widow of King Albert who had defended Belgium so gallantly in the Great War, had been held in great affection, despite doubts about her espousal of left-wing causes. She had survived into the sixties, and had gone to visit Chairman Mao. When I asked Mrs Van Rysbergen about rumours that the Queen had had some hand in Albert's mysterious death in the 1930s, she was more dubious. (The King, an excellent mountaineer, had allegedly fallen to his death while climbing along on an easy slope in the Ardennes). 'I don't think she was directly involved. But he was certainly murdered, and she may have encouraged them indirectly by her behaviour, for she had lovers—more than one.' She attributed the King's death to a plot by leftist Walloon republicans, and on that chauvinistic note I bid her goodbye, crossed to the tram station and bought a ticket for Nieuport's Albert Memorial—the end of the trench lines and the start of my journey. The tram ran west along the flat coast, amidst a desolate grey seascape with the Channel breakers rolling in to a monotonous reception by endless deserted tower blocks of summer holiday flats. Nearing Nieuport, the sand-dunes were scattered with concrete pillboxes, mostly of Second War vintage. I alighted alone at the Albert Memorial—a vast circular edifice with an equestrian statue of the gallant monarch in the middle.

On the wall, a saintly stele depicted his Queen, Elizabeth, bandaging a wounded soldier's hand. The pious scene was in some contrast to the tales I had heard of her amorous adventures, and her jaunts behind the Iron and Bamboo Curtains, but then, truth can never be encapsulated in memorials.

The monument overlooked the complex of locks which had been opened by the Belgians in the dark days of the Yser battle. The

Germans should have been forewarned of these aquatic tactics, for during a pre-war meeting with Queen Wilhelmina of the Netherlands, the Kaiser had boasted that his guardsmen were all over six and a half feet tall. 'Very impressive', murmured the Queen, 'and when we open our dikes the waters are ten feet high'. Wisely, the Kaiser had refrained from attacking the Dutch, but their Flemish cousins were of a similar mind.

Crossing the footbridges over the Yser and its canals I resolutely faced south, and, thinking of Mao's dictum that the longest journey starts with a single step, I set out. I had only walked a few metres along the road when I came across my first war cemetery, near the village of Ramskapelle. The graves were chiefly British. Impressed as ever by the enormous care lavished on these war cemeteries by the Commonwealth War Graves Commission, I flicked through the visitors' book and was struck by the most frequently used word, often written by young people: 'Vrede', 'Fried', 'Paix', 'Shalom', 'Peace'.

Rounding the next corner I came upon a friendly farmer repairing his driveway. Both of us speaking in fractured French, he told me that the line of coastal defences which the Germans had built in the last war ran across his land. When I asked him if he ever found any First War relics he gestured and replied: 'Mais non—this was all water'. His farm, and all the others in the area, had been built since 1918, after previous farms had all been 'totally destroyed'.

Marching on, I began to observe the landscape with the clarity and closeness which is the walker's advantage over the motorist. Farms were indeed thick on the ground—Belgium and the Netherlands being the most densely-populated countries in Europe. Between the farms were flat fields stretching endlessly away to the horizon. The light industry of the coast soon gave way to a pastoral environment, and the smell of seaweed surrendered to fertilizer. Irrigation ditches, filled with tall reeds and green algae, ran along roads as straight and monotonous as Roman highways. The fields were full of maize and beet, interspersed with red cows, a few pigs and some scattered sheep. Gulls and peewits flitted between the livestock making the mournful landscape chiller yet with their eerie cries. The level roads made walking easy at first, and they gave the impression of causeways laid over marshland—which indeed is what they are.

Three kilometres brought me to Ramskapelle village, preceded by a large Belgian military cemetery whose French inscriptions reflected the historical Walloon dominance which has now eroded. A plaque in the centre of the village, records in both languages its 'heroic defence' on

October 31, 1914, by the 16th Battalion of French foot Chasseurs and the Belgian 3rd Regiment 'with cannon and bayonet'.

As I set out on the 5km stretch to the next village of Perwyze, traffic on the road began to build up. I was constantly being buffeted two paces backwards by the wind of a passing lorry, executing a sort of soft-shoe shuffle from the road to the grass verge and back again. After reaching Perwyze I began to feel the first symptoms of fatigue and sore feet, but plodded on, looking for a left-hand turning which would lead me to the former Belgian front lines. I found this and ended up at a chapel near the village of Oud-Stuivekenskerke which had been fortified with concrete and turned into a strongpoint where it had seen action in October 1914 and again at the end of the war in 1918. A tablet commemorated the priest, a splendid example of the Church Militant, who had donned a uniform to defend his parish. By now I was tiring rapidly, and thirst and hunger had turned my legs to the consistency of jelly.

The road back led me on to the old railway line, along which the Belgians had hung on by the skin of their teeth as occasional ruined concrete bunkers attested. The rail ran straight toward Dixmude and the distant spire of the Free Flemish tower.

This massive memorial, 84 metres high, was erected to commemorate the Flemish dead of the Yser, and became a shrine to Flemish nationalism with its slogan emblazoned in the form of a cross:

$$A$$
$$V\ V\ K$$
$$V$$

('All for Flanders, Flanders for Christ'). The tower was blown up in 1946 by unknown saboteurs but was rebuilt bigger and better than before. Since then it has been adopted by the wilder fringes of the Flemish and European right-wing. In recent years our own home-grown British fascists have begun to make the cross-channel trip to join their friends from France, Belgium and Germany in annual rallies which are held here every summer.

One of the symbols of Flemish nationalism, emblazoned on the monument alongside peace slogans and their flag of a rampant lion, is a seagull in flight. A macabre little incident as I entered the memorial ground seemed to sum up the sterility of chauvinism. On a neatly-trimmed privet hedge at the memorial gate lay a seagull, its wings tidily folded. Thinking it was merely resting after doing battle with the winds, I reached out a tentative finger to touch it and was surprised when it rocked stiffly on its perch: it was as dead as its distant cousin the dodo.

I went round the memorial museum, with its sad collection of torn and faded flags, its sepia photographs, and its yellowing documents in an incomprehensible language. A high-speed lift whisked me to the top of the cross-shaped tower, where windows gave all round views over the landscape until it was shrouded in the mist.

I bought picnic provisions in Dixmude and consumed them in the market place, dominated by a statue of General Jacques, who held Dixmude against the Germans until they took the burning ruins. With darkness drawing in, I was pleased to board a bus back to Ostend, my tired limbs trembling. I had walked 20 kilometres, which I smugly considered not bad for an unfit beginner, but I was daunted by the distance I still had to cover.

5. 'Wipers'

Far, far from Wipers I long to be,
Where German snipers can't snipe at me.
Damp is my dug-out,
Cold are my feet
Waiting for the whizz-bangs
To send me to sleep.

Soldiers' song

Thwarted by the Belgian wall of water, the Germans turned their attention to the south, to the old cloth trading town of Ypres. Among the flat plains of Flanders, any slight rise counts as a hill, and to the east of Ypres is a horseshoe of slopes which the Allied commanders believed had to be held if Ypres itself was not to fall, and Ypres, they thought, was the key to the sea. And so it was ordained that this sleepy old town, wrapped in centuries of neglect and still dreaming of its ancient glories, should be the storm centre of four years of uninterrupted carnage.

The geography of the slopes around Ypres dictated the outline of the salient or bulge in the front which the British were to hold with such terrible tenacity. The shape of the salient ensured that every inch of it was within range of the raking German guns—not only from the front, but enfiladed from either side. No wonder that the men in the salient felt sometimes that their every move was monitored by the eagle eyes of the enemy and marked by a downpour of flying steel:

L. C. Stewart, Royal Garrison Artillery:

From the sand dunes of Belgium, from where on a clear day it was possible to discern the coastline of England on the horizon, we were moved down to the mud and squalor of the Ypres sector, where as many horses and men were drowned in the mud as were killed by gunfire. The railhead for the Ypres sector was Poperinghe and it was from there, at midnight, that the leave trains departed,

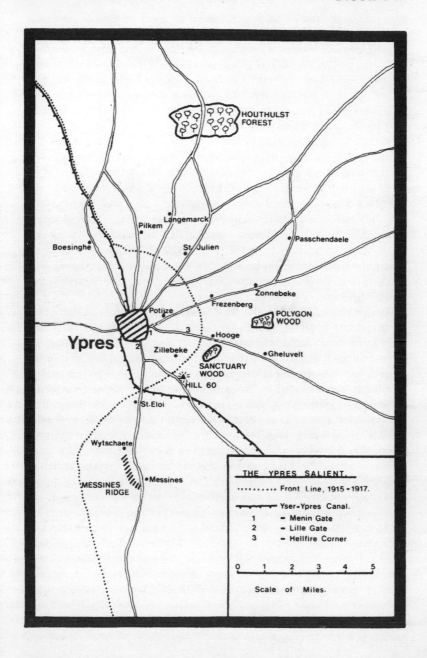

HOUTHULST FOREST

Langemarck
Pilkem
Boesinghe
St Julien
Passchendaele

Zonnebeke
Potijze
Frezenberg
POLYGON WOOD

Ypres
1
3
Hooge
2
Zillebeke
Gheluvelt
SANCTUARY WOOD
HILL 60

St.Eloi

Wytschaete

MESSINES RIDGE
Messines

THE YPRES SALIENT.

··········· Front Line, 1915 – 1917.

▼▼▼▼▼ Yser–Ypres Canal.

1 — Menin Gate
2 — Lille Gate
3 — Hellfire Corner

0   1   2   3   4   5

Scale of Miles.

taking the troops back to England for fourteen days. At the same time, the German leave trains departed from their railhead at Roulers. It seemed a very cruel fate that, having survived the front line, troops were killed while entraining for leave so one of our guns was detached and taken as far forward as to be within range of Roulers. A message was dropped over the enemy lines saying that if he would leave our leave trains alone we would do the same for his: no leave trains were ever hit by gunfire after that.

But before the lines hardened around Ypres a savage struggle was waged for possession of the city between the exhausted remnants of the BEF and five reserve Corps of Falkenhayn's army—previously un-blooded. These consisted chiefly of student cadets and old reservists, but they fought no less bravely than the élite troops who had surged forward in August, and inexorably the BEF were pressed backwards down the slopes towards Ypres. The Kaiser himself appeared at the Front, the first of many optimistic trips to the trenches that the supreme warlord would make to witness a final breakthrough by his armies that was destined never to occur.

By the end of October the BEF were at their last gasp; there then occurred one of those seemingly miraculous reversals of fortune that were to become characteristic of the war. For no apparent reason, the German attack seemed to run out of steam—a localized British counter-attack, by 368 members of the 2nd Battalion, the Worcestershire Regiment, commanded by Brigadier-General Fitzclarence, succeeded in recapturing the vital village of Gheluvelt, only a few miles from the gates of Ypres. This success set up a chain reaction, and other British units which had been sliding to defeat, rallied, stood their ground, and even counter-attacked. Even the intervention of the crack German unit, the Prussian Guards, failed to break the stiffening resistance.

Desperately the Kaiser and his commanders hurled five more Corps into the battle, and on November 11 and 12 the Germans attacked again from all directions. But the British Corps Commander, Haig, who had ridden up the soon-to-be-notorious Menin road out of Ypres on a personal inspection tour, had ordered the construction of the first permanent defence lines—bunkers linked with barbed wire; and against this wall and the withering BEF rifle fire the German attack shrivelled and died. The gallant Fitzclarence was killed leading a counter-attack by the Guards, Haig's First Corps had lost more than half its original strength, and the BEF as a whole had lost over 50,000 men, but at the cost of these losses Ypres had been saved. The Germans had lost half as many men again. The first Battle of Ypres was over, but the worst was yet to come.

6. The Trenches

> I have no complaint whatever to make about the response to my appeals for men. But I shall want more men and still more, until the enemy is crushed.
>
> *Lord Kitchener, November 10, 1914*

As the chill of autumn 1914 turned into the cold of winter, the realization sank in to the belligerent nations and governments that the war they had entered into in the summer would not be of short duration. Lord Kitchener, the British War Minister, had been among the first to express the opinion, at a Cabinet meeting, that the war would last as long as five years. The Cabinet responded by launching a recruiting campaign, using the famous posters of Kitchener's head and pointing finger above a demanding '*Your Country Needs You*'. 300,000 men joined the colours at a shilling a day during the first month of war. Another 450,000 joined up in September, and not less than 100,000 men joined each month thereafter until February.

The recruitment followed a similar pattern: signing on at the HQ of one's chosen unit, a few weeks' wait at home, then assignment to a training camp in Britain, followed by embarkation to France a few months later:

F. H. Jones:

Although I could have stayed at Napiers as we would be full of war work I had a go. Unfortunately (or perhaps fortunately), they would not take me as then they were fussy about eyesight and I could not pass the test. A week or two later I was given the opportunity to go in the Army as shorthand writer and I eagerly accepted the offer. I was rushed out to France right away.

Arthur A. Lamb, Pte, 2nd Lt, Lt. Capt, Hertfordshire Regiment, (Territorials), later 11th Battalion Royal Sussex Regiment, then 7th Manchester Regiment:

I enlisted in May 1915 at Hitchin Corn Exchange, where Colonel Rhodes was enlisting the Territorials of the Hertfordshire Regiment. I was seventeen and a half and you were supposed to be nineteen, so the Recruiting Officer asked; 'Are you sure about your age?' and sent me outside to 'think about it'. I came back in, told him I was nineteen and was accepted at once. I joined the depot at Hertford and started military training. Then I was posted to Stamford and Peterborough. There was an awful lot of route marching—you had to march 20 miles a day with 130 lbs of equipment which got you tremendously fit. My motive for joining up was pure patriotism. I had been a pacifist in 1914, but when I considered the rape of Belgium I altered my ideas a bit.

Montague Henry Tutt, Pte "C" Co, 20th Battalion, Public Schools Brigade. Later 2nd Lt. 1/5 Lancashire Regiment:

In September 1914 I enlisted to fight the war to end all wars. Since then I have become a committed Christian and I wouldn't fight in a war again. My father was a land surveyor in Ampthill, and I was on my way to London to train as a surveyor when war broke out. I enlisted in the Public Schools Brigade, but was sent away and told to wait. Later I was called for . . .

And it was not only the men of Britain who answered their country's call. In the far-flung reaches of Empire, men rallied to the 'Old Country' without hesitation:

Philip Leslie Ibbetson, Sgt. Major. Australian Imperial Forces (killed in action near Péronne, September 29, 1918, aged 27):

I enlisted on September 1, 1914 in the State of Queensland, Australia. My mate Jack Whensley and I came down from the back blocks of Queensland for a bit of a holiday in Brisbane and decided to join the Navy. We went down to the enlisting depot after spending eight or nine pounds on a new rig-out, which, as things turned out, we wore for one day. I passed with flying colours, but Jack didn't succeed, having hammer toes. So as he could not get in, I pulled out. We then decided to try the Army. Next morning we strolled up to Victoria barracks, saw a doctor and were both sworn in for the duration of the war, and four months after . . .

But for Philip Ibbetson, those four months would never arrive.

Wilfred Blaber, Pte then Lt., Inns of Court Regiment, then 22nd London Regiment:

I was living in Chile when the First World War broke out. I came home, incidentally paying my own fare, and joined the Inns of Court Regiment . . .

Meanwhile, at the Front, the outlines of the trench systems that were to govern the following four years of war were hardening. The armies faced each other across the barren soil of No Man's Land, which was sometimes 50 yards wide and sometimes half a mile or more. Isolated dug-outs and strongpoints were linked by trenches with barbed wire barriers in front of them. In turn, these front line trenches were connected with the rear by more shallow communication trenches, and further back there were two or more lines of reserve trenches. At intervals along the trenches, 'saps' were dug into No Man's Land at right-angles to the front line to act as listening posts, observation points or sniper's nests.

The trenches were not straight lines—to isolate possible enemy attacks, and minimize the blasts of exploding shells, 'firebays' were constructed at regular five-yard intervals, so that the trench lines from above look like the turreted battlements of a medieval castle.

The trench system, once fixed, very soon became a permanent world of its own—not surprisingly, since the trench lines were not to move, except in isolated sectors, for the next two and a half years.

From the North Sea coast at Nieuport the line ran due south to Dixmude, bulged out around the Ypres salient, then ran south-west to Mt. Kemmel, and south through the mining area around Lens, Lille and Loos, down across the open Artois countryside around Arras and on over the rolling chalky slopes of the River Somme. The line changed directions around Roye and Noyon, snaking south-east along the River Aisne, and then due east across the Champagne plains around Reims, before bulging up into another allied salient around Verdun and the Argonne forest. To the south was a German salient around St. Mihiel, and finally the line ran along the Franco-German frontier through the Vosges Mountains where the terrain was unsuitable for heavy fighting, before reaching the Swiss border near Belfort. All told it snaked and staggered for 400 miles, and on this wall of wire, Europe's youth was to crucify itself for sixteen sad and savage seasons.

The Belgians held the top 40 miles of the allied line north of Ypres, the British-held the next 90 miles, though this was to be progressively extended southwards as the pressure on the French intensified—and the French held the rest.

Theoretically, the ideal front line trench was seven feet deep, and four to five feet wide, with a parapet and firestep built on the side facing the enemy, and "parados" built on the "safe" side. Also on the 'safe' side were the dug-outs, usually occupied by officers only, while other ranks slept out in all weathers on the firestep, and took their chances that a stray shell or grenade would not turn their fitful dozing into eternal rest. The floor of a trench was an open ditch covered with wooden duckboards, though in wet sectors (and most of them *were* wet) these were often submerged in mud and water. The walls were built up with sandbags. You put your head "over the top" at your own risk, for vigilant snipers were often ready to mark the slightest movement with a fatal shot:

Pte. Joe R. Foster, Youth Training Corps 252nd Infantry Battalion:

Once I was standing in a trench next to this man. I turned round to speak to him and couldn't get a reply. He had been shot straight between the eyes. A sniper had got him.

The landscape all looked the same to us—mud. We slept in mud. We made little crevices in the sides of the trench and got in there. We were up to our thighs in mud so we didn't get much sleep at all. We were being strafed the whole time, so what sleep can you have?

Another frequent danger in the front line was the unheralded arrival of German artillery: either a dreaded 'Minnie'—'Minenwerfer' or 'Mine thrower'—or a heavy shell nicknamed 'Jack Johnson' after the American Negro boxer, because of the large amounts of black smoke they emitted. Other notorious shells were known as 'Whizz-bangs' and '5.9s'.

When we got into the front line our first casualties were from a 'Minnie'. One fell in a firebay. When the noise died down, we heard faint cries for help as though from a long way off. The platoon Sergeant came along and trod on a sandbag, and when they took it away a man's face was revealed. We were able to dig him and the others out and send them away for treatment.

(Lamb)

But there were a few palliatives to relieve the fears and the constant sleeplessness; these were chiefly rest periods just behind the front lines, food, and drink.

Army cooking has never been *haute cuisine*, and the standards on the Western Front were perforce rudimentary: food was cooked just behind the front and brought up the communication trenches in large canisters strapped to the backs of men detailed for the duty:

> We lived on hard biscuits and bully beef. We softened the biscuits by dipping them in shellhole water until they brought proper water carts up the front. We carried our 'Dixie' cans around on the back of our belts; cutting up the beef and cooking it over fires we made with sticks at the bottom of the trenches. I don't know whether this was against strict rules and regulations because there weren't any out there—you could do what you liked just to survive, but how any of us survived I do not know.
>
> *(Foster)*

Rifleman Sidney Thacker, 16th Rifle Brigade:

> We used to have hard biscuits and bully beef. We dipped the biscuits in water or tea, and if we didn't have that we crunched them up. We carried kidney shaped dixie tins on our haversack, which was hung under our packs and bounced on the bum.

Sgt. Jim Haddock, 24th London Regiment, (The Queen's) Territorials:

> We couldn't do much cooking, but there was Maconochie, a stew that was very nice—better than any you can find in the shops today. We seldom got bread. If water was short we took it from the shellholes and boiled it.
>
> Bacon was our favourite food because it was easily cooked and didn't make much smoke to attract snipers. Another favourite was known as 'Sandbag pudding', a duff made of suet and fruit boiled in empty sandbags. You got bits of the fibre sticking to it.
>
> *(Lamb)*

We were jolly thirsty and hungry as we had had nothing for 24 hours—the smell of dead men was too strong to eat anything where we had been. We foraged round and found a tin of condensed milk, some biscuits and a tin of bully beef. We made a kind of porridge mess and ate as much as we could . . .

(Ibbetson)

Alcohol in the trenches was strictly forbidden, with the exception of the traditional daily tot of rum.

We were given a tot of rum every day at 'Stand-To' as dawn was breaking. The first time we went into action we were given too much and some of the men were staggering around drunk. If there was a teetotaller in the unit, the issuing Sergeant would drink his tot.

(Lamb)

If it hadn't been for the rum I don't think any of us could have carried on as it put new life and courage into all of us.

(Ibbetson)

A. W. Hancox, 31370, Royal Garrison Artillery:

It was the practice to issue a tot of rum each day with the rations, the number of tots being added together to agree with the signed statement on the ration chit. Eventually each company or detachment acquired a container, a gallon jar, in which was kept tomorrow's issue.

The French, as befits a gastronomic nation, allowed their poilus— (literally 'Hairy Ones', the French equivalent of 'Tommies')—the luxury of Pinard or rough red wine, and sometimes before an attack this was spiked by an admixture of ether and rum.

But even in the perverted world of the trenches, built to serve death rather than life, existence evolved a routine. This included brief periods of leave, a reprieve for the condemned, which might mean going back to 'Blighty' for a reunion with friends and family, and a dip back into the increasingly distant world of the Home Front. But more often it was just a brief rest in a village or town behind the lines entailing plenty of sleep, trips to an estaminet, and perhaps flirtations with local girls.

This was how a typical day in the trenches ran:

After the dawn 'Stand-To' we would wait for breakfast. You usually saved some hot tea to shave with. Breakfast usually consisted of bacon, bread and tea, with a little tinned jam if you were lucky. When we had heavy casualties we got more because even if we had lost half our men they still sent up food for a whole company, so there was more than enough rations to go round. We also carried our own iron rations—hard tack biscuits and bully beef.

During the day you put up a couple of sentries to watch the front, while the rest of us ate and tried to sleep. The trenches were normally waterlogged, even in summer. They acted as drains, being under the earth's surface. You could sleep on the firestep in between the sentries, or you could dig out a cave at the back under the parados. If you were fortunate there was sometimes space in a large dug-out where the officers were. The midday meal was normally stew, you also got a supper which was a mixture of whatever was going. At night things got busy, with wiring, raids, and patrols.

You were supposed to spend four days in the front line, four days in support, and four days resting at the rear. But sometimes we went 16 days in the front line without relief. That was most uncomfortable because it meant you couldn't take your boots off, or change your clothes for over a fortnight. When the whole battalion was taken out of the line we would go into villages in the rear and find a farm where the officers would be billeted in the farmhouse and the men in the barns. If you were lucky you got a bath. They once took over the local brewery and turned it into a laundry and bathhouse. You would go into the big brewing vats which were filled with hot water, and you put your underclothes in with you and washed them too. When they were lice-ridden we got a candle and ran it along the seams of our vests, and you would hear 'pop-pop' as the nits burned. One very kind person at home sent me a new invention called a lice protection belt. It worked so well that it drove one lot of lice down to my socks, and the rest up to my neck, and when the chemical wore off they all returned to where they had been before.

(Lamb)

Lice were, of course, the literal bugbear of the men fighting at the Western Front. Decency and failing memory compelled many of the veterans I interviewed to draw a veil over this, one of the most un-pleasant aspects of trench life. But it is as well to remember George Orwell's comment, made when he was serving in the trenches of the Spanish Civil War, that every soldier, from Caesar to the Somme, has had lice crawling over his testicles.

We all had lice of course, we called them 'Chats' and cleaning them out was known as 'Chatting'. They got into the lining of your shirt. We scraped the seams with our old jack-knives to get rid of them but it was no good. They always came back.

(Foster)

Washing a shirt, even in hot water, did not make it vermin-proof, but there was one way of obtaining a few days' respite and that was by using petrol. It was possible to remove the shirt, steep it in a bucket of petrol, run your fingers down the seams to remove the lice eggs and put it on again in a relatively short time. Mind, it was a bit smelly for a time, but what a relief.

(Hancox)

Leave was an even greater relief, and the limited entertainments that accompanied it, however simple, were an added bonus:

While at rest camped beside the River Ancre near the Somme, I and my comrades practised a novel form of angling; we threw Mills Bomb grenades into the water. When they exploded stunned fish floated to the top to be scooped out for supper. Strictly against regulations of course—improper use of ammunition.

Class differences persisted behind the lines—troops had ordinary baths, but officers could choose between Russian or Turkish varieties. At rear estaminets ... we would watch the Danny La Rues of the day doing female impersonations. Besides the glimpses of feminine clothing, which we all hungered for, we also enjoyed the standard café provisions—*oeufs*, *pommes* and *vin*. I formed a liaison with one Gabrielle, proprietress of an estaminet in, I think, Poperinghe. I once saved her from 'A fate worse than death' at the hands of a British soldier, and ever after was treated to a free glass of wine whenever I was passing through.

Elsewhere, bathing soldiers were once surprised naked when a bevy of French girls arrived selling wares from trays. The girls didn't seem put out by the lewd threats of assault and breaches of their lines, nor by the display of the weapons by which the assaults were to be effected!

(Lamb)

Lice were not the only animal enemy of the front line men: the trenches were also infested by rats, which grew as fat as cats by gorging on the many corpses which were lying around:

> The Jocks used to organize rat hunts in the trenches; they would spear them with bayonets, and even throw their rifles at them.
>
> *(Foster)*

Some men even kept pets—a German corporal named Adolf Hitler took a fox-terrier under his wing when it jumped into his trench from No Man's Land. He christened it 'Fuchsl' and had to teach it German, as it had previously obviously belonged to a British soldier. The animal was later stolen, and the loss of this companion contributed materially to the future Führer's already substantial store of bitterness.

The insanitary conditions had obvious consequences:

> When I was suffering from a bad bout of dysentery I had to go into a shellhole to change my trousers. There was a German corpse in the hole, and while I was changing I had the eerie experience of finding the eyes in that emaciated face following me round like the eyes in an old master painting in a gallery.
>
> *(Lamb)*

A constant complaint of the English fighting men was the inadequacy of the British dug-outs and fortified positions compared to their German counterparts. But this reflected a difference in the psychology and planning of the two High Commands.

The Germans, surveying their position at the end of 1914, realized that they had failed to knock out France and now had to live with their nightmare of a war on two fronts. The new Commander-in-Chief, Falkenhayn, was in favour of continuing his strategy of driving for the Channel ports and cutting the British from their home bases. But he was overruled by the 'Easterners'—Hindenburg and Ludendorff, who, buoyed up by the triumph of Tannenberg, were convinced that they could smash Russia for good. They advocated a defensive posture on the Western Front, while troops and resources were diverted to the east. The Kaiser agreed with their arguments and Falkenhayn was overruled.

As a result, the Germans dug in more deeply on their heights overlooking the Allies and awaited the coming of spring and the expected Allied onslaughts—they were not to be disappointed.

In contrast, the Allied commanders in their comfortable châteaux behind the lines were reluctant to abandon the strategic thinking in which they had been schooled: they could not grasp the idea that their cherished open warfare was no longer possible, that technology had reached a stage of stalemate—and that mere men were no match for barbed wire and machine guns. It was to take more than two years of wasted life for the lesson to sink in, but by then it was too late—a generation had been sacrificed.

But for the men in the lines, the trenches were a novelty: they swiftly christened the muddy channels with names of their own; in the Ypres sector, for example, the Tommies called their new living quarters and their roads such names as 'China Wall', 'Sterling Castle', 'Jasper Avenue', 'New Cut', 'Tank Trap'.

Very soon the geography of hell was mapped by army cartographers, and on the trench maps that were issued to the troops, the killing grounds became standard map references. Examples of British names for German trenches in the Ypres sector: 'Impudence Trench', 'Imperial Trench', 'Impact Trench', 'Impartial Trench', 'Imperfect Trench'. British lines were sketched out in blue, in the vaguest detail in case the maps fell into enemy hands. German trenches were marked in red: for danger? But the impression of Teutonic strength given by these maps is not wholly wrong:

> When we occupied trenches, we slept in the saps that Jerry had dug underground. They had wire bunks and were really comfortable. The Germans always took more trouble than we did—they were twice as efficient as us at everything. All their actions were done according to the book, with precision.
>
> *(Thacker)*

> I went into a deep dug-out in the Schwaben Redoubt on the Somme. It was huge, like a mansion. There was even evidence of women having been there.
>
> *(Lamb)*

Impressed by the strength of the German defences, Captain Lamb pressed for more use of concrete in building British dug-outs in his sector. He was unsuccessful.

The French were even more reluctant than the British to dig in. The idea of grubbing into the earth like a species of rodent ran directly counter to the doctrine of the *attaque à outrance* still, despite the losses of the Frontier battles of the summer, deeply imbued in the French military mind. In addition, their British Allies complained whenever they took over a section of French trench, that the *poilus* were none-too-fussy about personal hygiene.

> We went into billets where the French had been, and, I am afraid to say, got lousy very quickly, which we had never been before.
>
> *(Tutt)*

> We approached the [Vimy] ridge by a communication trench across the rear slope which we knew as Zouave Valley [Zouaves = French-Algerian troops]. We all stood on the firestep and the French then stood down and departed and we were on our own. At dawn we looked around and found the trenches and dug-outs to be in a pretty dirty condition and I understood why it had been called Zouave Valley.
>
> *(Blaber)*

In general, the Allies were inclined to regard the trenches as a temporary nuisance—a mere hitch on the open road to victory. The Germans knew better and—dug deeper.

If the main daily business in the trenches was waiting, fetching and carrying, trying to snatch sleep, and fending off the bureaucratic requirements of the Army: weapons inspections, casualty reports, supply forms; the main business of the night was fighting—apart from big offensives, the only time when one had a chance of getting to grips with the elusive enemy was if patrols clashed in No Man's Land under cover of darkness.

Conditions were grim beyond belief.

> The trenches were flooded waist-deep. We stood in that waist-deep water for three weeks, and it was freezing. There was the danger of trench feet [swelling caused by prolonged immersion in water], and the men had to rub a sort of fat or whale oil on their feet to prevent it. Lots of the blighters avoided doing that because they knew that if they got trench feet they would be sent back down the line. It was part of my job to make sure that it got put on.
>
> *(Haddock)*

There were many who cracked under the strain. The wonder is that they were so few. For those who could not take it, the sanctions were drastic:

Field Punishment Number One was a euphemism for crucifixion on a gun wheel, carried out day after day when the sun was at its hottest. One man I knew was strapped to the wheel day after day for a fortnight.

(Lamb)

In the early days of the war it was the practice to tie delinquents to a gun wheel for one or two periods each day. Later, conditions didn't permit of this luxury, and other ways were found with which to extract the forfeit.

(Hancox)

There was a wide range of offences which merited the ultimate sanction: death by a firing squad composed of the guilty man's comrades, though often these executions were carried out in a quiet rear area so that the morale of the front line men did not suffer. Offences qualifying included desertion, cowardice, mutiny and sleeping on duty. Sometimes men did not wait for an enemy bullet to do the job for them—they turned their own guns on themselves and sustained a self-inflicted wound. These 'SIs' were not popular with their stouter-hearted comrades:

One man had nine wound stripes and he had never even been in the line—they were all 'SIs'. This time he had put his hip out by deliberately falling out of a train. So when we were lowering him into the cellars where the dressing station was located, the corporal said to let go of the ropes—and he landed with a hell of a bump.

(Thacker)

By Christmas 1914, the Western Front was frozen in a rigid deadlock. The summer hopes of a speedy end to the war seemed to the shivering men in the trenches to belong to another age.

On Christmas Eve, a strange silence fell over the trenches. Men, mellowed by extra rations of food, drink and cigars, sentimentally thought of their distant homes, and soon a strange sound was heard from the German lines—the strains of the carol 'Silent Night' lifted into the evening air. These were followed by shouts, not of hostility but of Seasonal fraternity. Within minutes the unthinkable was happening. Figures, few at first, but soon becoming numerous, stole out into No Man's Land.

Spontaneously, all enmity forgotten, enemies embraced, swapped snapshots and souvenirs, photographed each other, and even organized an impromptu soccer game. On those involved this display of human solidarity and brotherhood had an indelible effect. The unofficial truce lasted all through Christmas Day, but when the British Higher Command heard of the fraternization the units who had taken part were withdrawn from the front line and the killing resumed. It was to be another four years of death and destruction before the two sides were again permitted to regard each other as human beings.

Part Three
The Fights of 'Fifteen'

7. Gas

Gas. GAS! Quick boys—An ecstasy of fumbling,
Fitting the clumsy helmets just in time;
But someone still was yelling out and stumbling
And floundering like a man in fire or lime . . .

Wilfred Owen, 'Dulce et decorum est'

Sir John French, who was still Commander of the BEF, and his second in command and prospective successor, Sir Douglas Haig, were champing at the bit as the New Year opened, as befitted the cavalrymen they were.

Their chosen target for an attack against the enemy was the village of Neuve Chapelle near the Franco-Belgian border. In this section of the line, trenches had not been dug as the ground was too water-logged. The Germans were defending the village in positions made up of piled sandbags: opposite them, the British were in a similar case:

Arthur Greig, Pte. 2nd Battalion, London Scottish Regiment—Territorials:

Near Givenchy we were manning what we called 'grousebutts'— horseshoe-shaped emplacements made of piled sandbags with a corporal and eight men in each one. They were spaced out at 50-yard intervals.

Although the BEF had been numerically strengthened since the desperate days of August with the influx of Territorial battalions, and several new Indian and Canadian regular units, it was still lamentably short of guns, so essential in softening up the ground prior to any attack. Nevertheless Haig, who was in charge of the battle planning, scraped together 60 batteries of light field artillery and 120 heavier siege guns. The BEF, greatly enlarged, had been divided into two Armies, First and Second, instead of two Corps as hitherto.

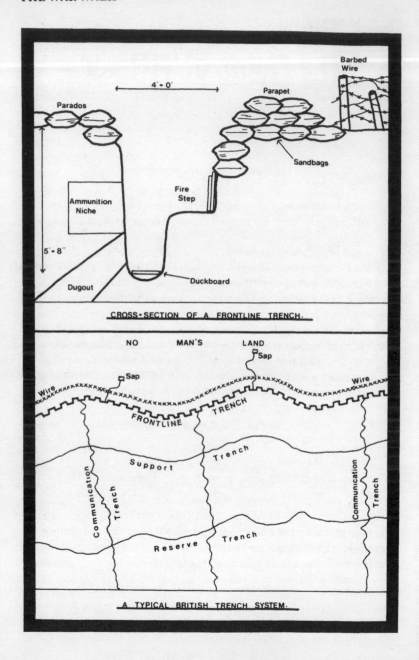

CROSS-SECTION OF A FRONTLINE TRENCH.

A TYPICAL BRITISH TRENCH SYSTEM.

On March 10 Haig's First Army threw nearly fifty battalions against the village, preceded by a half-hour artillery barrage. The German defences consisted of only six companies, supported by a mere twelve machine guns. The short bombardment, coupled with the overwhelming local superiority of numbers, enabled the British to achieve their first objective, and the German front lines were quickly overrun, Neuve Chapelle village being taken within 45 minutes. Seemingly surprised by their early success, the British paused for a fatal five hours, giving the Germans time to recover from the shock and organize a further line of defence.

Then, too late, Haig gave a characteristic order to press on with the attack 'regardless of loss'. As with so many subsequent actions, loss was all that was achieved: 583 officers, and more than 12,000 other ranks. On a narrow 4,000 yard front, the British had gained just 1,200 yards. On March 13, running short of artillery ammunition, Haig gave the order to break off the battle.

The Germans hastily learned the lesson of the battle: that something more than sandbags were needed to stop a determined advance—quickly they began to dig the deep dug-outs or *Wohngraben* for which they were to become notorious. Snug in these caverns, their troops could comfortably survive all but the most ferocious artillery barrage. The British, however, learned little, and pressed on with more of the same.

Two months after Neuve Chapelle—on May 9—the British attacked at nearby 'Aubers Ridge', another of the misnamed slight rises in the uniform flatness of Flanders. The attack went forward in support of a much larger French assault further south in Artois.

But the Germans were ready for it, and the artillery support was much weaker than at Neuve Chapelle. Seeing a solid wall of khaki bearing down on them, German officers gave the order to 'Fire—until the barrels burst'—and the attack was stopped in its tracks before the day was out. The British losses were nearly as bad as at Neuve-Chapelle, and for far less gain: 145 officers, and nearly 10,000 men. The shortage of artillery shells, and the poor quality of the ammunition that was supplied, which left the strong German defences almost untouched, was blamed by the British Staff for the failure.

> At Aubers we never even left our lines because although the initial attack went all right, there was no artillery support because we just didn't have the guns or ammunition.

(Greig)

Undaunted, six days later, Haig was at it again, in the same area. For ten days he slogged away around the village of Festubert (May 15–25), but the result was the same: a few yards of ground gained, but 710 officers and 16,000 men lost.

These three battles, for all their casualties, were but apéritifs to the main meals of the guns that were to come. They were dwarfed, too, by simultaneous attacks organized by Joffre and Foch near Arras and in Champagne which cost colossal casualties without the hint of a breakthrough. The Arras offensive, which gained the villages of La Targette and Neuville St Vaast and precious little else, took over 102,000 French lives. That September in Champagne, 143,500 fell.

Gas had made its very first appearance on the Western Front when the Germans fired rudimentary gas shells near Neuve Chapelle in the autumn of 1914. But the wind blew away the fumes and no one noticed. The German inventors went back to their drawing-boards, and one of them, Huber, due to a shell shortage, decided to put the gas in cylinders. After successful trials on the Eastern Front, the gas was released on the unsuspecting allies on April 22 in the 2nd Battle of Ypres, the only major German offensive in 1915.

This attack, which is described elsewhere in the book, can be summarized baldly—thousands of crazed fugitives fled in a headlong rush to escape the terrifying clouds of green smoke, and only by superhuman efforts did the British and Canadians manage to seal a four-mile gap torn in the French lines.

This first gas used was chlorine, and the Germans went on to develop phosgene—fired from shells at the height of the Verdun battles—and later the most deadly variant of all—mustard gas, the effects of which were unforgettable for the unfortunate troops who came into contact with the noxious stuff:

The Germans invented mustard gas, which was terrible stuff. Shells threw this awful liquid out, and if it happened in the dark and you put your hand in it and then touched your eyes you wouldn't know anything about it at first, but by first light you would be blind. The shells made a 'Pop' as they went off and gas always sounded different from other shells. It had a terrible effect—all your skin peeled off, and some men even lost their testicles. I think it made the eyelids swell up. We would join the blinded men together in long lines by making them put their hands on the shoulders of the man in front and take them to the rear. Eventually everyone was issued with gas masks.

(Thacker)

The German gas attacks quickly made them objects of vilification, as the pious tones of Sir Arthur Conan Doyle, in his war history, indicate: 'It is with a feeling of loathing that the chronicler turns to narrate the next episode of the war, in which the Germans, foiled in fair fighting, stole away a few miles of ground by the Arts of the murderer. So long as military history is written, the poisoning of Langemarck will be recorded as an incident by which warfare was degraded, and a great army, which had been long honoured as the finest fighting force in the world, became in a single day an object of horror and contempt.'

'I say, chaps', one can imagine Sir Arthur protesting, 'Steady on—this isn't cricket'. Cricket or not, the British had to deal with its effects, which were drastic . . .

Hector Macdonald, 4th Battalion, Cameronians (Territorials):

At about 10 a.m. one day, information was received that the Germans had made a gas attack on the Canadians at Ypres. Arrangements were immediately made for us being made available to accompany the Division on a 'forced march' to the salient. We marched at about four miles an hour for nine hours, during which time we covered about 36 miles. We rested for ten minutes at the end of each hour, at the roadside with our feet up. It was a very strenuous matter, carrying a rifle, pack, 250 rounds of ammunition, etc. Next morning we made contact with many of the men who were gassed. It was a pathetic sight, many of them were lying at the roadside with foam pouring from their mouth and gasping for breath . . .

Gas had an insidious effect, similar to pneumonia, with its victims slowly drowning as their lungs filled with fluid. Those who survived initial attacks were often lifetime martyrs to bronchial disease, nurtured in the dark smogs of urban England.

Pinched into a salient within the Ypres salient, the British tried counter-attacks to retake the villages they had lost, but this only resulted in more casualties. The Germans, for their part, renewed their offensive in May, preceded with more gas attacks, but the allies were by now wise to their tricks, and held firm.

All this fighting had finally finished the flower of the old regular army, and their place in the line was—despite the distrust of Lord Kitchener for 'weekend soldiers'—increasingly being taken by the Territorial Army. The 'Terriers', a professional militia raised as a result of Lord Haldane's pre-war army reforms, now proved their worth, and stuffy old veterans reported with wonder that at Ypres and Aubers the 'Terriers' had performed as well as the Regulars.

Kitchener remained unconvinced and went grimly on with the methodical training of the vast numbers of raw recruits who had answered his call to arms in 1914. These 'New Armies' would not be ready for action until the summer of 1916, but the bloodying they then received on the Somme blotted out the losses of 1915, bad though they were.

The thinning of the regular ranks often led to 'Terriers' and reserves being rushed forward in some haste, and using unorthodox means of transport:

Sgt. John Larrad, 2122, 1st Battalion, 18th London Regiment, London Irish Rifles:

The journey from Le Havre in French railway trucks [Hommes 40, Chevaux 8], to Cassel; thence we marched as reserves for Neuve Chapelle, and were issued with stinking goatskin coats en route. The ride from Voormezele to St. Venant was made in a fleet of open-topped buses. Mine was a No. 16 Cricklewood-Victoria on which I must, so many times before have been a passenger. Headed by our Irish pipers to Bethune and from there our first experience in the front line. We were on our own at Festubert—the terrain was too wet for trenches. We took enough scrapes to fill the sandbags for a low wall. It was impossible to stand erect. Many German dead were buried in the floor, and as it began to dry out the shape of the bodies became clearly visible. We were in and out (mostly in) of the trenches at Givenchy, they were quite deep, especially in the mud. After 21 days of this we had to scrape the socks off our feet. One spot known as the Orchard was not a health resort. The Germans were only a few feet away and were digging underneath. It's all right when you can hear them, but not when they stop. One night an RE officer came along saying 'No firing, no firing. There's a large working party up in front.' But in the morning it was all our wiring which had gone!

We went over on a French liner, from Southampton to Le Havre, then entrained, went up the line and detrained at St. Omer. The other year I went across with my son by coach and hovercraft—it had all changed but I recognized the central square.

From there we went up the line to Festubert-Givenchy, where we had our baptism of fire. We took over the line which was just water-logged ditches, with sandbag breastworks.

All Sir John French had was one battery of guns to support four divisions. What they would do was fire off a barrage, then saddle up and go off to another part of the line and fire off some more so that the Jerries thought that we had many more guns than we actually possessed.

We were mingled with the Regulars holding the line, and as we went into the trenches we lost our officer—a subaltern—a sniper got him. That was our first death, and some of us began to wonder what we were in for. It gave us a bit of a shock.

The opposing front lines at that point were 150 yards apart. We spent a fortnight at the front, then withdrew to reserve, and finally went to the rear for a rest. On May 25 we went up the line again. We had orders to regain a bit of the line that had been lost—a section of about 50 yards—at Festubert. We took a few yards of the front line but couldn't get into the communication trenches. That's where my Lance-Corporal, Keyworth, won his VC. He was throwing bombs and shooting at the Jerries as they came up the communication trenches.

At that time we were still wearing cloth caps and I got a shot right through the middle of my cap. I felt something singeing my close cropped hair, and I took off the cap to see that a bullet had gone right through the middle of the lamb of our regimental cap badge, the Lamb and Flag. One inch lower and I would have been a goner. Ten minutes later the same sniper got me through the shoulder. I was bending forward at the time, and felt a burning sensation go through me. I felt blood and thought to myself 'I've been hit'. The bullet went through my chest and out my back.

It was terrible out there—one man was shot through the privates and he was dying in agony. Keyworth and three others were the only ones from our section of 15 men who came through unscathed.

Then 'B' Company under the command of Captain Figg—I think he was the elder brother of the Lieutenant who was killed when we entered the line—got in further along the trench and bombed their way up. He got the DSO for that. I got back to a dressing station and the doctor told me I'd been lucky—the bullet had passed within half an inch of the main artery to the heart—I think that was my lucky day.

(Haddock)

It is interesting to compare this retrospective account of an action on the last day of the Battle of Festubert with the contemporary citation for L/Cpl. Leonard Keyworth's VC:

'. . .Keyworth's battalion, having already made a successful assault on part of the German line, determined to follow up the success with a bombing attack. Seventy-five bomb-throwers advanced to attack from a small British trench less than 40 yards from the enemy's front-line trenches.

But though the distance was short, the ground in between had been so badly cut up by shellfire they could not progress very rapidly and before they were half-way across, the majority had already fallen before withering rifle and machine-gun fire. But the rest, undismayed by the fate of their comrades, came bravely on.

Halting a few yards from the parapet, Keyworth began to throw his bombs. Then, springing to the top of the parapet itself, he took aim at the Germans beneath him and rained his deadly missiles on them with the most murderous effect.

When his stock was exhausted, he replenished it from the bag of some dead comrade and returned to the attack. For two hours he continued thus, hurling, it is computed, 150 bombs on the panic-stricken Huns, until the trench was a veritable shambles, choked with the bodies of the dead and shrieking mutilated wretches who presented an easy prey.

Marvellous to relate, though out of the 74 comrades, no less than 58 were killed or wounded, and though he was continually standing fully exposed at the top of the parapet, so near to the Germans that they could well-nigh have touched him with the muzzles of their rifles, Keyworth escaped without a scratch . . .' He was killed in action later in the war.

The shell shortage referred to by Jim Haddock, coupled with the long casualty lists of that spring, caused a major scandal at home. The energetic Lloyd George was appointed Minister of Munitions, and he drafted in armies of women to work in the arsenals. The nation, shaken by the seriousness of war, braced itself grimly for more sacrifice.

8. Loos

If any question why we died
Tell them—because our fathers lied.

Rudyard Kipling
(whose only son, John, fell at Loos)

Further sacrifices were not long in coming: impelled by the insistence of Joffre, the French Commander-in-Chief, who was himself committed to another grand attack in Champagne with fourteen divisions, the British generals, ignoring the lessons of Aubers and Neuve Chapelle, reluctantly agreed to a major attack with six divisions near the mining village of Loos, in the same industrial area as the rest of that year's fighting.

Even the customarily optimistic Haig, whose First Army would carry out the assault, was dubious of success. He had surveyed the area, and agreed with his subordinate, Sir Henry Rawlinson, that the sector—'as flat as my palm' and, pitted with German strongpoints set up in collieries—was entirely unsuitable. Besides, the Welsh wizard, Lloyd George, had not had time to conjure up the munitions necessary to back up the infantry—guns and shells were still in critically (not to say criminally)—short supply.

But several pressing reasons compelled the British to agree to the attack: the Germans had launched a massive offensive on the Eastern Front, and the Russian ally had lost 750,000 men. A British overseas operation, which had been designed to sidestep the stalemate in France and attack Germany's soft underbelly, Turkey, had gone awry. The bid to force the Dardanelles Strait at Gallipoli had been a bloody failure. But, Joffre, as the Allies' senior partner, was able to exert heavy pressure to wreak his will. Haig overcame his doubts by deciding that he could beat the Germans at their own game by using poison gas in place of the missing artillery. The attack was fixed for September 25.

The preliminary artillery bombardment started on September 21, but the shells were so sparse that it had little effect. The gas—150 tons of chlorine in 5,000 cylinders—was of little use, as the wind was not strong enough to carry it over No Man's Land, and it hung around the British lines in a foggy miasma, poisoning some of the attacking troops. Two of Haig's divisional commanders whom we shall meet again, Horne and Gough, nevertheless persisted with their attacks in the face of all advice. Their men advanced, with hopeless courage, into the mouths of the waiting machine guns, which swept the oncoming lines with leisurely but deadly ease. Scottish soldiers were prominent in these attacks; one of them was Arthur Greig:

At Loos we filled the gap between the 1st and 2nd Brigades as part of a reserve force commanded by Lt.-Col. E. W. B. Green of the Royal Sussex Regiment, by Le Rutoire farm. As usual we were at the bottom of the slope attacking the Germans at the top. The night before the attack we dug a forward trench in No Man's Land that more than halved the distance that we would have to cover.

It was a dawn attack, and my first time for going over the top. I had a feeling of fatalism, I realized that many men would be hit but I did not think that I would be one. The other men varied, some were quite eager to go, whereas others of course did not like the idea one bit. We were dressed in tartan kilts and Glengarry caps—later we got khaki aprons to hide the tartan; helmets had not been issued.

We attacked in extended order in half sections. At first there was not a great deal of enemy fire but it got worse as we approached the enemy lines. We came up to the wire which had not been cut by the artillery—I never knew a case in the whole war when it was cut. The Germans had excellently-sited and very accurate machine-guns, which were always the key factor in their defences. So we were pinned down and had to lie prone for hours until the 51st Highland Division broke through on the flank, and came round to the rear of the enemy, and the Germans in front of us put up their hands and surrendered.

The Germans, by the way, were wearing soft caps like us—not the famous 'Pickelhaube'. Incidentally, our equipment at that time was a short Mark IV Lee Enfield rifle with 150 rounds of ammunition in ten webbing pouches hung around our belts. Sometimes we had a bandolier slung over our shoulders with a further 150 rounds which was generally enough.

Our officer, Lindsay-Renton, opened fire as soon as he saw the

Germans get up, and killed two of them. Then there was a general shout of 'They're surrendering'. We sent the Germans to the rear and got into their trenches which were much deeper than ours, with real dug-outs which we hadn't developed at that time. (The French were even more loath to dig in than we were, their trenches were like ditches, with straw at the bottom which collected all sorts of vermin). The trenches remained in British hands and by the evening we were taken out of the lines and moved north to Auchy near the Hohenzollern Redoubt.

(Greig)

The main success for the British was in the southern and central parts of the front where an advance of 8,000 yards was made, and Loos itself and a strongpoint under a slagheap known as the Hohenzollern Redoubt were taken. Unfortunately the reserves which could have exploited this limited success were not at hand.

The British Commander-in-Chief, Sir John French, had three infantry divisions—including the Guards—in reserve, but they were sixteen miles to the rear, and when Haig needed them most they were not to be had.

The British commanders then made a bad situation worse by marching the raw reserves up by night, and flinging them pell-mell into battle on the following day, the 26th. By then it was too late—the Germans had reinforced their defence and were forewarned and forearmed. Bloody British losses were the only tangible result, and when the battle was broken off a few days later the casualty list stood at nearly 60,000— the same figure as on the dreadful first day of the Somme, a battle which has gone down in history in a way that the equally futile Loos has not.

The battle did have one important repercussion, however, for it led to the dismissal of French and his replacement as Commander-in-Chief by Sir Douglas Haig. My father was on Haig's staff, so let him tell the story:

Haig asked that the Guards division, which was in GHQ reserve, should be placed in Army reserve so that they were available for use immediately a breakthrough had taken place. French would not agree, beyond saying that if the battle went well and the troops were wanted they would be handed over to him. One can see French's point of view as well, as of course we were very short of troops and he did not have a very big reserve, and should the Germans have attacked on another front he might have wanted his reserves to plug that hole.

However, as it proved, Haig was right. On the first day the battle went well and he needed more troops to extend his gain. Unfortunately the reserves were not deployed as he had wanted and two fresh divisions, just out from England, and the Guards division, had to march through shell-swept ground to try and extend the attack.

They were too late, however, and after two or three days the battle had to be cut off. Haig was, of course, upset. Some weeks later, his Chief of Staff, General Butler, was in London, staying at the Berkeley Hotel. Haig had sent to him, at his request (after seeing the Secretary—Kitchener—at the War Office), all the correspondence which had taken place between Haig and French. (I remember the last letter from French which said 'this correspondence must now cease'). This was taken by Butler to the War Office and I believe was the cause of the replacement of French as Commander-in-Chief by Haig, which happened shortly afterwards.

(Jones)

This slightly underhand intrigue was unfortunately only too typical of the Cavalry Commander who was now to control the destinies of the millions of men employed in and behind the Western Front. Haig, a dour Scottish aristocrat, reserved and taciturn was never averse to a bit of backstairs whispering, if he saw it as his duty, and if it happened also to advance the career of Douglas Haig. Well, that was just an added bonus.

Haig has been a subject of continual controversy ever since the war. The pro-and-contra arguments are not only the preserve of military historians—several of the veterans interviewed for this book cursed him quite naturally as 'Butcher Haig'. Others said that he did his best.

The execration of him immediately after the war went too far, and he was badly maligned in the memoirs of his inveterate enemy and fellow Celt, Lloyd George, whom Haig privately called 'a cur'.

Haig ignored these attacks with stoical dignity, devoting the few years left to him after the war to the foundation of the British Legion, to look after the welfare and interests of those who had served under him. This tireless and unselfish work went a long way towards refuting the charge of his enemies that he was uncaring and unmindful of the horrendous sufferings of his men.

Inevitably there was a reaction to the abuse, and in modern times the historian John Terraine has devoted a one-man cottage industry to

Haig's rehabilitation. Starting with a revisionist biography, Terraine has continued with a series of books of impeccable scholarship, refuting the more careless calumnies of Haig's many critics. However, he can paint the lily, and comes perilously close to suggesting that Haig was another Caesar or Napoleon—'a man in a classic mould'. He was not. The man was a product of his age and class, i.e. a rigid, hidebound soldier, severely limited in vision and imagination. A gallant gentleman certainly, but not a military genius.

The final judgement, as so often, probably lies between the extremes of apologists and assailants: Haig showed stoic determination to hang on where others faltered. Thanks to factors beyond his control—the British sea blockade of Germany and the United States entry to the war—he hung on longer than his enemy, and that was enough. His dogged, terrier-like tenacity could be admirable in adversity, such as his 'backs to the wall' call during the darkest moment of the great German offensives in 1918, but the same quality proved dreadfully costly in men's lives when he persisted with his bulldog battering at unbreached defences on the Somme and at Passchendaele.

The immovable centre of Haig's philosophy was his unshakeable commitment to the strategy of a breakthrough on the Western Front. Like some latter-day Arthurian Knight, he pursued the elusive Grail of a Western victory across a dozen blood-drenched battlegrounds and over a million broken bodies. He was aided and abetted by the Chief of the Imperial General Staff, Sir William Robertson, 'Wully', a grim figure who had risen from the ranks to be appointed to his post at the same time as Haig. Together, this duo came to dominate British policy in the same way as their German counterparts Hindenburg and Ludendorff. Robertson was eventually eased out of office, but Haig— thanks in part to good contacts in the Royal Family—stayed put firmly to the bitter end. His reign meant that all other fronts—Macedonia, Italy, the Middle East—remained essentially sideshows. The decision, for good or ill, would be sought and found in the West.

9. Into the Salient

She, moon-like, draws her own far-moving tide
Of sorrow and memory; toward her, each alone,
Glide the dark dreams that seek an English grave.

Laurence Binyon, 'Ypres'

My journey to the infamous Ypres salient was made against the background of another war—albeit infinitely smaller than the great holocaust of 1914–18. A few days before I left, Argentina invaded the Falkland Islands, and despite the distance in time and space from the Western Front, the echoes were soon to be heard . . . The papers printed recollections of the previous Falklands battle in 1914, when a Naval Squadron under Admiral Sturdee destroyed the small German flotilla of Admiral Graf Spee.

On the land, the conditions under which British and Argentinian soldiers fought duplicated the horrors of the Western Front in an uncanny way: news reports carried stories of troops cowering in slit trenches, cold and soaking. Men went sick with that characteristic Great War complaint—trench feet.

For example, 'The Times' *Diary reported on June 11, 1982:*

Trench foot, which threatens our troops in the Falklands is an irritating condition which was all-too-familiar in the First World War. It is the traditional enemy of troops involved in trench warfare where the feet are exposed to cold and wet, and the blood supply and circulation are affected by tight boots and lack of opportunity to exercise. The bacterial invasion thus encouraged caused swelling, ulceration and great discomfort. During the First War, 1,000 cases were reported among the men of the 1st Division, between December 1914 and February 1915 alone. It was worse in the Ypres salient, where the ground was very wet and conditions resembled those in the Falklands. In the First War men wore thigh-length waders, or two pairs of socks with large boots, but the best protection of all was thought to be a mixture of tallow, boric acid and whale oil rubbed into the feet . . . A battalion used ten gallons of whale oil a day, but the mixture smelled vile.

Pacifists protested at the slaughter of young men in defence of a small overseas territory. Crowds waved Union Jacks in patriotic exuberance. A generation conditioned to peace was bloodied and burned. Young men went over the top to die in the face of machine-gun nests. Popular newspapers misquoted Rupert Brooke. The imagery of lines, break-throughs, encirclements, comradeship and rough humour was employed all over again. It seemed as though the seventy intervening years had gone for naught as I revisited again the scene of that first and seminal slaughterhouse.

I took up my journey where I had left off: at Dixmude. The roads to Ypres are flat and uninspiring; only the names carried echoes as I tramped through towns through which the British armies had marched on their way up to the line, singing, in the early days, the jaunty 'Tipperary', and later, cynically: 'Why did we join the army, why did we go to war, we'd rather be at home . . . living on the earnings of a whore'.

Poperinghe, where a young military chaplain, Tubby Clayton, estab-lished 'Toc H', a rest club, within whose walls all ranks were equal. Vlarmertinghe, the last base before the salient—and then, . . . 'Wipers' itself, the old cloth town, still living on its memories, no longer those of prosperity, but of death and desolation. The central square of Ypres, the Groot Markt, is dominated by the grandiose and beautiful Cloth Hall: ground to atoms by the guns, its restoration was only fully completed in the 1960s. It houses a large World War One museum, and as I browsed among the artifacts, a party of English schoolchildren swept in like a flock of chattering starlings. Their teacher had obviously prepared a History project on the Salient and the children scuttled among the exhibits, ticking off objects on a list. The exhibits themselves showed some surrealist contrasts; the muddy and rusted artifacts of battle reposed near a travelling tea service presented by Lady Haig as a peculiar tribute to her husband, Sir Douglas, unwitting architect of much of the carnage that the museum commemorated. His Field Marshal's cap also reposed in a glass case, with a symbolic small moth hole eating into the fabric.

My next journey took me along the ramparts of the Ypres citadel which still encircle the eastern and southern sides of the old town. Mostly restored, a small area has been left in the devastated state to which it had been reduced by continual bombardment by 1918. These massive walls housed many subterranean chambers, which were the most secure shelter for the troops defending the town and environs.

G. S. Muir, Canadian Army:

But we knew the salient, every trench and path of it. The end of the fourth day found us billeted in Ypres, HQ in the ramparts, that wall, 50 feet high and about 100 feet thick which runs nearly all round the city. It was made, I suppose, by simply throwing the earth out of the moat and then bricking it up on the outside. In this there were tunnels and dug-outs, which no shell could reach.

The ramparts bear the hallmark of the French military architect Vauban, perhaps the greatest builder of fortifications in European history. He it was, who was entrusted with the defence of the French frontier cities in the late seventeenth century, and we will meet his work at two other citadel cities which successfully held out against the German onslaught throughout the war—Arras and Verdun.

One can follow the great walls of the ramparts from the Menin Gate, a vast archway in white stone built to commemorate the myriads of men who passed through it on their way to the front, many never to return. Carved on panels are the names of 54,896 of these soldiers who died in the salient and have no known graves, though when their bodies are subsequently found, as some are to this day, (seven were discovered and reburied in 1982) the names are erased from the panels. The gate is the scene of a moving and unique nightly ceremony: the sounding of the Last Post on silver bugles presented to the town by the British Legion and the Old Contemptibles. The men of Ypres Fire Brigade carry out the ceremony each evening at 8 p.m. precisely. A few seconds before 8, two policemen stop the flow of traffic, turn to the arch and salute as two or three buglers play the haunting strains of the lament. Even to someone like myself, without a military background, the clear limpid notes falling through the evening air are almost unbearably poignant. You feel a host of ghosts behind you; you hope they approve and are at peace; you remember them.

The walk along the ramparts leads to another city entrance, the Lille Gate, whose medieval round turrets proclaim its origin. A small shed behind the gate is known as 'Plumer's Headquarters'. It was used as a signals office by this General's staff and some of his orders for the surprise attack at Messines Ridge, one of the few wholly successful Allied actions of the war, were transmitted from here.

After attending the Last Post I retired to bed, having planned a long walk for the next day, which would embrace the whole salient. The first station on my pilgrimage was to be a personal one, a visit to the grave of my uncle at Boesinghe, a village marking the northern extent of the salient where the British joined hands with the French and the Belgians.

I left Ypres by the northern road past the basin of the Ypres-Boesinghe canal, known to the wartime troops as Tattenham Corner, and perhaps more appropriately, Dead End. The road winds round another landmark, Salvation Corner, named after a Salvation Army hut placed at this spot. It then runs north past bungalow ribbon development until the first wayside cemetery marks the old fighting line. The next cemetery, Essex Farm, is situated close to a line of British blockhouses and dug-outs lining the Yperlee canal. These concrete shelters, some still used as storehouses by a local farm, had inspired some caustic comments in the cemetery visitors' book—'Scandalous, the way these historic bunkers are treated!' wrote one indignant traveller from peaceful Holland.

A grassy mound on the canal bank behind the cemetery marks the site of a wartime dressing station where Lt.-Col. John McRae, a Canadian medical officer, wrote one of the war's most famous poems:

> In Flanders fields the poppies grow
> Between the crosses, row on row.

Sadly, there were none of these flowers of remembrance to be seen.

Another six kilometres brought me to Boesinghe and the cemetery of Talana Farm. Luckily I had a trench map to guide me, and from this I located the exact site of the farm from which the cemetery takes its name. Originally a moated rectangle, what was once the farm is now a wood surrounded by a stagnant ditch. Bits of red brick among the undergrowth betrayed its former use. My uncle was killed in a typical small-scale action by his unit, the 1st London Rifle Brigade, on July 6, 1915, the attack on International Trench:

> The British found the trench choked with German dead and littered with letters and parcels. Evidently the mail had just arrived. Some kind of a meal had been in progress, for there was an abundance of hot coffee which was eagerly consumed by the

raiders who in addition fortified themselves with cigars. Thirty prisoners, mostly of the 215th Regiment (Schleswig-Holstein), were captured, together with two machine-gunes, two trench mortars and a considerable amount of trench stores . . .

But German machine-gun fire continued with unabated accuracy and by 11 a.m. the British casualties were becoming severe . . . At 3 p.m. a more deliberate counter-attack developed on the left. It was easily driven off, but two companies of the Hampshire Regt. who had been sent forward in support were stood-to in case of emergency. By 3.30 p.m. the shelling had become so severe that the old British front line had to be evacuated. The captured trenches received their share of the bombardment, under cover of which another effort was made at counter-attack on the left—the enemy endeavouring to work along a communication trench instead of advancing over the open.

This attack was checked and defeated—in part by the artillery, in part by 2nd Lt. C. A. Gould of the Somerset Light Infantry who, with his platoon sergeant and some of his men went to the help of a First Battalion post of three bombers, and engaged the enemy with them, whilst the remainder of the platoon worked feverishly at deepening and improving the trench. This was the last attempt at recapturing the position. Shortly after 5 p.m. the firing died down.

Late at night the captured ground was handed over to the 2nd Bn. Lancashire Fusiliers. The officers and men who had been engaged were, as they had every reason to be, in high spirits over their achievement. The Brigadier professed himself to be delighted . . .

But the gain of some seventy-five yards of ground on a frontage of three hundred yards had been made at the expense to the Somerset Light Infantry of one officer and 27 other ranks killed, 3 officers and 102 other ranks wounded and 5 men missing; to the First Battalion of Lt. Brandt, 2nd-Lts. Gibbs, Blair and Juckes and 33 other ranks killed, Capts. Downes and Ellis, 2nd-Lts. Bullock and Boyle and 176 other ranks wounded, and 37 missing; and it is safe to assume that the great majority if not all of the missing were killed. Congratulations were deservedly showered upon the survivors . . .

. . .but they did not include Ernest Jones who was one of the 33 'other ranks' who did not return.

After paying my respects, I moved on into the village and crossed the canal, using the trench map as my guide. The road layout has not changed from its 1914 grid, and little remains among the rebuilt farms and fields to bear witness to its grim ordeal as a wilderness of mud and fire where men and horses were blasted, drowned or frozen, where they suffered and survived, endured and died. My map showed that the German front line jutted out at this point in a promontory almost touching the British trenches, appropriately called Caesar's Nose. A small cemetery still bears this name.

The road carried me up over the gentle slope of Pilkem Ridge, one of the first objectives in the third Battle of Ypres, which came to bear the infamous name of Passchendaele. The ridge itself was gained by the British in savage fighting by the beginning of August 1917, before the battle became bogged down in a sea of liquid mud that gave it a peculiar quality of horror that stayed forever in the memory of its survivors and soon acquired the status of myth.

From Pilkem village I turned east towards Langemarck, a small town made infamous for the first use of poison gas by the Germans during the second Battle of Ypres on April 22, 1915. This sector was then held by French Algerian colonial troops. Around 5 p.m., after a peaceful spring day, a cloud of greenish-yellow fog was seen rolling across No Man's Land from the German lines. The gas enveloped a four-mile sector of the lines. Within minutes the terrified survivors of two divisions were pouring back across the Ypres canal. Behind them in the trenches lay their stricken comrades, their bodies twisted in the agony of asphyxiation. Hastily the Canadians and British on either side of the French lines squeezed together to stop the gap, and a major German breakthrough was foiled. But gas, in this case chlorine, introduced a new devilish element into the already horrific conditions. It unleashed a storm of fresh outrage against the inhuman methods of the Huns, but within a short while the Allies fought fire with fire and were producing their own supplies of gas.

L/Cpl. Edward Worrell, 4th Irish Dragoons:

I was present when the Germans used gas for the second time. It was on Whit Monday, 1915, at Wieltje on Pilkem ridge. The Northumbrian Division had come up all fresh into the line, and they were decimated by the gas. The only protection we had at first were four-by-two rifle-cleaning cloths with string ties on either end. You had to urinate on them, then tie them around your face, but they weren't effective at all. Later they issued pads with cotton gauze lining, then a mask with a nose-clip. None of them worked properly until we got hooded masks, which is still basically the same design in use today.

However, the initial attack at Langemarck secured the town for the Germans, and it remained in their hands until the latter phases of Passchendaele, when its ruins were captured on August 16, 1917. It was briefly retaken by the Germans in their Spring offensives of 1918, and when finally retaken, hardly a stone was left standing.

I turned off the main Langemarck-Pilkem road and headed by track into the heart of the salient. I was now traversing the Passchendaele battlefield, that ocean of almost indescribable terror and pity. I had prepared myself for the trip by reading a newly-published war diary, *Some Desperate Glory* by Edwin Campion Vaughan. The author describes, day by day, and minute by minute, the details of that living death. It is written in a matter-of-fact style that makes the dreadful truth all the more vivid. Here, among these peaceful green fields where cows slowly chomped their cud and regarded me with the incurious eyes of animals that accept all, Vaughan had fallen waist-deep into mud, had grabbed hold of a long-dead leg as a drowning man reaching for his last straw and then found it coming off in his hand. Throwing it away, he had struggled free, and within minutes was teaching a fellow officer how to play Patience! The gentle little brook which babbled under a culvert where I paused to rest was the Steen-beek—transformed by the guns into a vast lake, which had sucked whole armies under its red sea. Here Vaughan tried to jostle a slow man along, only to find that the trooper had just had his eyes and nose torn away by a shell. When he crossed the Steenbeek itself, Vaughan had almost slithered onto another corpse, its breast sheet-white in the shell-light.

I reached Vancouver crossroads, where the towering Canadian memorial stands, commemorating the containment of the 1915 gas attack and the 2,000 men who died in the action. The monument consists of a stone soldier in tin helmet bowed over his rifle. Coniferous trees, clipped into the shape of shells, surround it. Juniper bushes nearby are cut into the shape of shell-holes and craters. I pressed on and soon on my left saw the village of Passchendaele itself, an unremarkable place for such a hallowed name. The village tops a slight ridge which formed the outermost lip of the salient, gained by the Canadian Corps on November 6 1917, after the British Army had bled itself white crawling towards it through the sticky morass of the salient. On my right I could just discern the distant towers of Ypres, and it seemed wholly incredible that these few miles of humdrum pastoral meadow could possibly have once held all that horror.

At the bottom of Passchendaele ridge is Tyne Cot cemetery, the largest British war cemetery of all, containing nearly 12,000 graves. The great cross which crowns the cemetery is built above the largest of a complex of German blockhouses which were the most stubborn obstacle on the path to Passchendaele. As I sat, exhausted, at the cemetery entrance I read in the cemetery visitor's book an English schoolgirl's poignant question which was soon to be answered: 'Must more men die for the Falklands' freedom?'

I was then approached by another visitor, an Australian, who asked me to take his photograph against the backdrop of the cemetery. He turned out to be Graeme Hawkins, an airline pilot come to visit the places where his father had fought. We arranged to journey on together, and returned to Ypres via the village of Zonnebeke, many times taken and retaken as the tide of war swept over it and receded. The road rises over Frezenberg Ridge, one of the main sites for the guns defending Ypres, before entering the town under Menin Gate.

Exhausted by our exertions we spent the evening in continental-style drinking outside one of the cafés on the Ypres Groot Markt. Graeme regaled me with frightening tales of pilots collapsing with coronaries over the controls of their aircraft, and held forth on the delights of Bangkok's massage parlours.

His Belgian journey was by way of being a duty to his father, who had died the previous year, and he was keenly interested in the battlefields, and I packed him off to bed with some of my guidebooks and histories for company—Ypres not yet possessing many massage parlours.

The next day we set off for the southern part of the salient. Our objectives were two places which had once been the scenes of concentrated and savage fighting, of which traces can still be seen today—Hills 60 and 62. Once again, the word 'Hill' is a misnomer. Hill 60 was originally a mound thrown up by the excavation of the nearby Ypres-Comines railway in the nineteenth century. 'Sixty' indicates its height in metres. On the other side of the railway, which still functions today, were two mounds, known as the 'Caterpillar' and the 'Dump' to the British. Although these mounds were so small, they did give a commanding view north over Ypres and south along the Messines Ridge—for this reason, there were bitter struggles for their possession.

Hill 62 stands due east of Ypres, close to the hamlet of Hooge, whose château was a pivotal point in the fighting, both during the early battles for Ypres, and later, during Passchendaele. The late Baron de Vinckt rebuilt his ancestral home after the war and turned the shellholes into attractive ornamental ponds in the grounds. Sanctuary Wood was originally behind the lines and was so baptized because it was used as a place of rest and refuge for battle-shocked troops. As the tide of battle closed in around Ypres, however, the wood became part of the front lines and today it is the one place in the salient where trenches have been preserved as far as possible in their original condition.

Hill 60 was one of the earliest venues for mine warfare on the Western Front. Specially-raised groups of sappers, mostly miners in civilian life, were recruited thanks to the energetic efforts of a Tory MP turned Army officer named John Norton Griffiths. They were put to work in the Ypres salient, where the sodden, boggy soil and soggy clay made tunnelling conditions nightmarish. It was decided that mines would be used to take Hill 60 from the Germans who had wrested the position from the French in early fighting. Three shafts were accordingly driven forward.

The speed of digging was redoubled when it was realized that the Germans, too, were digging their own mines. The tunnellers became involved in a desperate race. Norton Griffiths—one of whose eccentricities was to tour the Western Front in his own Rolls-Royce—spurred on his 'clay kickers', as they were known, to ever greater efforts. At one point the tunnellers broke through into a German shaft and the two sides engaged in a brief skirmish in total darkness underground.

The officers in charge decided to lay and charge their mines and on the evening of April 17, 1915 six charges, totalling over 10,000 pounds of gunpowder and guncotton, were fired. One hundred and fifty Germans and two Royal Engineers were killed by the blasts. Debris was flung 300 feet into the air and scattered over a 300-yard radius. Infantry stormed the hill and occupied the mine craters. Despite repeated counter-attacks they held it until a German gas attack the following month drove them off the summit.

Hill 60 remained in German hands until June 1917, when the hill, and the Caterpillar mound across the railway, became the sites of the northernmost pair of the score of gigantic mines laid by the British in their successful attempt to literally blow the Germans off the whole Messines Ridge—the brilliant prelude to the disastrous Passchendaele campaign.

Work on these mines was in the hands of the 1st Australian Mining Company whose memorial stands on the Hill today. Just after 3 a.m. on the morning of June 7, 1917, nineteen of the Messines Ridge mines were fired simultaneously in an arc stretching for several miles along the southern part of the salient. The shock of the blast was heard by Lloyd George in Downing Street. Nearly a million pounds of high explosive ripped the heart from the Messines Ridge, overturning concrete block-houses like children's bricks and burying thousands of the ridge's defenders alive. As the infantry swept forward to take control, they were met by grown men blubbering like babies—unhinged by the horrific effects of being at the epicentre of a deafening earthquake. By seven in the morning, encountering practically no resistance, the villages of Messines and Wytschaete were in British hands. At one stroke the British had bitten off the whole southern sweep of the salient and established themselves on top of the high ground from which the Germans had slaughtered them at leisure for nearly three years.

The two Hill 60 craters can still be seen today, and the Caterpillar is particularly impressive. Nearly 300 feet across, almost circular, and fringed by trees, it looks an ideal spot for angling. No hint from the still, black 90-foot deep waters, that here in this crater ten German officers and 677 men were swallowed up forever.

Hill 60 is also rich in German-built bunkers, some broken down by war and time into their component concrete parts, but others pretty much in one piece, some having seen service in the Second War as well.

Sanctuary Wood and Hill 62, near Hooge, boasts a café-museum devoted to the war. The amiable owner will sell you beer and souvenirs with equal zest. Some of the relics, though, are of doubtful authenticity: a suspiciously modern-looking belt of machine-gun bullets for sale was admitted to be of Second War vintage. The café leads through to a museum, complete with perspective peepshow machines giving glimpses of atrocious pictures from the fighting.

Outside, in the woods behind, are the original trenches from the Vince Street-Jam Row sector. Helmets, howitzer shells, 'toffee apple' mortar bombs and other relics liberally scattered around testify to the fury of the fighting when the eastern part of the wood was in German hands and the western half was in the British lines. After a fierce German attack in June 1916, the Canadians counter-attacked and drove the Germans out of the vicinity, a feat commemorated by another Canadian memorial on nearby Mount Sorrel. The woods were shot to smithereens in the battles, but a few grey and aged speciments of original timber remain propped up here and there, riven and marked by shot, shell and shrapnel.

Part Four
The Watershed

10. Place of the Skull— Verdun

Who has not had a feeling of nostalgia for a place where he has endured great pain? . . . the fascination of a sombre lodestar. In the infinite, such stars—which we often imagine as dead—are burning. And everything that they touch is consumed by fire.

Georges Blond, 'Verdun'

In December 1915, the senior Allied Commander, Joffre, summoned his British junior partner, Haig, to a conference at the French GHQ at Chantilly, near Paris. The taciturn pair here laid their plans for the coming year.

The fearful slaughters of 1915—dwarfed only in retrospect by the more bloody shambles still to come—had not shaken their unbroken faith in an Allied victory to be secured by a breakthrough on the Western Front.

Joffre proposed, and Haig assented, to a joint effort on the River Somme, a co-ordinated Franco-British summer attack designed to break through into open country around Bapaume and end the stalemate of the trenches.

The spring would be spent in building up reserves of men and munitions, so that the attack would not again founder through lack of supplies. By then Kitchener's New Armies would be in the field, ready to prove their mettle and their still vibrant patriotism.

But the 'best-laid schemes o' mice and men gang aft a-gley', and the Allies failed to take into account what was happening over the hill in the enemy camp. Here Falkenhayn, riding high as Minister of War and Chief of the General Staff, had his own schemes for victory in the coming year.

As Haig and Joffre discussed their plans, Falkenhayn penned a memorandum to the Kaiser arguing that the French were the weak

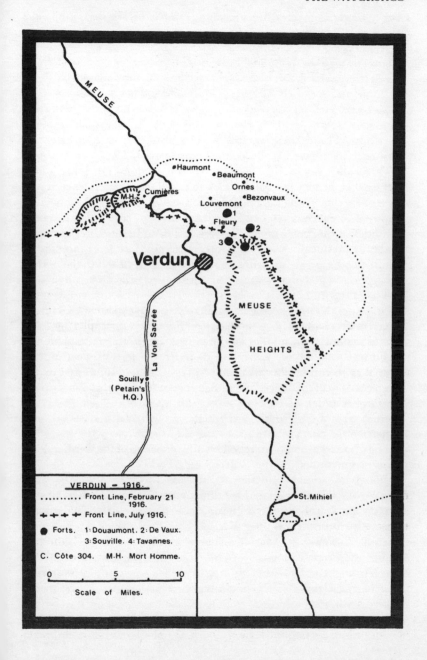

MEUSE

• Haumont
• Beaumont
Ornes
• Bezonvaux
M.H. • Cumières
C. • Louvemont
●1
Fleury ●2
3● ●4

Verdun

MEUSE

HEIGHTS

La Voie Sacrée

Souilly •
(Petain's
H.Q.)

• St.Mihiel

VERDUN — 1916.
·········· Front Line, February 21
1916.
+ + + + Front Line, July 1916.
● Forts. 1: Douaumont. 2: De Vaux.
3: Souville. 4: Tavannes.
C. Côte 304.   M.H. Mort Homme.

0   5   10
Scale   of   Miles.

sister among the Allies. By smashing France, he asserted, England's sword would be dashed from her grasp and she too would be forced to sue for peace.

His strategy for crippling France was to stage a limited German attack that would force the French into an unwinnable battle of attrition, and so slowly bleed her white and sap her will to resist. The place he selected for his cold, almost sadistic scheme, was the ancient French fortress of Verdun. The idea was not so much to take the town, but to force France to defend it at a heavy cost—and, for good historical reasons, Falkenhayn calculated that France would be prepared to pay.

This walled city, at the gateway to Germany in Lorraine, had a long and warlike history stretching back to pre-Roman times, when it had been burned by Attila, and later it had been a centre of Charlemagne's empire. More recently, it had formed the centrepiece of Vauban's chain of citadels protecting France's eastern frontiers. In short, it was a place of almost mythical, as well as strategic, significance to France, and it would not be given up without a furious struggle—just the sort of struggle that Falkenhayn wanted for his strategy of death by a thousand cuts.

On paper, Verdun seemed an unlikely spot to choose: it was ringed by a treble chain of forts and casements and surrounded by hilly, wooded country unsuitable for broad advances. But the apparently tough nut was hollow: Joffre had denuded the forts of most of their weaponry to equip other more hard-pressed fronts. Impressed by the rapid collapse of the Liège forts in Belgium in 1914, he had also stripped the forts of much of their garrison, and many of the soldiers in the Verdun area were elderly territorials, growing fat and sleepy in a hitherto quiet part of the front.

The attack was to be launched by nine divisions of the German Fifth Army, commanded by the Kaiser's eldest son, 'Little Willy' himself. Although the number of troops involved was planned to be quite modest, the Germans spared no effort in moving up their big guns for the coming attack. By the beginning of February 1916, 1,200 artillery pieces, including huge 'Big Bertha' siege guns, had been secretly assembled around the Verdun salient—the biggest-ever concentration of guns then known in history. Behind the guns, waiting in secretly-dug concrete shelters, known as 'Stollen' were the élite troops who were to spearhead the attack—72 battalions of first class, highly trained men.

Directly in the path of the coming attack, based in a small wood, the Bois des Caures, lay two battalions of French Chasseurs, unmounted cavalrymen, commanded by Lt.-Col. Emile Driant, son-in-law of

France's nineteenth-century would-be dictator General Boulanger, and himself a Parliamentary Deputy. The able and energetic Driant was only too well aware of the vulnerably weak state of the Verdun defences, and had striven in vain to alert the lethargic High Command to the danger. When Joffre stirred himself to take action it was already too late, and Driant was to pay the price of that tardiness with his own life.

After a delay caused by incessant rain and snow, the mighty German artillery bombardment opened on February 21. For nine hours, like booming flails, the big guns systematically worked over the French defences, thrashing and chopping the trenches, and pulverizing anything that moved.

At 4 p.m. preliminary patrols of German foot soldiers went in to probe the shattered enemy lines. To their surprise they were met in the Bois des Caures by a stiff resistance, organized by the imperturbable Driant. The guns opened up again, and the following day, waves of German infantry overwhelmed Driant's heroic band and the gallant Colonel was shot dead leading his surviving troops in a fighting retreat. But still, somehow, pockets of resistance remained.

As the Germans moved in to the forward villages defending Verdun on the right bank of the River Meuse, snipers opened up from the cellars of smashed houses. For the third time the guns spoke, and the remorseless grey tide rolled over tiny hamlets so smashed that their bricks were never to be put together again—Haumont, Beaumont and Louvemont fell.

The French resistance had delayed the German timetable, unfolding with mathematical precision, but nothing could disguise the fact that the attack was succeeding and Verdun itself was threatened: panic-stricken and shell-shocked troops appeared in its streets shouting 'Sauve qui peut!' But one massive obstacle barred the path—the huge hump of Fort Douaumont, largest and most modern of the defensive bastions and lynchpin of the Right Bank defences. So long as Douaumont remained in French hands, all was not lost. Thus far, the Fort had survived the devastating gunfire relatively unscathed. The shells had hardly dented its solid concrete and steel carapace.

But then the incredible happened—news spread that 'old father Douaumont' had fallen. The French government could not believe the rumours, and desperately denied them, but the report was true: individual patrols of scattered German units had entered the great Fort unchallenged and found it virtually deserted. One Pioneer Sergeant had rounded up most of its sparse garrison single-handed! Due to a farcical series of mistakes, the Fort had fallen. With Douaumont gone, the road to Verdun seemed open.

At this supreme crisis, even Papa Joffre was persuaded to bestir himself: his chief subordinate de Castelnau made a whirlwind tour of inspection, stiffened the flagging defences and recommended the appointment of General Henri Philippe Pétain to hold the town. Pétain was located pleasuring a mistress in a Paris hotel, and, in a new version of the Francis Drake bowls legend, agreed to accept the Command—the following morning.

Defending was what the pessimistic Pétain knew most about. Alone among France's generals, this cautious northerner, already an elderly man, rejected the prevailing offensive *à outrance* doctrine. He perceived that unprotected infantry could not prevail against artillery and machine guns. Like the peasant he was, he hoarded his soldiers' lives as though they were so many *sous*, saved up for a rainy day—no wonder the *poilus* loved him. As Pétain arrived on the scene, bringing order out of chaos, the German attack began to run into problems of its own making. Falkenhayn's meanness with men meant that the attacking forces were hard put to hold the ground they had won, particularly as losses from the French artillery on the left bank of the Meuse were mounting unacceptably.

Reluctantly, Falkenhayn gave the Crown Prince permission to extend the attack to the left bank, and took the first fateful step in escalating the battle beyond the strict limits he had set. More men would mean more casualties, and Falkenhayn's strategy of attrition would soon prove a two-edged sword that cut into his own hand: inflicting heavy losses on the enemy meant inflicting almost equally grievious casualties on his own side. His plan had unaccountably overlooked this fact.

As 'Little Willy' launched his men against their new goal, a hill on the left bank bearing the grim name of 'Le Mort Homme', Pétain was given a breathing space to organize the Verdun defence. He cleared the only safe road into the city, the route south-west to Bar-le-Duc, and scoured France for vehicles to provide the hard-pressed salient with men and supplies. Soon a non-stop two-way traffic was rolling along the little road, which was dubbed the *Voie Sacrée* (Sacred Way). Any truck which broke down was ruthlessly thrown into the ditch and cannibalized for spare parts. In the first week of March, 190,000 men poured in to strengthen Verdun, and Pétain devised a system of quick rotation so that no unit spent more than a few days stretch in the battle furnace.

Meanwhile the enclosed battlefield was becoming like a vision out of Dante. It was the first Great War battle to acquire those sinister characteristics that were to become so typical of the war: the blasted ground, the trenches and villages taken and retaken, and reduced to nothing but connected, stinking shellholes by the relentless battering of the guns. Major movements scaled down into localized hand-to-hand fighting were made more horrible and terrifying by the German use of a new weapon—the flamethrower. To the men of both sides, cowering in their holes, harried, as like as not, by their own guns, eating and sleeping in company with the corpses of their comrades for days and weeks on end, it began to seem that the real enemy was the battle itself, an inhuman machine of fire, iron and blood that required endless supplies of fresh young flesh to fuel its terrible engine.

By means of these nit-picking local actions, the Germans nibbled and tunnelled their way to the bald, blasted summit of Le Mort Homme by the end of March—only to find that the elusive French guns were still blazing at them from a neighbouring ridge, Côte 304, even further away from their alleged target of Verdun. April was largely devoted to clearing this festering spot—at the cost of ten thousand lives. The total battle casualties by May were well over 100,000 dead on each side—a figure which should have frightened Falkenhayn, who must have seen that he had created a Frankenstein's monster that was out of control. But this remote, mysterious man seemed to lack the will to pull out of a losing game. In truth, Verdun was becoming of mystical significance to the Germans as well, and taking it was, for them, becoming as vital as holding it was for the French. So Falkenhayn, like an obsessed gambler, pressed on, upping the stakes and wearily ordering a reluctant Crown Prince to take Verdun whatever the cost.

The fearful toll of battle was making an indelible and gloomy impression on Pétain as he watched the young conscripts stagger past his HQ on the Voie Sacrée like ghosts returning from hell. Now that the immediate danger had passed, France could afford to return to its aggressive old ways, and Pétain, whose rocklike calm—immortalized in the phrase *Ils ne passeront pas—on les aura*, ('They shall not pass—we'll get them')—had saved the day. He was booted up to a regional command and immediate control of Verdun was handed over to more dashing and ferocious generals, in the shape of a thrusting and confident artilleryman named Robert Nivelle, and the fierce Charles Mangin 'The Butcher', whose favourite troops were black Senegalese from France's West African colonies.

The savage struggle at Verdun had made enormous inroads into French manpower, and in May, Joffre told Haig that France could no longer play the leading role in the Somme attack, the brunt of the burden would now have to be borne by Britain. Moreover the date for the assault must be brought forward from August to July, and the main motive now was not so much the hoped-for breakthrough, but to take the strain of Verdun from French shoulders.

Back at Verdun itself, the focus of the fighting had switched back to the Right Bank, where the Germans were making a push on a narrow front towards another fort, Vaux. The Fort's Commander, Major Raynal, was determined that Vaux would not be another Douaumont—he would fight, and proceeded to do so. A protracted struggle went on in the fort's subterranean galleries and passages for a week in nightmarish conditions of heat and stench before the heroic garrison was forced by thirst to surrender. In a chivalrous gesture, the Crown Prince allowed Raynal to keep his sword in captivity in recognition of his courage, a privilege denied to another young officer taken prisoner near Douaumont—Charles de Gaulle.

The blocking of the advance for that vital seven days was enough—by the end of June, Falkenhayn was forced to withdraw men from Verdun and rush them to bolster the Eastern Front where a successful Russian general, Brusilov, had hit the Austrians with an offensive. The remaining men before Verdun were galvanized for a last desperate effort.

Using Vaux as a stepping-stone, on June 23 the Germans lunged forward on a three-mile narrow front. Their target was Fort Souville, the last bastion on the heights directly overlooking Verdun. If Souville fell, Verdun was doomed. For the occasion, the Germans had massed mysterious piles of shells marked with green crosses—they contained phosgene, a deadly new form of poison gas. But the gas clung to the bottom of the Verdun ravines in the humid summer air and its effects were nullified. Although the Germans, who were short of water as well as reserves, took the village of Fleury and a casement called Thiaumont, both of which changed hands many times during the battle, their great effort failed. Souville held, and the Kaiser, who had journeyed to his son's HQ in hopes of a breakthrough, went home empty-handed. A few days later the British struck on the Somme and the German pressure at Verdun loosened. But the Field Commander, Knobelsdorf, persuaded the Crown Prince to make one last do or die effort.

On the plateau before Souville the parched combatants flailed at each other like dying animals in the heavy heat. The Germans were being forced into an ever-narrower funnel because of their declining numbers, and their final bid, when it came on July 11, was launched on a front of yards rather than miles. The spearhead of the attack actually reached the glacis of Souville, but a handful of French defenders sallied forth under a Lt. Dupuy and beat them back.

These Germans had seen a tantalizing glimpse of Verdun in the distance—their goal; so near, but still so terribly far.

The Battle of Verdun would go on for another five months as the French under Nivelle and Mangin executed a series of well-planned counter-attacks to win back Douaumont and virtually all the ground they had lost, making it the longest battle in history. But the Germans had shot their bolt, and their total estimated losses of 282,323 were only slightly less than the 315,000 French dead.

If 1916 was the watershed of the war, the midway point of no return, beyond which nothing would or could ever be the same again, then Verdun, and more especially that last gasp attack on July 11, was the turning-point itself.

Had Souville fallen Verdun would have inevitably gone with it, and the effect of such a psychological disaster on the already shaky French morale would have been incalculable. But Verdun, thanks to Driant, Castelnau, Pétain, Brusilov, Raynal and Dupuy, and thousands of other nameless heroes who fought and died in the anonymous wilderness of fire, did not fall, and German hopes of victory received a mortal shock.

In the short term, then, the battle can be counted as a French win despite their greater losses, and the town has become the focus of mystical nationalism ever since.

But in the longer term, the grievous sufferings on the battlefield afflicted France in a way that may have eventually justified Falkenhayn—though years after his death—in 1940. The ghastly blood sacrifice bruised France's spirit where the more resilient Teutons brushed it aside.

The seepage of morale led, in 1917, to the mutiny of a great part of the French army, and formed the 'Maginot mentality'. Maginot himself was a sergeant who lost a leg at Verdun, and later, as Minister of War, forced through the construction of a greater Verdun—the Maginot Line behind whose impregnable walls France slumbered until rudely awakened by Manstein's tanks in 1940. A heroic generation held Verdun—just—but it could not be asked to do it again.

It is one of history's more brutal ironies that the chief hero of that generation, Pétain himself, should become the chief villain twenty years later when a nation crumbled and fell—and 'they'—finally—did 'pass'.

11. Hell Grown Cold—
Visiting Verdun

The slopes of the Mort Homme are covered with a forest of young firs, planted in the 1930s when all other attempts at cultivation had failed. The wind whistles through the trees and the birds sing, and that is all. It is the nearest thing to a desert in Europe. Nobody ever seems to visit it. Even lovers eschew the unchallenged privacy of its glades. The ghosts abound; it is one of the eeriest places in this world. A grown man will not willingly repeat the experience of getting lost in the labyrinth of firecuts that crisscross the deserted plantations . . . How much longer will the ghosts of Verdun continue to torment France? When will they be exorcised? Or will France have to wait until the eerie forests of the Mort Homme mature and are hewn down, and farms and happy villages once again populate its dead slopes?

Alistair Horne, 'The Price of Glory'

Of all the battlefields of the Great War none can make such a profound impression on the visitor as Verdun.

This place, whose very name is a symbol of sacrifice and suffering for France, preserves as in a timeless capsule countless reminders of those tragic, heroic and ghastly days. Wherever you travel on that concentrated killing-ground, whose total size does not exceed the area of London's parks, you are led back, time and time again, to the battle and forced, willy-nilly, to meditate on the madness of mankind.

Verdun is situated in the region of Lorraine, an out-of-the-way corner of unfashionable north-east France. Tucked away in a remote border area between France, Belgium, Germany and Luxembourg, it is near no major city and on few tourist itineraries. But those who do come—and they still do in a steady stream—know why they are there. The billboards outside the city proclaim: 'Visit the Battlefields and Museums', taking a shame-faced pride in Verdun's tragic claim to fame. But ironically it also calls itself the 'City of Peace' and a wall in the centre of the town sports a brightly-coloured series of murals painted by

L/Cpl. Leonard Keyworth (standing on right) with comrades of the 24th London Regiment (The Queen's)—displaying some of the aggression which won him the VC at Festubert in 1915

Trench tasks: a fatigue party carrying duckboards over a support trench. Cambrai, January 12, 1917. Note fixed bayonets and Verey light flare

Trench tasks: New Zealanders 'digging in'. They are joining up shell-holes to form a slit trench. Somme, September 15, 1916

Men of the Yorks and Lancs Regiment taking up wire for a night wiring party. Oppy, near Arras

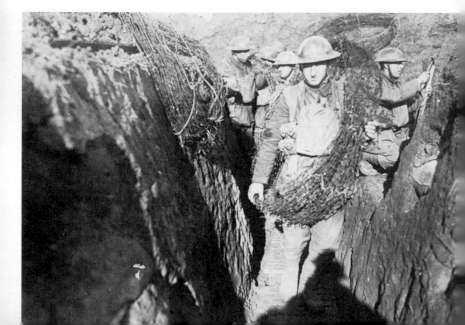

Trench treats: the rum ration. A tot of rum was served together with tea on most days and before battle

Serving stew. Every effort was made to bring hot meals to the front line in large canisters. Stew was a luxury, bully beef and biscuits a staple

British soldiers envied the luxury and depth of German dug-outs; here is a typical enemy forward communications HQ

The Germans carved these deep caves into the Chemin des Dames ridge on the Aisne. They emerged from them to take a murderous toll of the French, attacking in April 1917 in the disastrous Nivelle offensive. Picture taken in 1982

General Sir Henry Horne, Commander of the British First Army, addressing a parade to mark the anniversary of the outbreak of war; August 5, 1917, at his HQ, Château de Ranchicourt, near Arras

The Comtesse de Ranchicourt talking to the author outside the château, 1982. General Horne presented her with a horse in 1918. In 1940 Goering was billeted here, as was the author's father in the First World War

British Guards wiring party crossing remains of Yser–Ypres canal at
Boesinghe on makeshift bridge of duckboards and stretchers. Opening day of
the Battle of Passchendaele, July 31, 1917. German prisoners are being
escorted to rear, at left of picture

Battle of Langemarck (part of Passchendaele attack) –British soldiers watch
distant shellburst. Note phlegmatic pipesmokers on right. The corrugated
dug-out roof is still a feature on farms in the area. August 18, 1917

'Nothing can compare with the utter devastation and despair of the Passchendaele ridge.' L. C. Stewart, R.G.A. The ridge after Canadian capture of Passchendaele village. The hump on the horizon is the remains of the village church; November 1917

Air photograph of Beaumont Hamel sector. Distance lends detachment. This bird's-eye view clearly shows the 'battlemented' firebays in the front trenches, 'zigzag' support and communication trenches, and shell craters. Note white chalk spoil and T-shaped saps. (See diagram on page 44)

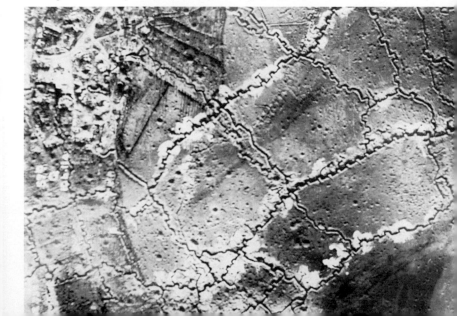

German wire near Beaumont Hamel, Somme, November 1916. Picture shows two of the chief hazards on the Western Front—metal and mud

Wire on the Western Front today

Verdun's schoolchildren on the theme—here a dove breaks missiles in its beak, there Verdun, city of the frontier, draws embattled east and west together in a reluctant embrace.

This contradiction characterizes the place. True, nearly 800,000 men were slaughtered here in one dreadful year, but that figure was the price paid for a sort of immortal glory—one found not only in the innumerable memorials which dot the battlefields, but also indelibly etched on the memories of those who were there, and handed down to their descendants. The potent legend of Verdun lives on, and the coach- and car-borne Germans and French who come to gaze at the scars of war serve to scratch the scab and keep it bloody and red. We are now at the point where fact becomes story, and history is dissolved into symbol and myth. Far from dying out with its survivors, Verdun looms larger as it fades into the past.

For the visitor, one way to approach the sacred battlefield is from either flank of what once was the Verdun salient—the French Ypres—a bulge of land jutting into the German lines on the banks of the River Meuse. The first fighting for possession of Verdun took place on the wings as the Germans struggled to push into the sides of the salient in 1915. Much of this tussle took the form of mine warfare. On the left flank, west of Verdun, lay the Butte of Vauquois, a hill on the edge of the Argonne Forest which was in 1914 topped by the village of Vauquois. No longer. The village was literally blown away in a series of gigantic underground explosions as French and Germans struggled savagely for possession of the strategic ridge. I visited Vauquois as I walked from Varennes in the Argonne towards Verdun. A steep ascent from the new Vauquois, a hamlet now nestling at the foot of the hill, led me to the edge of one of the deepest of the mine craters. Blown by the Germans in 1915, it claimed the lives of hundreds of Frenchmen. Gingerly, I made my way down from the lip of the crater to its centre, avoiding the rusty spikes of the *Frise de Cheval*—barbed wire entanglements which, almost uniquely, are still in place in Vauquois. The bottom of the crater, the 'plug' where the explosives were planted, was filled with old railway sleepers. The Butte of Vauquois is crowned with a tall monument to the combatants, together with a large tricolour floating on the breeze, and orientation tables to explain the layout of the battlefield. Precipitous paths wind around the rims of the craters which pit the place.

The 'twin' of Vauquois, another hill which became the scene of relentless mine warfare on the other side of Verdun, is the hill of Les Eparges, a spur jutting over the vast plain of the Woevre river. Unaccountably the French allowed the Germans to gain this strategic height early in the war, realized their mistake too late, and spent the rest of the war in prolonged and fruitless efforts to dislodge the unwelcome visitors. Eventually the exhausted *poilus* were replaced by the fresh blood of the 'Doughboys'—the Americans, who were allotted the St. Mihiel and Argonne sectors in 1918, and to them fell the honour of finally taking what was left of Les Epargues, though by then hill had largely been replaced by hole—so many mines had exploded in the subterranean struggle.

Today, Les Epargues is a beautiful and peaceful place. Like Verdun, it has been planted over with conifer trees which mercifully conceal the scars of war. Neat tracks wind through the forest, giving occasional views of the craters, and the vast panorama of the Woevre plain itself.

Luckily I had an aid to imagination, in the shape of *Storm of Steel*, a book published by the German writer Ernst Jünger who had been present in the fiercest phase of the 1915 fighting. Unlike most of the memoirists who penned their recollections of the war, Jünger positively gloried in the experience, both at the time and subsequently. He took a veritable delight in the business of soldiers killing and being killed, seeing it as a peak experience unattainable in the corrupt world of peace. Four years of service in élite units of the Western Front did not shake his joy, and it was a nice coincidence to read in the papers the week I visited his wartime haunts that the old warrior was still stirring controversy.

As recipient of Germany's premier literary award, the Goethe Prize, the 87-year-old Jünger faced a new storm of disapproval, and a boycott by the Social Democrats on the Frankfurt City Council who awarded the prize. His militarist creed, albeit mellowed by his experience of Nazi oppression and the death of his son in a Second World War 'suicide squad', still had the power to stir hatred.

Whatever one's views of Jünger's politics, *Storm of Steel* is an undeniably powerful and evocative work, as the following passage describing the Les Epargues fighting shows:

> Blood-stained fragments of equipment and flesh were caught on the bushes all round . . . a strange and oppressive sight that made me think of the red-backed shrike that spits its prey on the thorns . . . Right in our way lay a dead horse with gaping wounds and, beside it, smoking entrails . . . On the tortured ground lay the dead and dying that the attack had cost us, their faces towards the enemy and their grey coats scarcely visible against the ground. A gigantic fellow whose red beard was smeared with blood stared

into the sky, his fingers clutching the loose soil. Another, younger, lying in a shell-hole, stirred and turned over. The sallowness of death was already on his face. He did not seem to like our looking at him. With a listless movement he drew his cloak over his face and lay still. We had our first casualty. A shrapnel bullet had severed Fusilier Stoller's carotid artery. Three bandages were saturated instantly, and within a few seconds he had bled to death . . . My attention was caught by a sickly smell and a bundle hanging on the wire . . .

I found myself in front of a huddled-up corpse, a Frenchman, the putrid flesh, like the flesh of fishes, gleamed greenish-white through the rents in the uniform. I turned away and then started back in horror: close to me a figure cowered beside a tree. It wore the shining straps and belt of the French, and high upon its back there was still the loaded pack. Empty eye sockets and a few wisps of hair on the black and weathered skull told me that this was no living man. Another sat with the upper part of the body clapped down over the legs as though broken through the middle. All round lay dozens of corpses, putrefied, calcified, mummified, fixed in a ghastly dance of death. The French must have carried on for months without burying their fallen comrades . . . A trunk with head and neck shot away was clipped in among some riven woodwork. White cartilage shone out from the red and blackened flesh. It was hard to understand. Nearby a young fellow lay on his back, his glazed eyes and his fingers fixed in their last aim. It was a weird sensation to look into those dead and questioning eyes. It gave me a shudder that all through the war I never quite lost . . .

Notices around Les Epargues remind visitors that they are in a giant cemetery—although the graves are all unmarked. One wonders, and treads more lightly at the thought of how many hundreds of men lie forever entombed underfoot. Laid on the memorials are individual plaques, now sadly chipped and forgotten, placed by grieving relatives. A word that often recurs on these—*disparus*—is a poignant reminder that many of the men who fought here like the novelist Alain-Fourneir—simply vanished off the face of the earth—blown away, buried alive, or, as Jünger indicates, left in the open as carrion.

A third way to approach Verdun is the route that so many soldiers followed—many never to retrace their tracks. This is the infamous *Voie Sacrée*, the road to Bar-le-Duc, that was the only route into the town not vulnerable to the hungry German guns, and chosen by Pétain as the main line of supply.

Now a pleasant winding country road, the 'Sacred Way' is the only road in the whole of France to be excused the bureaucratic anonymous numbers which label the country's road grid—it is called "RNVS" (*Route Nationale—Voie Sacrée*). It is curiously empty—one almost expects to see the ghosts of the aged trucks, loaded with men and munitions, chugging forward into the carnage. Approaching Verdun, the road passes through Souilly, the village where Pétain established his HQ at the Mairie. The building is still there, complete with the flight of steps where Pétain's successor in the Verdun command, Nivelle, uttered his self-confident phrase 'We have the formula'—a formula which proved the following year to be just another recipe for death and mutiny, and almost plunged France into collapse and a repeat of the Russian Revolution.

The kilometre stones on the road are also different from those on other French roads—they bear a bronze French helmet of Great War vintage, wreathed in metal laurel leaves. Verdun is still a garrison town, boasting several large barracks—monuments not only to the innate conservatism of the French Army but also a reminder that for France, danger still lurks in the east. Memories last long here. Do they remember the arson of Attila's hordes? Or the subsequent attacks of the Prussians? Do they fear that once more, at some future date, Mongol hordes will sweep down to kill and burn?

Vauban's huge citadel, the nerve centre of the Verdun fortress, is not much used by the army today. Its damp, stalactite-hung corridors are now open to the public. Wandering through the underground chambers, we come across the skeletal iron beds of the soldiers who sheltered here in the dark, thankful for a few hours of rest and relief from the guns which thundered insistently but impotently outside Vauban's solid walls. One of the citadel's corridors contains a macabre reminder of one of France's most hallowed shrines—the tomb of the unknown soldier under the Arc de Triomphe in the heart of Paris. It was here in the citadel that the choice of the warrior was made. Eight coffins containing the remains of unidentified soldiers who had fallen at Verdun were collected and assembled on trestles. One of them was chosen at random, and amidst all the pomp and panoply that the French nation is capable of mustering, was shipped to Paris to lie forever in an unquiet grave under a flickering flame, and amidst the roar of the city's traffic. The other seven were buried with full honours in Verdun's chief cemetery. But replicas of coffins still lie on the trestles, covered with plastic tricolours.

Verdun's main street is dominated by the massive Victory Monument—a sombre statue of a cloaked and helmeted Dark Ages warrior at the head of a wide flight of steps. The Town Hall contains a small war museum, and statues of France's marshals are plastered everywhere. Even some of the shops contain grim little souvenirs and the ubiquitous peepshow machines with three-D photographs of the war. The ugly twin towers of the cathedral lower over the city. Here, in the courtyard, the first shell fired in the battle exploded.

My base in Verdun was 'Les Charmettes', an old house on the outskirts of town on the right bank of the Meuse. It was the family home of Jean-François Valet, a French friend who was to take some of the pictures for my book. The house has links with the citadel, in that it was owned by Jean-François' great grandfather who built the extensions to the citadel during France's programme of intensive fortification at the end of the nineteenth century, when a renewal of war with Germany seemed all too likely. The house had changed little since those days—in the battle it was used as a French communications post and was surrounded by a huge earth mound. Inside, I found on a dusty shelf some glass plate photographs of the *Belle époque* before the war. These evocative, Proustian plates showed a world lost: ladies in high-necked dresses sit daintily in sun-kissed gardens; fencers, waxed moustaches quivering, pose with upraised épées, their hands on slim elegant hips. Jean-François' great-uncle, poses cockily—a medical student, he jauntily twists a fibula in his hand, happily unaware that gnawing tuberculosis bacilli were to take his life before the holocaust would swallow up his world.

More martial relics littered the house, a box of bullets, looking as good as new, a rusty bayonet used as a poker, and the nose-cones of shells, laid like sacrificial tributes before a weather-beaten statue of Ceres, goddess of the harvest, which stands in the garden.

The house is now used only as a holiday home by the Valet family, and its neglected air adds to the charm. Unpicked 'Mirabelle' plums and pears rot underfoot in the garden. Behind the high wall which surrounds the property, it almost seems as though time has stood still—trapped in the garden, a prisoner, like the solitary sheep which grazes among the yew trees and laurel bushes.

Last year, Jean-François' father started to renovate his old home—a new floor of tiles replaced the woodworm-eaten floorboards, an inside toilet and bathroom replaced a hosepipe and trips into the garden with a spade. With this onset of mod cons, the house gained a future—but lost a past—and a lot of character.

I devoted several leisurely days to a thorough exploration of the battlefield beginning at the place where the Germans had started, at the northern end, the Bois des Caures, where the gallant Col. Driant made his last stand. So I walked along the road which winds out of the town, following the meanderings of the Meuse. The road passes through the villages which fell like ninepins beneath the cannonball of the original German attack—Bras, Vacherauville, Samogneux, Brabant.

At Bras, the battlefield claimed what may have been its final victim—General Karl Stulpnagel, German Military Governor of Paris in the Second World War. Here, where a small road leads down to the east canal of the Meuse, the General, a veteran of Verdun, chose to die. The year was 1944, in the weeks following the abortive July Plot to kill Hitler. Stulpnagel was the most successful of those unhappy conspirators—his men had actually succeeded in taking over Paris in the wake of Stauffenberg's bomb and had rounded up all the SS men in the city. When news came through that the plot in Germany had misfired, the SS were freed, and Stulpnagel returned to Germany to face the music. He stopped his car at Bras, and minutes later his chauffeur heard a shot and found the General floating in the canal. But the job had been botched, and Stulpnagel, who had only succeeded in shooting out his eyes, was fished out, patched up in a Verdun hospital, and sent home to an ignominious and terrifying end on a Gestapo gallows.

Beyond Brabant I passed a German cemetery where young men from the Federal Republic were carefully tending the graves. At Samogneux, I turned off the main road along a lonely little-used road that was signposted to Haumont, the first of Verdun's nine 'Ghost' villages—hamlets that were totally destroyed in the battle and never rebuilt or reclaimed by their scattered inhabitants. The road soon ran into the forest.

The forest of Verdun is not like other woodlands; no ancient groves with a past going back to the mists of time here: this forest is primarily an act of 'cover up'. In 1918, the end of the war found the previously peaceful cultivated land looking like a lunar landscape, complete with craters, a spider's web of trenches, and iron debris that yielded 30 tons of metal an acre for ten years. The topsoil had literally disappeared—blasted, burned and bombed away. By 1923 it was clear that any attempt to return the battlefield to normal agricultural cultivation was doomed, and France's Parliament designated the area as a state-owned forest.

During the 1930s, the battlefield on the Right Bank and the Mort Homme was planted with coniferous trees, primarily Austrian pines and spruce. The original deciduous woods, which covered one third of the surface area, were restored on their original sites, and in 1974 an intense programme was begun by the French Forestry Commission to plant indigenous beech trees and gradually return the whole area to deciduous woodland.

Notices remind visitors: 'These forests recalling sad memories are intended to be calm. Please turn off all transistor radios, don't use motor cycles on the forest paths, and don't shout.'

But to anyone sensitive to the special atmosphere, such rules are redundant; Verdun imposes its own sense of awe and respect.

As soon as you enter the greenery it is clear that this is no normal forest, glancing into the thick undergrowth on either side of the path you see that every inch of the ground is pitted and pockmarked by shell craters. Often you can see a trench winding away into the woods, and if you duck into the trees it will not be long before you stumble on some battlefield relic—a shell, a water bottle, hand grenades, barbed wire, or the occasional helmet. Even, in some places, a moss-encrusted fragment of human bone, Normally it is possible to identify the side which contributed the artifact—German grenades and water bottles are quite different from their distinctive French counterparts, but the bones could be anybody's—death took no sides.

The route I was following soon brought me to the site of Haumont village. The nine villages that were destroyed forever are oddly impressive. Most are commemorated by a tiny chapel built on the site of the former village church. The chapels are surrounded by a wall marking the old churchyard, and occasionally, former inhabitants of the village have been buried here. Outside the walls are the tumbled heaps of bricks and stones marking the houses of the village. At Haumont a bunker was constructed by the Germans from the stones; it exists still, skewed out of true by shellfire.

Haumont lay directly in the path of the first German attack on February 21, 1916. On February 22, the French defenders of the village, dazed by the mighty bombardment, had observed masses of grey-clad German infantry debouching out of the nearby trees of the Bois d'Haumont. They had turned their machine-guns on the enemy, who had temporarily withdrawn and called down an even heavier barrage. By three in the afternoon less than 500 men were left alive in the village and the Germans moved in for the kill. Their flamethrowers cleared out the last nests of resistance in the cellars of the shattered houses. The commander of the regiment holding Haumont, Lt.-Col. Bonviolle, made a hair's-breadth escape with 60 of his original 2,000 men, and Haumont was lost.

My next goal was the Bois de Caures itself, where Driant fought and died. The Colonel's Forward Command Post 'R2' almost miraculously survived the battle, and has been proudly preserved. A long concrete bunker in a clearing, it was from here that the Colonel organized his chain of redoubts that held up the German attack against overwhelming odds for those two vital first days of the battle. At length, with half his HQ destroyed by a direct hit from a heavy gun, and menaced with complete encirclement by German forces who had infiltrated on both his flanks, Driant ordered his surviving men to fall back. But they came under withering enfilade fire and Driant was shot through the head, dying within seconds. Only a couple of hundred of his original 1,200 men managed to find their way back to the French lines.

Close to the HQ is a monument to Driant's courageous Chasseurs, and nearby are some of their graves. A stele in the forest marks the spot where Driant himself died.

The next objective for the Germans, and for me, was another village, Beaumont. It fell on the following day, February 23, but once again only after a heroic defence by the French, whose machine-guns were only silenced when the hamlet's houses were brought down on top of them. The waves of attackers suffered such casualties that a German officer had to save the life of the French Commander from his angry men when the village finally succumbed. Beaumont today consists of a chapel-shrine, a graveyard where some pre-war tombs are preserved, and mounds of rubble where houses used to be.

Beaumont stands on a rise overlooking the crinkled mass of ravines that forms the right bank of the Meuse—down into the next ravine to the south and up again on the next rise, the forest track brought me to the site of the village of Louvemont. This insignificant place was of great strategic importance to the next stage of the German advance—the seizure of Fort Douaumont. Louvemont commanded a significant hill, the Côte de Poivre (Pepper Hill), and was the key to three vital ravines which all pointed south-east of the village, like the parallel prongs of a fork, towards the fabled fort itself.

The defenders of the village were not a coherent unit, but the scattered survivors of previous engagements who had found themselves lumped together in Louvemont. Dazed and battered, but still unbowed, these men braced themselves to face the German onslaught on the morning of February 25. First came the by-now-familiar flame-throwers. By one o'clock in the afternoon, their scorching tongues of liquid fire had theoretically licked out the opposition still lurking in the cellars of the village. But there still remained another dashing French colonel—each village seemed to boast one of these magnificent specimens in these desperate days. This one, Col. Theuriet, calmly ordered the remnants of his men to fix bayonets and counter-attack. The Germans were amazed when they saw the oncoming wall of 'horizon blue' led by Theuriet, calmly puffing a cigar! But such gallant gestures were in vain. Remorselessly, the inevitable machine-guns opened up, scything down the ranks and killing the colonel and all his officers, save one lieutenant who ordered a retreat. By three o'clock, Louvemont was finally in German hands, and with it fell the Côte de Poivre—the way to Douaumont lay open.

Like Haumont and Beaumont, Louvemont is off the beaten tourist tracks around Verdun, and no living soul is likely to disturb the musings of the solitary visitor. It is also probably the richest in relics—astoundingly, within a few stumbling steps of the wall which surrounds the chapel-shrine, I discovered a dug-out that had clearly once been the cellar of one of the village houses. Within it was the remains of a French soldier, or so I deduced from the pathetic evidence—the distinct metal gourd—which usually contained Pinard rather than water,—and next to it some bones—human vertebrae and a couple of ribs. With a chill shudder I moved on, picking my way between the unexploded shells lying about, until the remains of the houses petered out behind a deep trench that may once have formed a perimeter defence of the village.

The next day I followed the unrolling impetus of the German advance up to the village and Fort of Douaumont. The Fort fell first, in an astounding episode that is still the source of embarrassment and debate among French historians. Small patrols of German infantry, approaching the Fort on February 25 in disconnected groups, found themselves under the twin threat of destruction from the plunging shells of their own artillery and persistent machine-gun fire from the French who were still holding Douaumont village, just north of the Fort. To escape this harassment, one group of men hopped down into the Fort's moat, thinking, no doubt, to escape the frying pan by leaping into the fire. To their astonishment, the Fort's defenders took no notice of their intrusion, and, emboldened, they formed a human pyramid and their leader, Sergeant Kunze, squeezed in through an open casement. This intrepid man wasted no time in rounding up a substantial part of the garrison of elderly gunners and Territorial reservists, including the crew of the Fort's biggest gun, a 155-mm cannon. The sergeant was followed into the Fort by three German officers—Radtke, Haupt and

Brandis. The latter, an inveterate braggart, was sent back with the news and took the opportunity to claim that he had taken the Fort virtually single-handed. This legend, convincingly repudiated by Verdun's English historian, Alistair Horne, is still repeated by the guides who show the modern visitors round the Fort.

Stunned by the loss of their invulnerable Fort the French were—and are—inclined to attribute its fall to rank trickery by their opponents, and a French historian of the battle, Durassié, who was fighting nearby on the day, claims that German soldiers disguised themselves in the uniforms of French Zouaves and gained entry in the time-honoured way of the Trojan Horse. But the sad truth is that the French had only themselves to blame—the Fort had been denuded of troops and guns thanks to Joffre's commands early in the war, and frantic last-minute orders to reinforce it after the German attack never got through. This lapse was to cost France dear; it is estimated that 100,000 lives were lost in the repeated attempts to take the Fort before it was finally recaptured the following October.

By then, 'old father Douaumont', as the Germans called the Fort, had also become their graveyard: most disastrously on May 8 when some troops, brewing up coffee with explosive fuel, ignited flame-throwers which in turn touched off a magazine of 155-mm shells. Six hundred and fifty men perished in the blast, and many of the victims were walled up in one of the casements for all time. This catacomb is still commemorated by gigantic wreaths from Germany.

When the French finally retook the Fort it was a battered wreck; its concrete roof was laid open to the sky by the constant hammering of hundreds of tons of high-explosive shells. Today, visitors are led round the upper corridors of the Fort: its two underground galleries are permanently waterlogged and one shudders to think what gruesome remains would float up were they ever to be dredged.

In one room, a flickering permanent film show recounts the story of the battle over and over again. The chamber of the 155 cannon that was seized single-handed by Kunze, can still be seen. The machinery of the vast gun, like a huge piece of modern abstract sculpture, rusts quietly—its technically advanced machinery, which could raise and lower the gun turret, now mummified into permanent paralysis.

The Douaumont guides, veterans of the Second World War, for the original battle veterans have all faded away, crisply roll the gran-diloquent phrases around their lips, concentrating on the retaking of the Fort by Mangin's men without mentioning the awkward facts of how it was lost. Our guide had his own novel method of demonstrating what it felt like to be in Douaumont, as the shells burst outside. He casually lit a firecracker and tossed it into an empty casement; the hollow bang echoed, reverberating, around the walls, but somehow, it was not the real thing.

Outside, on the Fort's glacis, the cupolas of the guns with their solid steel cases and the observation domes which guided them can still be seen. Bullet and shell scars pock the massive metal with weird, intricate patterns. Idly, I knocked on one of the turrets. At once a female voice, belonging to a German girl tourist, replied 'Herein!' So it was all in vain, I thought . . . they are in possession once again!

Douaumont is the centre of the battlefield; within a few hundred yards of this spot are most of the memorials and the sites of the fiercest fighting. Around this area, the tide of battle rolled, receded, and swept up again and again. Natural features disappeared under the pulverizing rain of fire and steel. Stinking, corpse-clogged craters became the strongpoints where men lived and died. One such place has been preserved in all its grisly realism—the trench of bayonets.

This position was held by a regiment from France's Vendée department—the rural Royalist region on the west coast which maintained such a stubborn resistance to the elsewhere victorious French revolutionaries at the end of the eighteenth century. During the most savage phase of the summer fighting, when the French were struggling to maintain a toehold on the Right Bank heights, this regiment vanished from the face of the earth. After the war their trench was discovered, completely filled with soil. From the earth, at regular intervals, the muzzles of rifles protruded, complete with fixed bayonets. Under each rifle was a corpse: the men of the 137th Infantry Regiment had died at their posts, either entombed by the German bombardment, or respectfully buried by their victorious foes.

An American millionaire, impressed by this fabulous story, paid for the construction of a concrete shelter to encase the trench. It can still be seen, with the twisted rusting rifles still sticking up defiantly through the ground.

Just round the corner from the trench, overlooking Verdun's most hellish ravine, the Ravin de la Dame (nicknamed the Ravin de la Mort) is the supreme, towering memorial to this and every battle—the Douaumont Ossuary. This vast, cathedral-like structure is a charnal house without compare: a rounded white building with a huge tower at its centre, from which, nightly, a revolving beacon illuminates the battlefield.

The Ossuary is divided into a series of chambers, into which were heaped the remains of over 100,000 soldiers of both sides, whose shattered fragments could not be identified. The visitor can walk around the Ossuary, peering into the windows of each of these chambers at the ghastly sights within: skulls, leg bones, ribs, vertebrae, are stacked in piles like a vision from a nightmare.

Inside, the Ossuary resembles a church, with consecrated candles burning in the gloom. Everywhere are plaques of regiments and individuals who vanished at Verdun. At the base of the tower, a small souvenir shop sells books, and tasteless battle trophies—ashtrays, postcards, bookmarks, tea-towels. As you ascend the steps of the tower, at each floor, more is revealed. There is another of the ubiquitous peepshow rooms, as if the imagination were not sufficient to reconstruct the horrors. Tailor's dummies dressed in the uniforms of both sides, fading sepia pictures of the vanished villages, and examples of the mortars, rifles, grenades and other weapons that reaped the appalling harvest of death.

The viewing gallery at the top of the tower looks out over the 15,000 graves in the Ossuary cemetery—the biggest Great War cemetery. You notice, among the uniform rows of white crosses, spade-shaped Moslem and Jewish tombs—a reminder that France had to call on her colonies to provide much of the lifeblood which drenched this ground. This bird's-eye view also gives a clear impression of the shell-ravaged ground, in the hollows and hummocks surrounding the nearby Ouvrage de Thiaumont, a small strongpoint which changed hands no less than fourteen times during the battle.

Walking southwards and downhill from the Ossuary you find the site of the most hotly-contested of all the villages—Fleury, which fell, was retaken, fell and was captured again, time after time, until it was utterly obliterated. Even the rubble which had been the houses was ground to dust and mingled like mortar with the mud. All that remains today is a shrine, named *Notre Dame d'Europe* in the pious hope of reconciliation and final peace.

Next to Fleury, surrounded by field guns, is a modern museum with an imaginative layout. The centrepiece is a tableau showing a typical battlefield scene, complete with real earth and shellholes, wire and weapons, and an electronic board with winking neon lights picking out the tide of war, as it rose and fell, across the map.

A few yards further on you come to the crossroads of the Chapelle St. Fine, where a monument depicting a dead lion marks the high-water mark of the German advance, in July 1916. Just beyond the crossroads, hidden in the woods, the intrepid visitor will find Souville, oldest of the

Verdun forts and nearest to the city. The glacis of this fort, now overgrown with trees, is the place where, according to some historians, Germany finally lost all hope of winning the war. 'Here', in the words of France's wartime president, Poincaré, 'are the walls upon which broke the supreme hopes of Imperial Germany'.

For it was upon this glacis that a few scattered German soldiers assembled, as their last bid to take Verdun faltered and died. But inside the Fort were no timid Territorials, as at Douaumont five long and weary months before, but battle-hardened veterans who, as soon as they heard that Germans were on the Fort, burst forth and drove them back.

The Fort is deserted and its masonry mouldering now, but a bold visitor can still venture down the tunnel leading from the main entrance, and, risking life and limb from chunks of crumbling concrete, explore the dark corridors within. Only the occasional tweet of a bird breaks the silence as you try to locate the command rooms where Mangin masterminded the recapture of Douaumont.

Further along the road from Souville, to the west, lies Fort Vaux, Douaumont's tiny twin, where the thirst-crazed garrison of Raynal held the whole German army at bay for a vital week in June. In these narrow, fetid tunnels, which are open to the public, a grim struggle to the death was waged with rifle, grenade, and finally bare hands. In the end, Raynal despatched his last messenger pigeon to inform his superiors that he could resist no longer, and Vaux fell, but its resistance may well have spelled the difference between victory and defeat, by buying the French that most precious commodity—time.

Outside the fort, the wide moats, or fosse, are grassed over now, and the mind must make an effort to visualize that savage siege, and to picture the besiegers lowering their bags of grenades, and touching them off outside the casement windows.

The next day I devoted to a tour of the Left Bank of the Meuse—the infamous Mort Homme sector. Retracing my steps up the river to Samogneux, I turned left and crossed the Meuse, coming to the ruins of the village of Forges, which stands astride a brook of the same name, a tributary of the main river. A new Forges has arisen a few yards away from the ruins of the old. My family has connections with Forges as my wife's great-uncle, a young French infantryman, was stationed here after his call-up in the last months of the great battle:

Private Antoine Godde, 44th French Infantry Regiment:

In the autumn of 1916 we were stationed on one side of the river

Forges and the Germans were on the other, with the ruins of the village lying just behind the French lines. By this stage of the war there was a general feeling of being 'fed up' among us younger conscripts.

Those fed-up feelings, built up by the constant slow bleeding to which the French had been subjected at Verdun, was to culminate, the following year, in the mutinies of large parts of the French army in the wake of Nivelle's disastrous offensive on the Aisne.

From Forges, on a day of glorious early September sunshine, I set off along a farm track that wound slowly through the fields upwards towards the menacing woods which now envelop the Mort Homme hill. As I left the light and entered again the cool of the woodland shade, the path was blocked by a group of foresters leaning on their scythes and regarding the lonely hiker with curiosity. A friendly '*Jour M'sieur* was exchanged as I plodded past. They were to be the last human faces I was to see that day, for, as Horne tells us, no one today visits this place which was, for a few weeks in March and April 1916, the focus of the Verdun fighting and the centre of a horrified world's attention.

Once again, I was following the track of the German advance: on March 14, also a day of radiant sun, the fury of the German assault on Verdun was switched to the left bank and flung in a head-on attack against the Mort Homme. Boosted by new reserves, the Crown Prince's soldiers crawled like grey ants further and further up the gentle slopes, inching their way from shell-hole to bloody shell-hole. The French fought back with deadly tenacity and the artillery of both sides played a mortal game with the infantrymen cowering in their holes—lashing them with savage strokes, which killed, buried, resurrected and buried again. As the Germans approached the summit of the hill, they moved within range of the French batteries on a neighbouring hill, Côte 304. It was decided to extend the Mort Homme front to take out this poisonous thorn in the side of the advance, and on April 9, a simultaneous assault, backed by seventeen trainloads of artillery ammunition, was launched. Despite losses, the French line held, and German casualties began to approach those of their opponents. It was on this day that Pétain told his men: *Courage! On les aura!*

Frustrated, the Germans, with typical ingenuity, set to literally digging their way onto the elusive summit. It was the entrances to these tunnels, buried somewhere deep in the woods, that I was now seeking. At the crest of a ridge I turned off into the woods, following a trench. In some places, the thorny undergrowth was so thick that I turned round and literally butted my way through backwards using my behind as a blunt ram!

This could have been very dangerous, as I was soon to find; rounding a firebay, I was detained by a particularly troublesome strand of thorn, which clung to my anorak like a restraining hand. Turning to deal with it, I glimpsed from the corner of one eye a yawning hole in the ground literally at my feet—like the shaft of a colliery, it ran down into the earth for about 20 feet, the bottom being obscured by dead branches—this was my goal, the entrance of the tunnel that the Germans christened 'The Crown Prince's Tunnel' after their Royal General, although there is no evidence that 'Little Willy' ever ventured this far into the front line. Alone in the forest, well out of earshot of the nearest forester, I quaked to think of my fate should I have fallen down the shaft.

Persistent rain prevented offensive operations for the rest of April but by May the Germans were ready, and with a supreme effort they took Côte 304 and, by the end of the month, the Mort Homme summit itself, along with the village of Cumières which nestled in its shadow. But both sides had been exhausted by the struggle, and the Germans switched their attention back to the Right Bank, and the final, futile attacks of the summer.

Emerging from the woods again, I walked up to the hill's summit, where I sat and ate a picnic lunch in the clearing around the grim memorial with its immortal inscription: *Ils ne passeront pas*. Another hour's march brought me to the Côte 304, where another memorial, unveiled by Pétain in the 1930s, tells the visitor that 10,000 French gave their lives and blood to defend this one small hillock. Just as I arrived a coach pulled up, and disgorged a dozen French veterans—the aged survivors walked slowly about, poking at stones with their walking-sticks, and rheumy-eyed, reflected on the past, when they stood here and lived through hell.

The shadows were lengthening and I turned my face to the east and returned to Forges, passing the entrance to the other Mort Homme tunnel, which was named 'Gallwitz', after the German general who commanded the Left Bank sector. This tunnel, just off one of the main forest tracks, or *chemins*, was easier to locate than the 'Crown Prince' and in a better state of repair—the remains of wooden supports could still be seen, and the muddy impressions of the steps down which the grey-coated soldiers walked to their fate.

Stopping on the way back in Cumières, yet another of the nine vanished villages, I picked about in the well preserved ruins and found a door hinge and a fragment of kitchen pottery to take home: pieces of ordinary life elevated to the status of relics, as holy in their way as the official shrines which stand here now.

Following the forest *chemins* to the east, I emerged at length out of the woods again, and was rewarded by a magnificent view over the Meuse valley, with the grim forests of the Right Bank hills darkening the distant horizon, and the spire of the church of the new village of Forges in the middle ground. This pastoral scene could have been seen by a similar viewer in the nineteenth century and it almost seemed to me as I stumbled on tired legs through the clods of the field as if none of it had happened, the whole scene became new, fresh, harmonized as indeed it was . . . before they had the war.

I reached Forges, and sitting down on the banks of the brook that had once been the front line, rolled down my socks, removed my boots and gratefully bathed my feet in the chill running waters. It looked a good place to fish, I thought, as I placed my water bottle between two stones in the stream and waited for the wine inside to cool.

The next day, my last in Verdun, I devoted to an exploration of some of the places on the Right Bank where the tourists rarely go—the tiny fortifications which were just as vital to their defenders as the big ones, like Vaux and Douaumont, and to some of the almost impenetrable ravines which were so characteristic of the battle.

I set off in the pre-dawn dark, when chill mists were still hovering wraith-like among the buildings at the edge of town. Soon I was ascending a footpath leading up to the heights and my first goal hove into view: a deserted barracks, the Caserne Marceau, which came under German shellfire during their last-gasp attack in July. Tethered horses had run amuck, their torn entrails twisting in their hooves. The path led from here up past Souville to another fort, Tavannes, and a railway tunnel nearby where the French suffered one of their greatest disasters in the battle.

This occurred during September, when a temporary peace of exhaustion had settled on the weary combatants; the last German effort to take Verdun had failed, Falkenhayn had been sacked, to be replaced by the terrible twins, Hindenburg and Ludendorff, who had immediately called off the Verdun offensive, both calling the battlefield 'Hell'. The French were slowly recuperating and gathering their strength for the autumn when Pétain planned to mount a grand-slam counter-offensive.

The 1,400-yard Tavannes tunnel had served the French as a substitute fort—thousands of men had sought shelter and refuge here from the prowling demons of the open battlefield, but this time, there was to be no safety in their subterranean shafts. On September 4, a chance explosion set up a chain reaction among the munitions which shared the cramped space of the tunnel with exhausted and wounded men. The blast turned into a complete conflagration which did not burn out for three days. When it was quelled, 500 men were found to have perished.

The railway line—part of the route between Verdun and Metz—still runs today, and between trains I scrambled down and peered into the dark depths. The silence was all I heard.

From Tavannes I followed the footsteps of a Captain Delvert, who had left its shelter in May 1916 and found his way up to a concrete bunker in the Bois Fumin, a wood on the left flank of Fort Vaux. The Germans had just launched an operation code-named 'May Cup', to take the Fort and open the gateway to Verdun itself. Delvert was charged with defending his bunker 'R1' (for Retrenchment). Like Fort Vaux itself, Delvert and his single company were to hold out against the advance for a whole week.

I made my way into the sparse woods and located R1, now just a pile of stones on the edge of a small ravine. The other side of the ravine, from which his German tormentors strafed and shot at Delvert, looked absurdly close. There were a pile of relics at R1, but, curiously, all were made of leather: there were boots, belts and buckles, curled and lined with moss; I wondered about the fate of their former owners.

Leaving R1, I made a detour up the right flank of the battlefield to visit two more of the vanished villages, Bezonvaux and Ornes. The sun was now up and the straight road at the eastern edge of the forest disappeared into a heat haze; I now began to appreciate the worst factors of the Verdun climate; on days like this it exudes a foggy enervating miasma, a swampy muggy heat that breeds midges and mosquitoes by the million. Hordes of these winged fiends now took off and buzzed me in squadrons, so I was not in the best of humours when I trudged past the ruins of Vaux and its modern equivalent and found my way to the site of Bezonvaux. The foresters had been busy here and had levelled the trees all around, so that hardly a trace of the village remained, only an army of tree-stumps looking like truncated mortars.

I rejoined the road and tramped up towards Ornes, when by the side of a ploughed field I saw a small mound of shells. I counted 40 of them, and as the farmer's tractor swept round I asked him whether the formidable pile was still dangerous: 'Only if you throw them on a fire', I was told, and suiting the action to the word he spied another shell in the furrow he had just ploughed and hurled it with careless abandon onto the heap. I must admit to having flinched as the metal shellcases clanged together, and the farmer laughed a contemptuous snort of familiarity.

I arrived at Ornes, and found it to be the best-preserved of all the villages; several walls are still standing, and so are the outer walls and windows of the village church, with an iron cross erected on the site of the altar, and the pillars which once lined the aisle cut off at waist and knee level.

A rare French trench map of this sector which I had found at the Imperial War Museum had given me the exact location of the Front lines on May 23, 1916 when the Germans were limbering up for 'May Cup' and I had traced the trench lines on to a local Verdun map, which enabled me to have the imaginative experience of actually walking along the exact path of the lines, which led me back to Fort Douaumont and so round to the village of Douaumont.

Behind the village shrine, the ground descended sharply into the Ravin du Helly, and here I found the most incomparable collection of battlefield debris I had ever seen. Each step you take in this dank, mossy wood, is lined with the relics of war; within a few minutes I had found a machine-gun belt, a bayonet case, water bottles of both sides, still in a shiny state of preservation, and above all hundreds upon hundreds of discarded German 'potato masher' grenades—some with the rotted wooden handles and rubber fuse wiring still in place. Foot by foot I walked along the ravine, noticing in the earth of its steep sides, holes and bunkers in profusion. I was horrified, as I stepped and picked up a roll of rusty barbed wire, to find a human pelvis, and soon the rustle of rain in the trees made this sad necropolis more mournful than ever.

The ultimate note of realism was sounded as I was disturbed in my reveries by the unmistakable sound of a shot being fired at close quarters. But I pressed on, having heard that the French hunting season was opening that day and thinking that the *chasseurs* would blast their birds and pass on. But as I neared the end of the ravine the shooting increased in intensity and I was amazed when the single reports changed to the clatter of a machine-gun. Suddenly I remembered that I was close to the Wavrille shooting range, a long clearing carved out of the forest in front of Fort Douaumont where the French army tests its light arms every Monday and Tuesday. Absorbed in my search, I had not noticed the distinctive red *Danger de Mort* warning signs, with their grim death's-head motif, which warned off trespassers in three languages. Anxiety turned to alarm as the shots grew louder and I heard the singing whine of ricocheting bullets.

Then I heard the distinctive crack of a bullet striking wood near me, and heart pounding, I flung myself full-length on the damp earth—this was battle re-enactment with a vengeance. From my prone position I studied my map and discovered that I had been walking in the wrong direction down the ravine, and had inadvertently strayed into the woods which actually abutted the range. Clearly, a retreat was in order. Maintaining a very low profile indeed, I scrambled back down the valley and was inexpressibly relieved to find myself back in Douaumont once again.

This brush with danger was enough for one day, and I said a long goodbye to the battlefield as I walked, for the last time, past the gloomy, ugly, but imposing memorials which I knew would draw me back one day to walk again those haunted bloody slopes.

Stumbling down back towards the town, I saw a car parked to one side of the track; it seemed to be moving slightly—a startled female face in the back seat told me why; I had stumbled on a pair of illicit lovers who had chosen the field of death for their tryst.

12. Slaughter on the Somme

The men are in splendid spirits, several have said that they have never before been so instructed and informed of the nature of the operations before them. The wire has never been so well cut, nor the artillery preparations so thorough.

Sir Douglas Haig, 'Diary', June 30, 1916

You are about to attack the enemy with far greater numbers than he can oppose to you, supported by a huge number of guns. You are about to fight in one of the greatest battles in the world, and in the most just cause. Remember that the British Empire will anxiously watch your every move . . . Keep your heads, do your duty and you will utterly defeat the enemy.

Brigadier-General H. C. Rees, Commander 94th Infantry Brigade, Special order of the day, June 28, 1916

But I've a rendezvous with Death . . .
And I to my pledged word am true—
I shall not fail that rendezvous.

Alan Seeger, killed on the Somme, July 4, 1916

Crouched among thistle-tufts I've watched the glow
Of a blurred orange sunset flare and fade;
And I'm content. Tomorrow we must go
To take some cursed wood . . . O world God made!

Siegfried Sassoon, July 3, 1916

Two years in the making. Ten minutes in the destroying. That was our history.

John Harris, 'Covenant with Death'

Shortly after 7 a.m. on the morning of July 1, 1916, whistles blew in the French and British trenches astride the Albert-Bapaume road north of the River Somme and officers led their men over the top and into action.

A clear blue morning presaged a day of broiling heat. It was a day

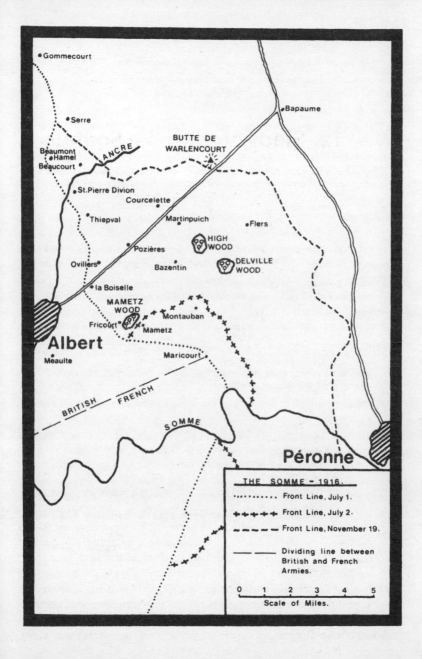

Gommecourt

Bapaume

Serre

BUTTE DE
WARLENCOURT

Beaumont
Hamel
Beaucourt

ANCRE

St.Pierre Divion

Courcelette

Thiepval

Martinpuich

Flers

Poziéres

HIGH
WOOD

Ovillers

Bazentin

DELVILLE
WOOD

la Boiselle

MAMETZ
WOOD

Fricourt

Montauban

Mametz

Albert

Méaulte

Maricourt

BRITISH   FRENCH

SOMME

Péronne

THE SOMME – 1916.

.... Front Line, July 1.

+++++ Front Line, July 2.

– – – Front Line, November 19.

—— Dividing line between
British and French
Armies.

0   1   2   3   4   5

Scale of Miles.

that was to prove the greatest disaster to British arms since the Battle of Hastings in 1066. When dusk finally fell on that first day, nearly 60,000 men were casualties, 20,000 of them were dead.

The men who suffered this appalling tragedy were those of Kitchener's vaunted New Armies. They were the cream of the country's youth, who had volunteered in droves in 1914 and had been two years in training for this morning and this hour.

The soldiers, many of whom were friends and colleagues in civilian life, who had enlisted collectively and had formed 'Pals' Battalions' from particular towns and firms, went over the top totally confident of victory.

The 18 Divisions' attack of 100,000 men had been preceded by a five-day artillery barrage by 1,573 guns. Their commanders assured the men that the enemy lines had ceased to exist—the Germans would have been pulverized into the ground and all the British would have to do would be to literally stroll across No Man's Land and occupy the blasted positions, to make way for the three Cavalry Divisions who were mounted behind the lines ready to sweep forward into the open ground around Bapaume. True, there was some confusion among the British generals as to whether the enemy wire had been completely cut and levelled, but what matter? There would be nobody behind the wire anyway:

William J. Smith, Gunner, 44th Siege Battery, Royal Garrison Artillery:

We were stationed near the village of Meaulte, close to Albert when the Somme battle began. A week before 1 July, a terrific artillery bombardment began. I was on a twelve-inch howitzer which was mounted on a railway. We were a two-gun battery. We hoisted the shells up to the breech by means of a winding gadget as they weighed 750 lbs. each. Then an officer put the fuses in, different fuses depending on the range, and five men manhandled the shell into the breech. Our maximum range was five miles, and the gun could fire a round every two minutes. The officer fired the gun by jerking a lanyard. I remember the first of July because it was such a lovely morning. The skylarks were singing on the Somme, and then a few minutes later there were all these humans trying to kill each other. There was a hospital in Meaulte mill and the word went round about the number of casualties there had been. From there we moved to Bray, on the river, and then to Montauban and Mametz wood as the battle progressed. The trees in the wood were just stumps, and the ground around just shellholes.

But all this immense weight of shellfire had not fatally damaged the enemy as the Allied Commanders fondly hoped; far from it. The Germans were by now past masters in the arts of fortification and digging in, and on the chalky slopes above the Somme they had spent two years constructing what Winston Churchill described as 'undoubtedly the strongest and most perfectly defended position in the world'. Their defences now consisted of a vast network of dug-outs, trenches, dormitories, and redoubts, dug in-depth along the ground and down into the earth, where they had carved out caverns in the chalk to depths of 40 feet.

The Germans had plenty of warning about the coming attack—from their eyrie-like lines they had watched as the New Armies were brought up into the Somme sector via Albert, the small town whose basilica, with its golden virgin knocked lop-sided by shellfire, was becoming a familiar landmark to the Tommies.

The Germans perfected a technique of rushing their machine-guns up and down from the dug-outs so that they would have plenty of time to mow down the attacking infantry as soon as the British bombardment lifted on zero day.

When the barrage opened, the Germans obediently scuttled below and sat out the storm, secure in the knowledge that even the heaviest shells could not penetrate their subterranean fastnesses. This fundamental failure by the British Command to realize the strength of the enemy defences, coupled with the imperfectly cut wire and the rigid, parade-ground manner in which the infantry attacked, were the main reasons for the horrible failure of the attack and the ghastly casualties which the first day brought. For their inability or unwillingness to comprehend this, and for their blindness, Haig and Rawlinson, respectively Commander-in-Chief and Commander of the Fourth Army, must be held eternally—and damningly—culpable. They turned a blind eye to reports from front line patrols which told of large areas of wire either uncut or imperfectly cut, preferring the optimistic noises made by their Corps and Divisional Commanders.

By the time that the Battle of the Somme opened we found ourselves at Gommecourt, on the extreme left of the Somme front. The night before the attack I took a patrol out into No Man's Land with long aluminium tubes filled with ammonal explosives. The tubes had fuses at one end which you lit with a match before getting away; they were just like the blue touchpapers on fireworks. We blew two gaps in the wire, and I was surprised that the Germans seemed to take no notice of us. The only reaction was a Verey light that was sent up from their reserve lines. The reason was that they had abandoned their front lines completely while our pre-battle artillery bombardment was in progress. They came back to man their machine-guns as soon as the artillery stopped and our infantry went over the top. On July 1 itself, I was at Battalion HQ and luckily didn't have to go over. But we knew things hadn't gone well. 7,000 men died in our sector and many of my friends didn't come back. The Westminsters lost heavily, attacking Gommecourt Wood on our left. They were caught by machine guns and never even got into the enemy front line trenches. They were badly mauled. The trouble was with the battle that the Generals persisted with the attack, which was sheer folly. Altogether it was a failure and we suffered heavy casualties on and after the first day.

(Greig)

To add to the tragedy of this sector, the two divisions' attack against Gommecourt which Mr Greig refers to was never intended to be successful: Gommecourt was a strongly-defended and fortified village redoubt and the attack on it had been mounted as a diversion, intended to draw enemy fire and attention away from the main body of the attack further south.

Reading from north to south along the British front the story of that first day was much the same—the men, heavily laden with wire, water bottle, belt, bayonet, rifle ammunition pouches, groundsheet, haversack, full mess tin, iron rations, spare socks and laces, sewing kit, gas helmets and goggles, field dressing and iodine, and often, digging tools or wire cutters—the whole weighing from 65 to 90 lbs.—left the trenches, and staggered, rather than advanced, towards the distant chalk spoil that marked the enemy lines, each man keeping at a regulation two-three paces from his neighbour and moving in fanned-out lines. They presented a perfect target to the German machine-gunners as they emerged from the dark and rubbed their eyes in disbelief.

Just under Gommecourt, the 8th Corps of General Hunter-Weston, (known as 'Hunter-Bunter' to his troops), faced the fortified village of Serre. The men headed obediently towards the gaps torn in the enemy wire—only to find German machine-guns trained on the self-same spots. The bodies accumulated on and around the wire, and by high noon, as a merciless sun beat down on the dying and the dead, an estimated 3,500 had become casualties in one division alone (the 31st) of this Corps. In the next sector, Hawthorn Ridge, the attack was supposed to be helped by the blasting of an enormous mine containing 45,000 lbs. of ammonal. It was originally planned to blow the mine at 3.30 a.m., but the plan changed and the mine was blown only ten minutes before zero hour, which gave the Germans more than enough time to recover from the shock of the blast, rush the crater and occupy its lip. Again the same story was repeated; mounds of bodies built up along the wire, and the succeeding waves of attackers found themselves unable to get forward, obstructed not only by the deadly thorned strands, but by the bullet-riddled corpses of their own comrades.

Next station down the line, opposite the village of Beaumont-Hamel, the Royal Newfoundland Regiment from Canada, attacked a German position called 'Y Ravine'. Within minutes, 710 men were lost. By night, Hunter-Weston's Corps had lost 14,000 men. Their only gain was a score of German prisoners. A temporary truce was called in this sector after dark for both sides to collect their wounded and dead.

In the next sector, Thiepval, the attackers faced one of their toughest nuts, but the men who went over the top were almost equal to their near-impossible task. They were the 36th (Ulster) Division, composed of Carson's pre-war Ulster Volunteers, and probably the most well-trained men in the whole army. The dour Protestants, celebrating the anniversary of the Battle of the Boyne, stormed out of Thiepval Wood and hurled themselves at the Schwaben Redoubt, a vast network of underground fortifications bristling with barbed wire and machine-guns. Within an hour the Inniskillings had advanced a mile, cleared Thiepval Ridge and captured the Redoubt. But almost all the officers were casualties, and while runners were sent to the rear for further orders, the Germans regrouped and struck back. Losses were enormous—by nightfall the division had lost 9,000 men—but they retained a precarious toehold on their hard-won gains. Thiepval village itself was to resist the British assaults for months to come.

As the line moved south, to where the British joined hands with their allies of Fayolle's Sixth French army, the only solid gains of the day were made: Congreve's 13th Corps surrounded the redoubt village of Fricourt—(known as 'Gibraltar' because of its rock-like strength)—seized Mametz, and moved on to Montauban, where they found most of the German defenders dead. Helped by more mine explosions, the villages of Ovillers and La Boisselle were rushed but not secured.

In the French sector, the day had gone reasonably well; learning from the experience of Verdun, French tactics had been more flexible and imaginative. Their heavier artillery had succeeded in pounding even the most powerful German positions to pieces, and when the infantry advanced, later in the day, it was in smaller groups, skilfully infiltrating the enemy lines. By the end of the day the French had advanced several miles, taken over 6,000 prisoners and were threatening the German-held town of Péronne. But they were unable to continue without the support of the British who were so bloodily bogged down on their left.

British losses on this single catastrophic day were worse than the French casualties in the worst month of the Verdun fighting. At the end of the day fewer than 2,000 enemy prisoners had been taken, and the Germans, outnumbered by eighteen divisions to six, or one regiment to each British division, had in most places held on to their original positions and recaptured several others.

The day had seen unparalleled acts of heroism from the men of the New Armies—typified by the famous story of Captain Wilfred Nevill, of the 8th East Surrey Regiment, who gave his men two footballs to kick into No Man's Land, as though the Somme was to be some sort of Wembley Cup Final writ large. Encouraging his wavering men as a torrent of fire burst upon them, Nevill was shot through the head as he neared the enemy front lines. His deed was lauded in England as the act of a sportsman, but ridiculed by earnest German propagandists as an example of English frivolity and idiocy.

The losses of the day in numbers had been horrible, but what, in the long run, was even worse was the effect on morale, both military and civilian. The First of July represented for England, in one terrible day, all the suffering that the French had found at Verdun. The battles represented a watershed—the last traces of the early carefree spirit of the war had gone for good—there would be no more heroics. From now on the men who moved into the trenches to replace the fallen would not see the war as a wonderful crusade, but as a bloody, deadly chore to be slogged through, and, if possible, survived. From now on there would be a growing alienation from the Home Front, still sustained in their glorious illusions by a patriotic press and censored letters, of which the following is an example:

Pte Harry Beale, 17th Royal Fusiliers:

Dear Uncle and Aunt,   20 May 1916
At last I am writing you a few lines to let you know how I am going on. Of course you know I have left dear old England, it does not seem possible I have been over here a month. The time goes very quickly. It is not so bad in France and the weather is something glorious at present, although we have had some rough weather and

no doubt you have had the same. I have nothing to grumble about. The food is very good for the Army, and we have not wanted for much.

We get up at 5.30, breakfast at 6.30, dinner at 12.30, tea 4.30. Of course, there are one or two canteens, and the YMCA refreshment bar. My address is PE 2279, 17th Royal Fusiliers, 33rd JBD APO/17, BEF, France. I shall be very pleased to have a line from you at any time. It's rather difficult to find any news as we are not allowed to say much, so will draw this to a close, hoping this will find you all well, with my best love and wishes to all.

From your ever-loving nephew.

Harry

A few weeks after this letter was written, the following notice from Harry Beale's Company Commander was sent to his parents: "I very much regret to report that your son, Private H. Beale, was killed in action, charging the enemy on July 27. He was a very gallant soldier and I wish to express my very deepest sympathy with you in your loss, as I am proud to have had the honour of commanding men like him".

This sort of message was becoming a commonplace as the war placed its deadly hand on every family in the land. The telegram boy on his bicycle became a dreaded figure as he brought the bare, bald news from the War Office, beginning: 'The Secretary of State for War very much regrets . . .', and subsequently, if the family were lucky, a letter from an officer of the dead man, describing, in heroic terms, the last hours of the deceased. Such messages were to become more and more frequent as the Battle of the Somme went on. For, almost incredibly, after a stunned pause on July 2, as the full extent of the previous day's disaster sank in, Haig pressed on with attacks on the following day, attempting to exploit the gains on the southern sector of the front.

Charles Quinnell, 9th Battalion, Royal Fusiliers:

In 1916 I was on the Somme for the big battle. On July 1, when the offensive opened, I was stationed in Aveluy wood, half a mile west of Thiepval. At that time it was a young wood full of saplings. I returned there last year (1980) and the saplings had grown up into enormous trees. In the wood we had a grandstand view of the battle. I have heard it said that the heavy artillery was standing wheel to wheel. That is a lie. The 18 pounder guns were 20 yards apart. There were also 4/5 howitzers and 12 inch naval guns mounted on railways. Before going into battle we were told that there would be no enemy wire left after our massive bombardment. But the German barbed wire was much thicker than ours, and the barbs were closer together—it was like trying to get through a thick thorn hedge. The wire was fixed on wooden posts, while we used iron stakes. Some genius issued us with wire cutters that were a yard long! And before we went over we were sent out on wiring parties in patrols of six to twelve men. The German wire 'sang' as soon as it was cut, and when they heard the twang the Germans sent up a Verey light and tried to shoot the wire cutters. As a result, very little of the wire was cut; the German wire was practically invincible. You couldn't climb over it or crawl through it. To attack was just sending men to their deaths. Each company in the battalion had a different job to do. Our objective was to capture a slag heap just short of Bapaume—but we didn't get anywhere near that. Our first target was the village of Ovillers. At dusk on July 1, we moved into trenches opposite Ovillers, and we found two Pioneers in the front line trench shooting at anything that moved in No Man's Land. We said: "You daft bastards ... that's our wounded you are shooting at."

On July 14, Haig gave permission for Rawlinson to use new tactics—a furious bombardment of only a few hours' duration, followed by a lightning night attack, on the southern sector towards Longueval Ridge. Twenty-thousand men were thrown into the attack and swept all before them, advancing through the twin villages of Bazentin le Grand and Bazentin le Petit and reaching the edges of High and Delville Woods. But then the usual story held up progress. Haig and the French had been sceptical of success and no reserves were available to exploit the gains. When they were finally found, the Germans had recovered from the punch and resistance stiffened, as the South Africans discovered when they were thrown in on the next day, to take Delville Wood, where young Harry Beale was to meet his death.

By this time, the weather had broken and the rains made the late summer and autumn on the Somme a misery of mud. Haig characteristically decided to maintain his slogging offensive throughout the autumn—perhaps the decision was not entirely his; he was under heavy French pressure to keep up the attack as the French were still unsure whether the enemy had definitely broken off his Verdun offensive, and the Somme was drawing off ever-increasing supplies of German manpower.

It must not be forgotten that the Germans, too, were suffering severely on the Somme: they lost over 100,000 men in July, compared with the British 158,736 and the French losses of 50,000, and in August and September lost 208,000 more. Indeed, Ludendorff, visiting the battlefield after he and Hindenburg had replaced the discredited Falkenhayn at the end of August, criticized his men for their too-dogged defence, which had cost them many lives. The German army had, remarked Ludendorff, been bled to a standstill. This perception was the prelude to the German decision to withdraw, early next year, to the formidable defences of the Hindenburg Line, which was to remain unbreached until the final weeks of the war.

A vivid impression of life at the front line in the Somme is given in the memoirs of an Australian signaller, Sgt.-Maj. Philip Ibbetson:

> I arrived with the left section at the new wagon lines which were the other side of Albert, about 2 p.m., got a bit of a snack from the New Zealanders we were to relieve and set off back for the right section. We eventually arrived at the Battery about midnight and all our kit and gear were dumped in the mud. Bdr. Young, the Signaller Bdr. met me and told me to crawl in his dug-out till morning. I was told that Fred was already up at the O.P. with the Major. Bdr. Young said he was going up in the morning to relieve Fred. I had only been asleep about half an hour when someone crashed in on top of us. It was Fred who had come down on the line which had broken, so he crawled in with us. We were crowded into the dug-out which was about the size of an ordinary dog kennel, so didn't get much sleep. About 4 a.m. we were called out as the O.P. line was broken. We set off for the O.P. which was about three miles away, and mended the line on the way, as it had broken in three places. We met the Major and his batman on the way carrying all their swag on a stretcher. We gave them a hand and left Bdr. Young at the O.P. We had an awful job getting Major Rygalls' swag through the mud but landed back at the Battery at last to find our dug-out had been blown in and most of our kit with it. We went to the cook-house to get some dinner as we had had no breakfast but were told all the food had been given out so had a smoke and tightened our belts. The line had broken again so out we went, arriving back in time for tea, a biscuit and a tin of bully each. No tea as it was a clear day so we could not light a fire.
>
> That night we set to work to build a dug-out and also a bit of a place to cook our own tucker. We got the two places finished about 3 o'clock in the morning and turned in for a good night's sleep. No

such luck as at 5 o'clock we were called out again as the damned line was broken. So out we went, mended it and arrived back for breakfast. This time as it was a misty day we got bacon and hot tea. After breakfast we thought we would run out another line so that if one got broken we should have a second line to fall back on. We set off carrying a mile of wire each, and got the job done about 4 p.m., we had missed dinner but managed to get our tea. As we had had no sleep for 56 hours and had been going all that time, we were clean foundered, I felt I did not care how many lines were broken, I had to have some sleep. We slept the clock twice round and did not wake until 4 p.m. the next afternoon. I was then called to the Major's dug-out telling me that two spooks were needed to go with the Liaison Officer to Battery HQ the next morning and as Fred and I were the lines men it was up to us to go. We set off with an officer called Ford (who was a rotter). We walked about six miles carrying a mile of wire and two telephones each and got to a disused dug-out about 100 yards behind the front line. We relieved the 22nd Battery spooks and as the line was broken when we arrived they said they would repair it on their way back.

This they did not do so we had to turn out and things were pretty warm. It took us about three hours to find the break and mend it and we got back to Battery HQ about 2 p.m. The line kept OK until about 7 p.m. From then on until 1 a.m. we were mending it continuously, got back and it kept good until 3 a.m., from 3 a.m. to 5 a.m. broken, mended again and remained good until we were relieved at 11 a.m.

We had six miles of mud in front of us and did not like the idea and felt pretty well knocked up. We had bneen in wet clothes for about a week, we were not allowed to light a fire to dry them, so used to dry them with the heat of our bodies at night only to get them soaking wet again the next day. However we made it back to the Battery about 3 p.m. to be told that all the battery lines were broken. By this time I was thoroughly fed up and if it had not been for Fred I should have deserted or done something rash, but Fred persuaded me to do nothing so damned foolish. So we each set off again on different lines. I mended mine and got back about 7 p.m. but Fred had not arrived. As he had the shortest way to go I could not understand why he was not back so set off on his line to find him. I had gone about a mile when I heard someone shouting. I went over to where the voice was coming from and there he was up to his waist in a muddy shell-hole and unable to move. I was in a fix as I knew if I left him to get help I should never be able to find him again. It took me the best part of two hours to lever him out but I managed it at last by making a kind of lever of our telephone wire and poles. When I did get him out he was too frozen to walk and as he weighed twelve stone I had a fine job carrying him through the mud back to the Battery.

I got him to bed and went to the Officers' cookhouse and pinched some warm tea and bread and butter and we had a good feed and felt better. The next day Bdr. Young telephoned to tell me to come up to the O.P. as he was coming down to the Battery. I was damned wild about it as Fred and I wanted to stay together. However Bdr. Young was senior to me so I could do nothing but obey. So up I went, I think on the whole it was better than the Battery, less mud and not so many lines to look after. As soon as I got there I set to work to build myself a dug-out. I made myself a hole just big enough to crawl into but I had to get out if I wanted to turn round. I used to see Fred every day as he used to be up at the O.P. or I was down at the Battery. I had been there a week when I heard two men were wanted to go to Battery HQ again. Fred came up the night before we were to go up and camped with me in my rabbit hole. It was one awful curse and Fred seemed funny that night and kept telling me who to send his papers to and his other possessions if he got killed.

As a rule he never mentioned being killed and was always full of plans he had made for after the war was over. I asked him what the hell was up with him, he said he was uneasy but did not know why. I said I would get another signaller to go in his place but he would not hear of it. We neither of us slept much that night as we were talking and smoking most of the night. We got up at 6 a.m., had breakfast and set off with an officer called Lloyd. He was the coolest man I had ever met, most of the coves did not like him but I admired him for his coolness under shell-fire. We arrived at Battery HQ about 11 a.m. and the line held good all day until about 7 o'clock at night. We were out nearly all night repairing the line and then were sitting round a fire with some Tommy engineers having a mug of tea and Fritz was dropping shells pretty close. I said we had better get a wriggle on. We had only gone about ten yards away when a 5.9 burst right in the centre of the file killing six men and wounding about a dozen others.

We were going back to help when a shell burst on top of a bank, burying us completely. We crawled out somewhat shaken and lost our telephones and tin hats. However we got back to Battery HQ about 6 a.m. and relief came without the line breaking. We had got a little way on the way home when I remembered I had left my telephone behind. So I set off back to get it and was only about 20 yards from Capt. Lloyd and Fred when a 5.9 burst right on top of them. When the smoke and dirt cleared away I saw them both lying in the shell hole. I thought dead at first but found Capt. Lloyd had a couple of pieces of shrapnel in his thigh and Fred a piece of shrapnel through the back of his ankle. Capt. Lloyd could walk so he made his way back to an advance dressing station and I carried Fred. I got him to the dressing station and they dressed his wound, which did not look too bad. As they were short of stretcher bearers, I took a hand with the stretcher to the clearing station at a place called Becordel. Fred seemed quite OK and in good spirits as I assured him he wouldn't lose his leg. I said goodbye and told him to get back to the Battery pretty damn quick, as I did not think he would ever get to England. I little thought it would be the last time I should see him.

I walked back to the O.P. and telephoned through to the Major to report casualties. He told me to evacuate the place and send the two telephonists down to the wagon lines and come down to the Battery. I set off with all my swags and met an Infantry L/Cpl. and a private and walked along with them. I was in the centre and they were giving me a hand with my swag when the Cpl. said: 'Here she comes DUCK'; we all ducked in the same shell-hole. I saw a blinding flash and then all went dark. When I came to I saw the Cpl. was lying near me with half his head blown off and the other private with a ghastly wound in his stomach but I was without a scratch. Of course I was shell-shocked but as we were quite close to a dressing station I got them both attended to but they both died straight away.

I then made my way to the Battery but I had the jumps very badly by this time. I reported the casualties to a Battery Officer and I was in such a rotten condition he told me to get to bed. I met Fred Lomas on the way and he told me to come with him to a sub-gun pit and he would fix me up. He gave me a water bottle full of rum and I got a proper skinful, I did not know where I was or anything, so Fred put me to bed. I woke up in the morning free of shell-shock but with a terrible thick head. We were at Guidicourt for a week and were then told we were going into action at Delville Wood, about three miles away. We shifted across all OK and

Verdun: the north fosse of Fort Vaux, whose heroic garrison delayed a German advance for a vital week in June 1916

The same view today

Verdun: the village of Ornes, one of nine hamlets destroyed for ever in 1916.
Note church on right

The church at Ornes today

Verdun: Command Post of Col. Emile Driant, killed leading the French defence in Bois des Caures, 1916

The Command Post today

Verdun: the Glacis of Fort Douaumont. In 1916, the key to Verdun's
defences. Taken by the Germans with ease, it cost France an estimated
100,000 lives to recapture. The machine gun on the summit (left) was
controlled from the observation dome (right)

Verdun: a rifle in the 'Trench of
Bayonets'

The tunnel of Tavannes, Verdun, used as a French fort and HQ. A chain of explosions on September 4, 1916, killed more than 500 men

The tunnel of Tavannes today

The 'Casemate Panard', part of the outer defences of Fort Souville, the final French bastion before Verdun which successfully resisted the last German attack in July 1916

Entrance shaft to a trench dug-out today

British troops in the ruins of Beaumont Hamel church with a large haul of 'potato masher' German grenades, May 1917

Monsieur André Coilliot with his private war museum, housed in his home at Beaurains, Arras. 1982

pulled in just behind the wood. All this time I expected to hear from Fred Alberts and could not understand why I had not had any word of him. We were only behind the wood four days when we were ordered to relieve a Tommy Battery in the front of the wood. As we had been in action about six weeks we were disappointed as we had expected to be going out of action for a spell any time. But we put in three more weeks at Delville Wood. It was quite a good place for me as I had very little work to do except to go up to Brigade HQ once a week to mend lines there.

At Brigade HQ we used to get a lot of shells coming over. I had the roof of my dug-out blown off one night and one day I was splitting a six-feet-long log when a shell lobbed off one end and burst all the skin off my fingers with the concussion. Every evening about 7 p.m. Fritz used to plaster shells all around the Battery and break all our lines. On the whole I had a good time, as I had a nice little dug-out to myself with a good fire and also my own telephone there. One evening I happened to hear a message coming through from Durisance HQ and got an awful shock when I heard that Gunner F. E. Alberts had died of wounds on November 16, 1916, the day he got wounded. I just about reckon it made a different person of me, from then on I always kept to myself and camped on my own, in fact became a regular mankind hater.

One of the men thrown into the battle in August was Arthur Lamb:

The casualties in the Somme battle had been so terrific that we were split up and sent off in batches to make up for those who had been lost. I was sent to the 11th Battalion, the Royal Sussex Regiment. I joined them at Beaussart near Beaumont-Hamel on the Somme. We moved into the line to relieve the Royal Naval Division, at Beaumont-Hamel, around the beginning of August. I remember it had been a very lovely summer, and it was a hot summer's evening when we went up. The fiercest fighting in the Somme battle had died down by this time, but there was still peripatetic fighting going on, here and there.

There was not much left of Beaumont-Hamel village except for a huge chalk pit. We moved about in the Somme area quite a bit, I remember being at Engelbelmer at one point.

We went into a full-scale brigade action to take the Stuff Redoubt, and instead of a dawn attack, which was usual, this was carried out at midday—I don't know why. We lost half the

Company killed. I was slightly wounded by shrapnel in the head; I did not know anything about it until I felt the blood trickling down under my steel helmet. I was able to carry on. We got into the German trenches and faced only slight resistance. Most of them were in their dug-outs and we raked them out. One lot wouldn't come out, so we had to push in a Mills bomb (hand grenade). They came out pretty fast after that! I found one of their officers who was dying. I offered to help but he just glared at me. I went through his pockets and found his name was Lt. Schulz, of the 113th (Badische) Infantry Regiment.

We sent their prisoners back, but we were very busy with our own wounded. We had to prepare for a counter-attack which meant turning the rear of the German trench into our front. We stayed there until late the next day when we were relieved by the Devons. On the way back we were being shelled, and one shell fell just in front of my group. When the smoke cleared, I saw that one of my best friends, Bill Gentle, of Baldock, had been wounded. One of his legs was shattered and he was covered with other wounds. I was trying to stay and help him, but a Major of the Devons threatened me with a revolver and told me to get out. He was quite right. I inquired at a Casualty Station about Bill two or three days later, when I was having my own wound attended to. I had presumed that he was dead, and I had an arrangement with Bill to tell our families if one of us got it. So I wrote to his mother; luckily, by the same post, she heard from a base hospital nurse that he was still alive. He survived the war, but died from the effects of his wounds four years later—I lived with him and his wife until he died.

After that action, we were kept in the reserve for the next attack on Thiepval, in mid-September. I was not allowed to keep a diary—I wish I had, but a lot of people kept them secretly. In our letters home we could not disclose where we were, though some developed a code. If they said: 'I've seen Albert recently', it meant that they were near the town of Albert.

On September 15, an entirely new aspect entered the world's warfare on the Somme: the tank.

These crude, but revolutionary machines had been developed in great secrecy and tested in Norfolk and Dorset. Haig, displaying for once some flair and imagination, insisted that fifty of the prototypes be brought into the battle, despite the scepticism of Asquith and Kitchener who thought them little more than mechanical toys. So primitive was the mechanism of the new vehicle that several of them broke down on their way to the front and only 32 were ready for action on the chosen day. Haig decided to employ 24 of the monsters in isolated groups supporting the infantry rather than use them as a single, formidable spearhead. But even in this scattered, penny-packet fashion, and although several were knocked out or bogged down, the tanks made an overwhelming impact on the German defenders. One of the men who was there, acting as a Scout Liaison Officer, was Geoffrey Muir:

It was just getting light in the sky at 6 a.m. and it had cleared up to be a bright clear dawn; at 6.15 it was all perfectly still, everything seemed to be waiting and holding its breath to let loose at 6.20. It was a clear, pink, cold dawn; standing in my trench I could see the shattered trees and church of Courcelette, a mile away on the German side, Pozières behind me, shattered ruins, and then I saw the vague shape of a blind tank—the first ones ever used. There they were, stationary, trying to hide in large shell craters, waiting for the moment to lumber forward.

It was 6.19 a.m., only one more minute; I felt a most intense excitement, I could hardly speak, the strain of waiting grew nearly unbearable.

Then a gun cracked the silence, another, more, a rattle of machine guns, more machine guns, thousands of rattling machine guns, puffs of smoke over the enemy's trenches, only about 200 yards off, the constant sighing, whizzing of shells overhead, one could not speak, thousands of guns of every size were firing full speed. The attack was to be on a six-mile front, we were in the centre more or less.

In a minute our men could be seen in the thickening haze of smoke marching in steady lines on, over to the enemy. A tank lumbered by, then my first two scouts came back: 'German front line taken, no serious opposition encountered'.

My position was alongside our only communication trench to the front, and soon the wounded began to come down. I saw about 500 wounded men pass me that morning from different regiments, also a great many prisoners.

Soon my other men came in, one only was wounded and he brought the report right back before going off to get his wounds dressed. The attack had gone very well, our objective was all gained, though we lost pretty heavily, nearly 400 men and about fourteen officers, all in about three hours.

. . .by the evening of the 15th, all our own particular work was over, for at 5 p.m. other troops came over us and went forward, taking the actual village of Courcelette, so that there were two attacks on the 15th, making a total advance of nearly three miles in places.

Apart from Courcelette, the village of Flers was also taken—by four surviving tanks, followed by cheering infantry.

The autumn rains made the mud still worse, and the ground was so churned by months of prolonged bombardment that it was almost impossible for men to move, let alone machines.

On November 13, the village stronghold of Beaumont-Hamel, one of the first objectives of July 1, finally fell. A week later, after 142 days of brutal attrition, Haig finally brought the offensive to an end. The Battle of the Somme had ground itself into the mud and the exhausted protagonists prepared to face a gloomy winter and a dark new year.

13. History has the set

... Where Edward Thomas brooded long
On death and beauty—till a bullet stopped his song.

Alun Lewis, 'All day it has rained'

Set in the heart of the Somme battle area it [the Thiepval memorial arch]
looks over those bloody ridges now empty, ridges which rise and fall like
the sound of a dark and swelling Bach prelude. Visitors still come in small
groups . . . On any day of the year men and women can still be seen, a few
old but most the sons and daughters of the war generation. They are
always silent and go first to one particular graveyard. Then they like to
walk over those broad chalk downlands, where space seems as long drawn
out as the steppes and where skylarks and poppies unnerve still as they did
sixty years ago. Frail and tiny these poppies seem to wither almost as soon
as they are picked. Even pressing cannot preserve them. So it is with the
memories of those who come to this countryside.

Denis Winter, 'Death's Men'

My trip to the Somme front was made in the company of a friend
Stephen Plaice who had already, as a poet, made and published his own
comment on the Great War:

TO THE YOUNG DEAD, 1914–18

Sleep deeper now that history has the set,
the last of all your comrades dead,
having lived the broader stretch and seen
the bee collect fifty summers in his sack.
And in those sprawling years having known
a woman's body age beside their own,
children's voices sing high and crack,
the extended quiet of the house
that little in old age disturbs,
even in the senile chair's deep recess
understood perhaps the migration of birds

and felt, unlike you, a gradual decline,
blending into the landscape of their lives.

While you in uniform with stony stares
have witnessed from cold public plinths
the wild fling of our great affairs,
heard us on each other's doorsteps peddle
the romantic software of our minds
and meddle with our little feelings,
pretending for them grand designs.
You have thought no doubt of sacrifice,
the great word that sustained you in the mud,
and of all those decent girls in your pockets
who married others when the grief had ebbed,
you have thought perhaps and reconsidered
since what you died for now itself is dead.

Still we approve your doomed platoon
trooping into the trenches of conviction,
for that authentic act remains
even if the words for which your lives
were wasted have grown meaningless.
Your youth forever framed in death
stiffens us a moment at the mantelpiece
and makes us wonder if we could forsake
all the warm refuges that are open to us
and storm forward to the ideal sacrifice.
But you too, watching us, you must regret
that you did not hesitate, grow old and love
imperfectly as we have done.

Just so. The voice of an intelligent and sympathetic modern man:
'What you died for now is dead'. That line sums it up; our plastic
throw-away, take-away society is completely alien to the Spartan values
for which the men of 1914–18 fought and died. What place does
'courage', 'comradeship', 'loyalty' and above all, 'sacrifice' have in the
'Me' world? Even the negative values have gone. What price the
'hateful Huns' and 'brutal Boche' when the Menin Road boasts an
Opel car showroom? The bewilderment on the faces of the aged survivors of the war when I asked them what they thought of the modern
world, was painful to behold. Without exception, all of them thought

things have got worse, and that selfishness had replaced sacrifice, profit had been placed before patriotism, loneliness before comradeship. Almost all of them shuddered before the face of the future, believing a Third World War to be not only likely, but inevitable. The sad forebodings of a played-out generation? The pessimism of elderly greybeards who have always shaken their heads at the goings-on of youth? I think not. They realized in their bones, which we know with our minds—that the war had been a turning point, at which civilization reached a high water mark, and then receded towards barbarism.

Our heads were full of such thoughts as we stood in the corridor of the Lille train, looking out at the unlovely country of the Pas-de-Calais. The towns we passed through were redolent of the war: St Omer, an important British rail-head, Hazebrouck, target of the second phase of Ludendorff's 1918 offensive, Armentières, where that unfortunate mademoiselle (who had not felt an amorous embrace for fifty years) came from, and which the Germans had briefly captured during that same offensive. Then we were behind what had been the German lines proper. Some of the little farms contained traces of the bunkers built by German slave-labour in the Second War, and the persistent resilience of the French peasant had converted them to cattle sheds.

Arriving at Arras, we were met by Jean-François Valet, my ebullient photographer friend, who drove us round a lightning tour of the town—like Ypres an old cloth city—whose architecture bore witness to the long Spanish influence and occupation when it had formed part of the Spanish Netherlands. Arras tapestries had once dominated the up-market rag trade, and rated a mention by the Bard when Hamlet stabs the hidden Polonius behind the Arras tapestry. Later claims to fame of the Artois capital included being the birthplace of the French revolutionary leader Maximilien Robespierre, the 'seagreen incorruptible', whose puritanical sway ended in his own execution and a slackening of the Terror he had propounded. The house of his birth still stands, in a narrow street close to the Arras Bishops' Palace and the little square where the Arras guillotine had stood during the Revolution.

Arras also has two impressive squares, with architecture in the Flemish and Spanish styles—the Place des Héros and the Place de Ville. The Town Hall is particularly magnificent. Most of the buildings, like the Hôtel de Ville, were pounded to pieces in the First War, when Arras, like Ypres, formed a bulge in the German lines. In his war diary, written a few days before he was killed in action at Arras, the English poet Edward Thomas describes his view of the shattered town . . . 'Beautiful was Arras yesterday coming down from Beaurains and seeing Town Hall ruins white in sun like a thick smoke beginning to curl'.

The buildings, of course, had been meticulously and lovingly restored to their former glory. Arras had also had a brief moment of glory in the Second War—being the scene for a forlorn-hope counter-offensive by ancient British Matilda tanks against the Waffen SS during the victorious German drive to the sea in 1940. The city had grown with the years, and Jean-François was temporarily staying at an appro-priately bleak and windy modern structure at the edge of town—an old people's hospital. A structure so anonymous that it did not even have a name, just a title, V 208, after the standardized design of the build-ings. It was a terminal place in every sense of the word. One side of the service flat where we were staying looked out over flat fields, the other gave onto a view of the hospital laundry, where flag-like sheets, stained with geriatric blood and excreta, sailed past on a moving belt to be abluted in giant washing machines. Momentarily I doubted Stephen's poetic insistence on the joy of growing old, if it led to this . . .

The next day, we were up early to start our walk. Jean-François took us out onto the main Arras-Lille road. The road drove east past a Highland Infantry memorial that is an exact copy of the cairn erected at Culloden. We parted company at a point where a new motorway flew over the road, bearing traffic for Calais and the coast. We took a track leading up to the village of Bailleul-sur-Berthoult, scene of one of the Allied thrusts in the Battle of Arras in 1917. Our target was the infamous Vimy Ridge, whose capture had been the main aim—success-fully realized by the Canadians—of the offensive north of Arras. Passing through the village, the old trench map I was using told me that during the war, railway track had rolled north parallel with the road and sure enough it was still there. I was struck, not for the first time, not by how much, but by how little the countryside of the battlefields has changed. The towns have grown round the edges, of course, and roads have widened—but they still follow the old course, and the villages, although blasted off the map, were rebuilt on their former lines—no bigger, no smaller; their survival, a tribute to human tenacity.

We plodded along the railway embankment until the woods on the slopes leading up to Vimy Ridge came in view across the railway line, crossed the tracks at the village of Farbus, and headed up into the trees. The track led upwards quite steeply—we were on the 'German' side of the ridge and this soon became apparent when we gained the ridgeback. This was lined with a string of bunkers made of reinforced concrete.

Their solidity, surviving 66 years, was sufficient evidence of Germanic construction.

There then occurred what was, to say the least, a remarkable coincidence. Examining the bunkers, several of which had been completely stove in by shells, we started to speculate as to exactly when reinforced concrete had been invented, and by whom. We came to the conclusion that it had probably been the late nineteenth century. A couple of hours later, after descending the ridge to the village of Neuville St. Vaast, we saw across the main street of the village a plaque with a man's head and shoulders. Curious, we crossed the road and read that the house had been the birthplace of one François Hennibecque, inventor of reinforced concrete.

We emerged on the far side of the ridge near Thelus and were picking our way along the edge of heavily clodded ploughed fields, which yielded, at every few paces, heavy twisted shards of rusty steel—the iron harvest of the war, still reaped year after year.

Later, we transferred to the Arras sector to prepare for the British offensive there in April 1917. It was there that we came under fire for the first time. We were stationed at a village called Thelus just under Vimy Ridge when the Canadians captured the ridge. We were spotted by the Germans and a Jerry shell burst just in front of our gun. Luckily the next one was a dud. I saw it coming down, a black spot in the air. Then we were allowed to take cover in dug-outs. Next morning, the Royal Engineers came up and started to repair the railway which had been cut by the shelling, so we had to start firing the next day again—talk about having the wind up! We were sleeping in a former Jerry dug-out, it was very deep and the walls were lined with wood. That night some more shells came over and one burst just outside our front door. Gunner Bob Fretton was standing just inside and a splinter went through his chest, killing him. He was the only fatality in our unit.

(Smith)

We dropped back down through the woods again, to the small town of Vimy itself. Here suburbia was beginning to elbow out pastoralism. We passed through a street in which showy Citröens and big Renaults were parked, shining in immaculately-kept bordered driveways. 'Tupperware country'. The violent past seemed buried deep . . .

Once we were halfway up Vimy Ridge and we had to dig trenches to shelter from machine guns. We started digging and found the bodies of Canadian soldiers who had died there the year before when they stormed the ridge. I think they must have been buried alive by shells because they still had their watches and personal effects on them. Their clothes were still intact but the bodies were like porridge—that's what happens to human beings who have been in the ground for twelve or eighteen months.

(Thacker)

It took a violent leap of the imagination to envisage scenes like that as we marched through the tidy village streets, incongruous in our big boots and paramilitary outdoor gear. Already dehydrated, we paused in a café for a beer and a map consultation to plan the next steps.

Leaving the village, we headed back up into the woods again which covered the steepest points of the ridge (the description 'ridge' is something of a misnomer: it is said that Haig himself, arriving at the foot of the ridge in his staff car, inquired 'But where is it?'. In truth, it is nowhere much more than a gentle undulation).

We stopped to eat a picnic lunch by a tiny Canadian cemetery, Petit Vimy. I was struck by the more homely epitaphs on the graves here— nearly all of men killed in the taking of the ridge on April 10, 1917. One which hit home with its simple but moving naïvety, read: 'He would give his last meal to a hungry dog and go without himself'. Not a bad passport to take into eternity. In contrast, the British epitaphs in most of the cemeteries we visited were as clipped as the grass around: 'Always missed', 'Gone, but not forgotten', 'Died for us'.

Replete, we were ready for a stiffish climb through La Folie Wood, one of the main objectives of the Canadian attack. At the summit, a ride had been cut through the woods leading straight to the vast Canadian monument, unveiled in 1936 by the ill-fated King Edward VIII, who had served in the trenches, albeit in a slightly protected position:

A rather round-shouldered young Lieutenant in the Grenadiers came to my office and asked me where he was to report. I recognized him at once and told him no one was to come through our office and directed him to General Haig. I saw him many times later and he grew into a fine upright looking soldier. He was seconded to the First Corps who at that time were under the command of Sir Charles Munroe. Having such an important person under him, made Sir Charles cautious and he issued instructions that the Prince of Wales had to have someone with him if he went out. The Prince got over this by using a bicycle by which he could go to danger spots with no one to interfere and without the restraining hand of his C.O.

(Jones)

The memorial built on Hill 145, highpoint of the ridge, is the sort of massive architecture favoured in the inter-war years, equally popular with Hitler and Stalin, and I think of it as a totalitarian art. As we approached it, we could see the trenches and almost overlapping shell-holes in the woods on either side of the track. The white stone memorial itself stands on a square of grass hummocked with shellshot, and bears exaggerated notices warning off the unwary visitor. The memorial consists of two huge parallel pillars, surrounded and surmounted by outsize statues of weeping women. Only from the esplanade of the memorial do you get some idea of why the ridge was such an important strongpoint. To the north-east, a view of the flat plains extends to the red brick and slag heaps of the mining town of Lens. On a clear day, one can see the next important promontory to rise above the Flanders plain—the Messines Ridge.

Like Messines, Vimy was the scene of much mine warfare:

In the summer of 1917, we went down to Vimy Ridge, which the Canadians had taken. There were lots of skulls and skeletons about from Frenchmen who had occupied it the year before. It stank. We could see Lens in the distance beyond the German lines, but never reached it. Lots of mining went on there. On one occasion we heard a swishing noise and we were sure that Jerry was mining underneath us. We got in touch with a Royal Engineers Officer and told him. He went down a sap to listen, but came up again without hearing anything. Just when we were talking about it in a dug-out, a stone jar of rum on the table was knocked over . . . and the swishing stopped. We realized that the wind had made the noise as it passed over the open top of the jar. Another time when the Germans were mining, they sent over lots of 'Minenwerfers' to cover the noise. We were due to go back for a rest, and we knew that a German mine was about to go off, so we left only skeleton sentries in the trench concerned. We were relieved by the Civil Service Rifles. We told them where the mine was due to go up and when, but they didn't believe us. I remember that they all had their Christmas parcels with them. We marched back 15 kilometres to rest, and we had just reached our destination when the mine went

117

up. We had to turn round and march straight back again to hold the line. About 20–30 men were buried alive. We were there another ten days before being relieved again.

(Haddock)

The C.O. sent for all officers and told us that we had to go back to the front line as the Bosche had put in an attack on that part that we had recently vacated and that we were to put in an immediate counter-attack.

We paraded and started to retrace our steps, all feeling fed up that our few days rest had been denied and I know that I wondered if I would be lucky enough to get a blighty one. We were passed by ammunition limbers galloping by at a hell for leather rate, and although an inspiring sight in retrospect, it didn't do much to cheer me on the way.

When we reached the communication trench leading up to the reserve line on the rear slope of the ridge, the C.O. sent for me and said: 'Get me in touch with the front line somehow'. I saluted and said 'Yes Sir', and wondered how on earth I was going to be able to do it.

However I detailed (a lovely word 'detailed') my Corporal to come with me to pick up wire and a telephone set and together we started off up the trench towards the front line. There was a certain amount of shelling going on but it was not uncomfortably near and as we proceeded up the trench, we tapped into old wire already there hoping to find one that was alive with someone on the other end.

After various tries we found a line which, praise be, was alive and when I asked who and where they were, found that they were another London Regiment in the front line. I asked if they would take my messages and as they agreed, we started with great relief to retrace our steps and report our success to the C.O.

I was emotionally drained by this time when the Boche suddenly opened up with everything he had in the way of artillery and all hell seemed to be let loose over the Zouave Valley, shrapnel, heavy stuff, the lot, presumably to stop any reinforcements.

It frightened the life out of me when I heard a heavy shell called a Jack Johnson coming too close for comfort.

As we were at the entrance to a dug-out, we both flung ourselves down its steps into pitch darkness only to realize that it was occupied by troops all talking a foreign language!

I immediately decided that I was not going to go down fighting but would pack my war effort in and go to Germany.

It was then that somebody called me 'Bach' and I suddenly realized that we had fallen into a squad of South Wales miners engaged in tunnelling under the Hun trenches, returning the compliment, so to speak.

By this time dawn was approaching and the shelling had eased off, so the Corporal and I scuttled down the communication trench and I was able to report to the C.O. that he was in touch with the front line. I felt very bucked with myself and felt sure that the C.O. would recommend me for a Military Cross! But all he said was: 'You have taken a damned long time about it!'

(Blaber)

The memorial is surrounded by the 240-acre Canadian memorial park which contains a section of the original front line trenches, preserved for posterity. Even the sandbags lining the trench walls are still there, but are now made of concrete. Concrete duckboards run along the floors of the trenches. Underneath the trench lines are four layers of tunnels—originally they amounted to over 22 miles of subway. The topmost level, which is open to the public in the summer months, is around 20 feet underground. The second level is 75 feet down, and the last two even deeper. The lowest level contained a narrow-gauge underground railway used to bring up ammunition to the Front, and reputedly, a whole train—forever halted at its final terminal. The tunnels, lit by electric light, also contained Brigade and Battalion HQs, casualty stations, ammunition stores, plus accommodation for men. The labyrinth was bomb- but not gas-proof.

It is an eerie experience to climb out of the Canadian trenches and stroll a few yards across the greensward to the German front lines. One can hardly conceive of the horror of hand-to-hand fighting which these few square feet of ground once contained. Only the lunar landscape, with its huge mine craters, looks in any way unnatural. The trenches themselves, in their unreally-preserved neatness, seem a little too pretty.

We left the ridge and crossed the motorway via a modern bridge to the village of Neuville-St.-Vaast. Like Vimy, this was originally in the French sector too, the scene of savage fighting in the early years of the war, and was aptly described in the diary of one French front-line soldier as 'a charnal house'. Initially captured by the Germans during their drive into France in 1914, it was recaptured by the French under the brutal General Mangin, 'the Butcher', in June 1915. One of those killed in the retaking was the young sculptor Henri Gaudier-Brzeska, the 'Savage Messiah' of Ken Russell's film. Gaudier had been one of the founders of the artistic movement, Vorticism, which, in its magazine *Blast* had tried to blow away all the formal artistic niceties of the pre-war world. When war came, many of its members, like their Italian counterparts, the Futurists, joined up, eager to put their ideals of speed, violence, and iconoclasm into practice. Their intellectual mentor, the philosopher T. E. Hulme, fell at Nieuport. Others, like the artist and satirist Wyndham Lewis, survived to espouse Fascism in the 1930s. Gaudier wrote from the trenches a few days before his death:

> I have been fighting for two months and I can now gauge the intensity of life. Human masses teem and move, are destroyed and crop up again. Horses are worn out in three weeks, die by the roadside. Dogs wander, are destroyed, and others come along. With all the destruction that works around us, nothing is changed, even superficially. Life is the same strength, the moving agent that permits the small individual to assert himself. The bursting shells, the volleys, wire entanglements, projectiles, motors, the chaos of battle do not alter in the least the outline of the hill we are besieging. A company of partridges scuttle along before our very trench. It would be folly to seek artistic emotions amid these little works of ours. This paltry mechanism, which serves as a purge to over-numerous humanity. This war is a great remedy. In the individual it kills arrogance, self-esteem, pride. It takes away from the masses numbers upon numbers of unimportant units, whose economic activities become noxious as the recent trade crises have shown us. My views on sculpture remain absolutely the same, it is the vortex of will, of decision, that begins.

Nearby, at Notre Dame de La Lorette, the French have built another ossuary for their dead; a mini-Douaumont; it contains 7,000 graves.

We left the village and crossed the ploughed fields towards the main Arras-Béthune road. We were traversing the original German lines, an in-depth defensive position that became notorious as the 'Labyrinth', and withstood repeated Allied attacks until the breakthrough in the Battle of Arras. On the road is an enormous German graveyard, known originally as the 'Concentration cemetery', since German corpses were brought from all over France to be interred here. Acres and acres of black metal crosses stretch away to the horizon.

This place, too, has literary associations; Henry Williamson, author of *Tarka the Otter*, became obsessed with the cemetery which he saw as a futile symbol of the hatreds dividing Europe. A veteran of the Western Front, he returned again and again to brood here, and it recurs in many of his novels.

We turned homewards, and soon encountered the depressing suburbs of Arras. The edges of towns always have a dark, desolate feel about them: they are landscapes of loss. The detritus, literal and metaphorical seem to collect here. We saw the hindquarters of a dead dog, shoved in a cardboard box and discarded on waste land behind a garage.

The next day we explored the main battleground of Arras itself. Appropriately enough we approached this via the town's municipal cemetery, and then passed out of the town along the main railway line to Lille. Much of the battlefield is being swallowed up and concreted over by the city's expansion. A new bus depot covers the trench lines from which the British launched their attack on Easter Sunday, 1917. By a coincidence, the weather which met us was the same that faced the men as they moved forward then: squalls of snow drove in our faces as we trudged along the railway embankment to Railway Triangle, a tiny piece of land which took many lives, before it was absorbed by the British attack. We turned south along a farm track, and began to see the scars of war: the shells excavated by the farmers and piled along the fields. Most of these were British, and had been fired in the bombardment that preceded the offensive. The number of duds still dug up testify both to the intensity of the fire and the muddy conditions, as the shells often failed to explode on impact, plopping harmlessly into the soft and churned-up soil. One of the artillerymen behind the barrage on that day was the English poet Edward Thomas, whose tomb we were due to visit that afternoon.

He had been on duty at an artillery observation post in a suburb of Arras when the blast of a shell had stopped his heart, (and his watch) at 7.36 a.m. on April 9, the first hour of the offensive. The diary he scribbled in the last days before he was killed gives a vivid, poetic picture of a landscape still recognizable today, despite the creeping encroachment of urbanization: the large fields, the larks, living their precarious lives despite the destruction all around them, the bitter cold, and the troops, huddling for warmth in the ruins of the mean red-brick houses.

Thomas' battery was raining shells on a German strongpoint known as Telegraph Hill—today a hardly-discernible rise in the fields crowned by a small wood. After passing through the village of Tilloy-les-Moufflaines, we strode up to the hill in the teeth of a blinding snow-storm. Once among the shelter of the trees, the evidence of German occupation was clear: a line of concrete bunkers sunk in the earth, a shaft with steps built into it—and the shell craters of the British barrage which finally dislodged the defenders. Descending to the Arras-Bapaume road, we made our way over to Agny where Thomas' body lies—under an anonymous headstone among many others.

We then returned to the Arras suburb of Beaurains where we had arranged a meeting with the local expert on World War One, M. André Coilliot, an extraordinary figure who has converted his own house and garden into a private museum of both wars. He was slightly discon-certed by our dishevelled appearance, but soon put us at our ease. He greeted us in his hallway, which is lined with glass cases containing every imaginable British military medal and decoration, together with the cap badges and insignia of virtually every British unit in the two wars. Ushering us into his 'study', he proudly showed us the rest of his museum: glass cases containing tailor's dummies in the uniforms of all countries involved in the war; weapons, such as shells, grenades, rifles, machine-guns and enormous maps displaying the dispositions of every unit that took part in the battles of the Somme and Arras. A narrow passage wound around the cases and into a reconstruction of a trench dug-out, lined with sandbags and complete with original signposts. On we went, into what had clearly once been M. Coilliot's back garden. It was now covered with a large shed, containing an enormous German anti-tank gun of Second World War vintage, a photographic gallery, and more battlefield relics—rusty helmets, mortars, howitzer shells, flags, contemporary books and magazines.

To call M. Coilliot a militarist fanatic would not perhaps be a compliment, but it is nevertheless true. The place reeked of the enthus-iasm of a small boy who had never, as he freely admitted, seen any action. But one could only admire his industry in amassing this huge and comprehensive collection. Some men sell their lives for women or drink, some for politics, bingo, pigeon fancying, or football—but M. Coilliot's all-embracing obsession was for war and weapons. A senior railway official by trade, M. Coilliot had devoted a large part of his life since his boyhood to his harmless, but single-minded hobby. He had even paid for the private publication of a history of Arras under the German occupation in the Second World War.

Of Madame Coilliot there was no sign. We got the impression that she was confined to her kitchen, besieged by her husband's ever encroaching army of militaria. Seated at his war desk amidst the museum, M. Coilliot invited us to share a bottle of wine while we picked his brains. It turned out that he was the Arras representative, and the only civilian on a committee of generals of a French organization called *Souvenir de France* whose symbol, a naked sword against the tricolour, accurately summed up its objectives; to foster a sense of France's glorious past, to preserve its battlefields, and to inculcate French youth with patriotic values.

M. Coilliot was proud of the fact that the kids who accompanied him on his pilgrimages to the Somme and Verdun included girls as well as boys. He also told us that the German Army held the most fascination for his youthful acolytes, because of the 'discipline', but he did not think there was any danger of neo-Nazism infecting his members. At that moment the phone rang on his desk. Answering it, M. Coilliot visibly stiffened to attention: 'Oui, mon Colonel', he rasped, 'A vos ordres, mon Colonel . . ., mais certainement, mon Colonel'. Replacing the receiver, he proudly told us that the colonel in command of the Arras garrison had been his caller. The Army wanted M. Coilliot's help in mounting an exhibition on the World Wars at Vauban's Arras citadel. We also called upon his expertise in another field—to give us a timetable of the local trains which would enable us to plot our exploration of the Somme the next day. Then, with his tips and admonitions ringing in our ears, we bid him *au revoir*.

We were up in dawn's early light next day to take a local train to the heart of the Somme battlefield—Beaucourt-sur-Ancre—the blood-stained village in the valley of the Ancre whose capture had been one of the objectives on July 1, 1916. It had not been achieved.

The writer and humorist A. P. Herbert was one of those who fought here, and later wrote in a poem, *Beaucourt Revisited*:

I wandered up to Beaucourt;
I took the river track,
And saw the lines we lived in,
Before the Boche went back . . .
And I said, there is still the river, and still the stiff, stark trees:
To treasure here our story, but there are only these;
But under the white wood crosses, the dead men answered low,
The new men know not Beaucourt, but we are here—we know.

The first thing I noticed as we stepped from the train was a garish poster on a farmhouse wall advertising a local disco. The names of the two bands playing seemed strangely appropriate: 'Holocaust' and 'Armageddon'.

We trudged up the road to Beaumont-Hamel village. As always on the battlefields, I was struck by the peace and stillness. The Somme is a particularly isolated place. It is inconceivable that so much blood, tears and treasure could have been expended to secure this unremarkable patch of north French farmland.

Out in the fields you could be anywhere in Home Counties England. Some things are constant, like the cry of the larks which the men heard and remembered as a defiant counterpoint to the cacophony of the guns. Otherwise the scene is idyllic, without being beautiful; gently undulating ploughed fields, a few sparse woods, and a pleasant brook called the Ancre babbles past. Utterly impossible to conceive that this pastoral place could have turned, in the autumn of 1916, into a quag-mire which sucked down men, guns and the ambitions of nations into its all-engulfing maw. Beaumont-Hamel was deserted except for a farmer on a tractor.

The war poet Wilfred Owen supped his fill of the horrors of this village in the grim winter 1916–17, and in a brief period of later tranquillity wrote to a friend with a pungent comment about another poet, Lord Tennyson, who was fond of glorifying war, yet complained of never finding happiness:

> I can quite believe he never knew happiness for one moment as I have; but as for misery was he ever frozen alive with dead men for comforters? Did he ever hear the moaning at the bar, not at twilight and evening bell only but at dawn, noon, and night, eating and sleeping, watching and waking, always the close moaning of the Bar?—Tennyson, it seems, was always a great child. So should I have been but for Beaumont-Hamel.

A stony path led from the village to 'Y' Ravine, which led in turn to the Newfoundland Memorial Park, an area similar to the Vimy Park and also beautifully maintained by the Canadians. The 80-acre park encloses the area fought over by the Royal Newfoundland Regiment on July 1.

They went into action following the detonation of the massive mine under nearby Hawthorn Ridge, creating a crater 150 yards wide and 80 feet deep. The Hawthorn crater is hidden among trees and hard to find. It is also being gradually filled in with debris.

Another mine left the greatest crater still preserved on the Western

Front, known as the Lochnagar crater, which was bought by an Englishman, Richard Dunning, and is preserved outside the village of La Boisselle. The crater is 300 feet across, and 90 feet deep, and was caused by the largest mine exploded before the battle. The blast from the 60,000 pounds of explosives was felt for hundreds of miles around.

The park contains cemeteries and artificially-preserved trenches, but its bare, sparse grass acres do give some idea of what No Man's Land was like. The area is replete with battle debris. The old German front line, dominated by the statue of a kilted Highlander of the 51st Highland Division, who took Beaumont-Hamel at last in the autumn of 1916, is filled with howitzer and trench mortar shells, ripped open by blast like gigantic pea pods. The curly iron stakes which once held the barbed wire on which the British were caught and cut down in waves, still stand as mute witnesses to the slaughter. In the middle of the park stands a more macabre memorial: the so-called 'tree of death', a petrified skeleton of the only surviving original tree left in the wilderness. The Caribou memorial, baying defiantly towards the German lines, dominates the scene on top of an old dug-out mound. The memorial sparked a discussion on the aesthetic qualities of war monuments. Stephen held that the memorials of this war should have been more in keeping with the technological nature of the conflict: he favoured futurist shapes and abstract mechanical constructions, rather than traditional statues of meditating soldiers and weeping women.

Leaving the park we dropped down with the road into the valley of the Ancre through the village of Hamel, and back over the river itself, where the rainbow flash of a kingfisher surprised and pleased us. The road climbed again on the south side of the valley, where the monument to the 36th Ulster Division crowned the slope.

The history of the Ulstermen is one of the more tragic episodes of the Somme battle. Recruited *en masse* from the Ulster Volunteers, the civilian militia raised by Sir Edward Carson to resist Irish Home Rule in the years before the First World War, these Ulster Protestants patriotically joined up en bloc in August 1914, and turned from fighting their Catholic cousins to fighting alongside them. There was intense rivalry between the two faiths on July 1, as to which should be the first to reach their objectives. Unfortunately for the Ulstermen, their targets were the almost impregnable German strongpoints of Thiepval village and the Schwaben Redoubt—heavily fortified positions consisting not only of deeply-wired trenches, but of underground tunnels and galleries cut through the Somme chalk, which the Germans had been strengthening and building up for years. It was not an easy nut to crack, even for the tough and hardy Inniskillins. But somehow they managed to flush the Germans out of the redoubt and hang on along the wire, despite dreadful losses and a woeful lack of reinforcements. Thiepval itself proved too much, and was not captured until September.

Many of the 5,500 Ulstermen who died that day lie in the two cemeteries of Connaught Road and Mill Road. The latter is built over the redoubt itself and some of the headstones are laid flat because of the continued subsidence caused by the crumbling caverns of the underground fortress. Passing by the memorial tower we found a rusty British Mills bomb grenade in the copse behind it, and struggled across the metal-littered ploughed field to Mill Road cemetery. The visitors' book was remarkable for the number of Ulster people who still make the long trip out to pay homage to their dead. July 1 was long kept as a day of mourning in Ulster, and there were dark suspicions that the British authorities had deliberately let the recalcitrant Protestants go to their deaths, so that, decimated, they would provide no opposition to Home Rule after the war. The slogan most often written in the book is 'No Surrender!', the Ulster Protestant rallying cry since 1690. I added a line from the war poet Ivor Gurney, who ended his days in a lunatic asylum: 'An end to pain'.

We moved on to the handful of houses that are all that remains of Thiepval, the fortified redoubt village which was the centrepoint of the Somme battle. Behind the hamlet stands the huge red-brick Thiepval memorial to the missing. This colossal arch, built on the site of Thiepval Château which dominates the Somme area from its high position at the top of a ridge, is the work of Sir Edwin Lutyens. On the memorial's panels are inscribed the names of 73,412 men who died in the Somme battles and have no known graves. Time has taken its toll of Sir Edwin's work, and entry to the memorial was forbidden owing to the risk of falling bricks adding to the battlefield's casualty roll.

We left the road and took a track eastwards towards Courcelette, picking up muddy fragments of bone and iron on our way, as we passed the site of Mouquet ('Mucky') farm, forward HQ of the defending German army in the battle.

> After another day we moved back again out of reserve, for our companies had had a very bad time, having been called in to reinforce the front line and had undergone some very heavy shelling. During these two days the scouts had done a lot too, in the way of reconnoitring all the ground and we had been right through the village of Courcelette, finishing dug-outs for HQ, etc., for we

were to go up there the next time we came in. This time we only went back about a mile to a place called Sausage Valley; this had been a German support line and was full of good dug-outs which we occupied.

We stayed here for several days and on October 21, we moved up to Courcelette, and lodged in a dug-out about 30 yards away from HQ. We arrived at dusk and when night fell, it was so pitchy dark, that several men lost themselves trying to find HQ from our dug-out, and such was the shelling that a number of men, though they knew the way and ran across, were killed; there was no time between the shells, they just were bursting all ways.

All that night, the scouts were kept very busy, guiding men up to the trenches, and guiding our companies. We were working hard; no sooner did a man come back from doing one thing than he went out again. Most of the work was guiding for no one knew the way anywhere, and several times an officer or a party of men would come and ask for a guide to take him to some place quite out of our own area, as he was lost. We never disappointed these people if there was a man who could take them to their destination.

Early in the morning, our snipers went up to the front to see what could be done and a little later, I went up also, on duty, to go out to a German dug-out about 500 yards in front of our line and about the same distance from theirs, to see what was in it.

As it was now broad daylight, it was necessary to take great care in covering the open ground from our line to the dug-out, but luckily it stood on a slight rise which lay between the two lines, so that if we kept very low, we were out of sight of the enemy for a little distance and the last few yards, we covered (there were three of us) at a run in full view of the Germans. This dug-out lay on the West Miraumont Road, in the high bank.

When we got down there, we found very little but one dead German and one wounded one, whom we bound up with a field-dressing; I also found a watch and a pocket knife, which I took.

We then ran from the dug-out and got into a shellhole on the rising ground to have a look at the enemy's trench. But he soon saw us and we had to get out pretty quick as he began to shell the spot very accurately.

We then came back and handed in a report on the dug-out and gave up some papers we had found. We sent a stretcher for the German. We stayed here for one more day and carried on some of the usual guiding, etc., and then were relieved by the 52nd

Battalion, and we struggled out on the early morning of October 4; it was raining and very muddy and we were all pretty tired for we had had no real sleep for two days and nights.

(Muir)

Crossing the straight Albert-Bapaume road, we made for Martin-puich, another key village, and two nearby woods, High Wood and Delville ('Devils') Wood, where the South Africans won death and glory.

The South African Brigade, fresh to the fighting, were thrown into the Somme battle on July 15, a fortnight after the struggle opened. Their orders were to take the wood, which was heavily held by entrenched Germans. In two days of savage fighting they cleared the wood, but at a terrible cost. Of 121 officers and 3,032 men who went in, only 29 officers and 751 men emerged. Their exploits are commemorated by several moving monuments, including a Voortrekker cross marking the Brigade's dug-out HQ. Rides cut through the wood bear British names like Buchanan Street and Rotten Row.

Neighbouring High Wood is also something of a literary landmark, for it was during an attack here in late July that the poet Robert Graves, received near-fatal wounds from an exploding shell. Given up for dead he struggled to survive, and despite his death being reported in *The Times* on his 21st birthday he is still, at the time of writing, happily among us.

Other lesser luminaries like Jim Haddock, have their memories of the wood:

When we came out of Vimy, we went into training on the Somme. We were using models of trenches designed to simulate our real objectives. We were stationed in High Wood and it was there in the summer of 1917 that we saw our first tanks. The Jerries put up their hands at once when they saw them, they were so scared. But they couldn't get the cavalry up in time—if they had done that, we might have broken through and the war would have ended then. We all believed that each attack would lead to a breakthrough. All the men had visions of victory—they were fed up with trench warfare.

For Wilfred Blaber, the memories were painful ones:

In August 1916, I left Vimy to go to the Somme show. The roads were so crowded and it was so hot that we decided to march at night. We were not allowed to ask directions so one night we got lost. I did not know about it until the C.O. said: 'Blaber, we've taken the wrong road'. I thought that was a good moment to hop off on leave, but I was back in time to get wounded, which happened on September 21 at High Wood. I was following a tank too closely which was hit by a shell, and I was scattered with fragments. I was taken back to England, but the hospitals were so crowded there that I was shipped out to France again!

High Wood today is in private hands and as it has never been properly cleared of munitions it is allegedly dangerous, but curiosity got too much for us, so braving gamekeepers, we climbed through the wire and wandered at will through the thick trees.

After a look at the villages of Bazentin les Grand and Petit, we visited Flat Iron Copse cemetery on the edge of Mametz Wood, where Graves' friend and fellow poet. Siegfried Sassoon, distinguished himself and won the nickname 'Mad Jack' for his lone bombing raids on German trenches.

Do you remember the dark months you held the sector at Mametz—
The nights you watched and wired and dug and piled sandbags on parapets
Do you remember the rats; and the stench
Of corpses rotting in the front line trench—
And dawn coming, dirty-white, and chill with a hopeless rain?

—He asked in one poem.

Flat Iron Copse cemetery contains another literary name which brought us up short: William Shakespeare.

A quick dip into Mametz Wood revealed a trench in excellent condition, and relics so numerous that the battle for the trench could almost be reconstructed: here a German grenade, there a British one, here an old boot, there a rusty spade. But the shafts of evening sunlight slanting through the trees told us that evening, and our last train home, was fast approaching, so we turned weary footsteps round and 'towards our distant rest began to trudge' (Owen).

Tramping back through Martinpuich, I remembered the opening lines of another poem—by Graves:

> Near Martinpuich that night of hell
> Two men were struck by the same shell
> Together tumbling in one heap
> Senseless and limp like slaughtered sheep.

But the peaceful country road in the gentle evening sun reminded me of nothing so much as the quiet country lanes near my Hertfordshire home.

We retraced our steps through Courcelette and took a track northwards over the undulating downland which petered out at a lonely cemetery, which takes its name from a hard-fought line during the September battles: Regina Trench. Only a few dedicated pilgrims made the march up to this isolated, windswept spot. Yet it was as tidy, as hallowed, as all the rest. Moved, I wrote: 'Lonely, seldom visited, they keep the quiet comradeship of the dead'.

As the dying sun cast long shadows across the furrows, we saw on the slopes the clear lines of trenches carved out in white chalk patches, like smears on a school blackboard. And ever, always laid reverently at the sides of the fields by the cautious hands of the Somme peasantry: the shell shards of war, the constant kilometre markers on these untaken roads.

Reaching the village of Grandcourt, we turned left along the Ancre, moving westwards and following road and rail, until calves and thighs were aching and twitching from tiredness. I recognized the marshy area from a trench map I was carrying, and again remarked on the exactness with which the devastated landscape had been reconstructed after the wind of war had passed. Even the unmanned station shed into which we flopped to await the homeward train had been on the same site in 1916.

The following day I devoted to another personal quest. I knew that my father had been stationed during the war at a château near Arras, called Ranchicourt. Jean-François had located the château, and the chatelaine, the Comtesse de Ranchicourt who, it turned out, remembered both the days of British occupation in the First World War and a brief period of German occupation in the Second.

We arrived at the château, a magnificent if dilapidated building standing in its own park of enormous, dripping trees. The Comtesses' lady companion greeted us at the front door and ushered us into the library, a deliciously decayed but ornate chamber, complete with slow ticking ormulu clock, and oil portraits of the Comtesse's aristocratic ancestors frowning down from the walls.

When the Comtesse herself came in, she proved to be a small but sprightly lady, as old as the century. In answer to our eager questions she became steadily more voluble and forthcoming—yes, she remembered the days when her home had been the HQ of the British First Army commanded by General Horne . . . 'LORD Horne!', she reproved me, giving Haig's promoted artilleryman his post-war title.

Pausing only to shoo away her cat as he dug lazy paws into a no-doubt valuable but already ragged tapestry-covered chair, the Comtesse produced a treasured volume of photographs illustrating those days of 1917. On one occasion the parkland at the rear of the château had been filled with armed men come to hold a service 'celebrating' the fourth anniversary of the war's outbreak. Horne was there, addressing the men from a Union-Jack draped platform, greeting the President of Portugal on a visit to his countrymen at the Allied Front, and saluting a march past.

My father had been a shorthand writer on Horne's staff, and I vaguely hoped that the Comtesse would show us round the château and point out the British officers' bedrooms, but she explained that the staff had conducted its work from huts in the grounds. Most of the senior officers had signed their photographs in her album, including Horne's right-hand man, Major-General Sir Warren Hastings Anderson, a special favourite of my father's who rose in the Army after the war. Indeed, only the unhappy accident of his being carried off by a chill prevented him from commanding the British Army in the Second World War.

My father left a description of how the Army's Staff 'fought' a battle from the château:

> We had a busy time at First Army. A day's work usually commenced at 8 a.m. and continued until about 11 p.m. except for meals. Of course when there was any action the hours were much longer. I well recall the 9th April, 1918, when the Germans attacked the Portuguese.

(The Battle of the Lys, Ludendorff's 'Operation Georgette', the second phase of his great spring offensives in 1918).

> There were two Portuguese Divisions in France and they happened to be in our Army. When the Germans attacked they made a tremendous advance. [Even capturing the previously safe town of Armentières and threatening the Channel ports—this was the occasion of Haig's famous 'Backs to the Wall' exhortation].

Generals Horne, Anderson and I were in the operations office from the time the first report arrived—about 5 a.m.—until very late at night or rather early the following morning, receiving messages, sending messages, stopping gaps, arranging for divisions to be moved to the places where they were most wanted, sending up more artillery . . .

[A speciality of Horne's was the invention of the Creeping Barrage, a technique which was very effective unless shells fell short and killed some of our own troops advancing behind it.]

Keeping in close touch with the Royal Flying Corps, etc . . ., in fact fighting the battle until the gaps were closed and the danger passed. Horne went to inspect troops after the position became a little easier. I was of course taking orders all the time, reporting after telephone calls, etc. This is where my shorthand proved of great value.

The Comtesse proudly showed us a photo of herself as a seventeen-year-old girl mounted on a magnificent black horse which she told us had been a personal present to her from Horne. When Jean-François asked her to pose for photos outside the château, she agreed after donning a battered brown felt hat to go with her unpretentious old clothes.

The Comtesse pointed to one of the chairs in the library and described how it had once housed the ample posterior of Hermann Goering, who had been briefly billeted at Ranchicourt during Germany's lightning dash through France in May 1940. The old lady vividly described how the First World War flyer turned Luftwaffe Overlord, had chortled as he listened to a French Radio smugly assuring its audience that the Germans were still behind the Meuse!

The Comtesse had clearly been deeply shocked by the latter occupation, especially, she told us, by the Nazis' 'Socialism'—which consisted of billeting the ordinary soldiers in the château while their officers roughed it in the grounds. 'And', she added with a wistful twinkle, 'The first thing they all did when they got here was to strip off their clothes and shower—I have never seen so many naked men in my life!'

As we took our leave, my attention was caught by an unmistakable picture in the hall, a Breughel which the Comtesse assured us was an original. I expressed surprise that the picture had escaped the attention of Goering, the supreme art thief—but perhaps he had been in too much of a hurry.

The Comtesse seemed to have survived two world wars and a lifetime of social and political upheaval with equanimity. Perhaps survival was inherent in her family's long history. But she was an elderly and childless lady, a Socialist Government had come to power in France, and although she was still, in feudal style, Mayoress of her tiny village, it was clear that she mistrusted the future. Local gossip had it that she was selling off some of the endless vistas of land that stretched behind the château and investing in Parisian real estate. The shadows of tomorrow, as well as yesterday, lie deep over Ranchicourt.

Part Five
New Blood

14. The Butcher's Bill—Aisne and Arras

The offensive alone can give victory; the defensive gives only defeat and shame.

General Robert Nivelle

We saw fire on the tragic slopes
Where the flood-tide of France's early gain,
Big with wrecked promise and abandoned hopes,
Broke in a surf of blood along the Aisne.

Alan Seeger, 'The Aisne'

'He's a cheery old card', grunted Harry to Jack,
As they slogged up to Arras with rifle and pack.
—But he did for them both by his plan of attack.

Siegfried Sassoon, 'The General'

The tall forest towers;
Its cloudy foliage lowers
Ahead, shelf above shelf:
Its silence I hear and obey
That I may lose my way
And myself.

Edward Thomas (killed at Arras, April 9, 1917), 'Lights Out'

The summer and autumn of 1916 saw a wholesale changing of the guard among the High Commands of the adversaries. On June 6, Kitchener, his work as Minister of War largely completed by the raising of the New Armies, died when HMS *Hampshire* was sunk by a mine *en route* to Russia. On August 20, Falkenhayn was dismissed by an increasingly powerless Kaiser, as an impoverished Germany moved closer to a virtual military dictatorship under the control of Ludendorff. On November 20, the Emperor Franz-Josef of Austria-Hungary, whose reign had begun in revolution in 1848, died, two years before another revolution finally engulfed his ramshackle empire. On December 6, Asquith, the British Premier, was replaced in a Cabinet coup by a Coalition Government headed by Lloyd George and dedicated to a more ruthless and efficient prosecution of the war. Six days later, Joffre, whose reputation for sang-froid had long outlived its usefulness, was made a Marshal and booted upstairs, to be replaced as French Commander-in-Chief by the aggressive and arrogant Nivelle. Finally, as the year ended, Rasputin, the hypnotic Holy Man who had gained such a baleful influence over the Russian royal family by his healing powers, was murdered by a court coterie as Russia sunk into ever-greater corruption and chaos. Just before he died, Rasputin had prophesied that the Tsar would lose his crown within six months.

For the first time since the war began, voices began to be raised demanding peace: Lord Lansdowne, a Conservative Cabinet Minister, put forward a memorandum proposing that peace negotiations be considered, and America's president, Woodrow Wilson, issued a note inviting the belligerents to state their war aims as a pre-condition to a peace conference. He also proposed a post-war League of Nations to maintain universal peace. In France, pacifist agitation which had caused several strikes in vital war industries, began to spread to the armed forces, with soldiers on leave encouraged to desert, and Left-wing newspapers being distributed in the trenches.

But for the moment, the warriors had the upper hand and they laid their war plans for the coming year: as usual, the Allies intended to attack in the west.

The increasingly sceptical French and British governments were temporarily dazzled and captivated by the ambitious plans propounded by France's new Commander, Nivelle. This officer, fresh from the triumphant recapture of Douaumont at Verdun, proposed to repeat his storming tactics on a grander scale and so end the war at a stroke. The attack, Nivelle insisted, must be made with the utmost speed and with violence, élan, force and fury. Nivelle, aided and abetted by his Lieutenants, 'Butcher' Mangin and his Chief-of-Staff, d'Alenson, who was dying of tuberculosis and wanted the war to be won before he quit the scene, had an exceptionally persuasive manner. Cocky and confident, he assured his Government that his offensive would work where all others had failed.

In January 1917 he came to London and made a favourable impression, even on Lloyd George who was, as ever, mistrustful of seeking victory in the trenches. Nivelle, a Huguenot with a British mother, spoke fluent English and was able to persuade the stolid Haig to play second fiddle to his grand offensive with a preliminary British attack around Arras.

Nivelle's chosen ground for his grand slam was bizarre: he proposed to hit the Germans along the River Aisne, striking northwards with more than a million men and 5,000 guns. He would seize the strategic Chemin des Dames ridge, north of the river and sweep onwards, within 48 hours, past Laon into the open country beyond the German lines. The shock of such an immediate breakthrough, he argued, would bring the Germans to their knees.

The fly in the ointment of this optimistic scenario was that few places along the Western Front were less promising for an attack. The ground above the Aisne was steep and open, an uphill slog at the best of times. In addition, the whole area was honeycombed with in-depth German defences as formidable as those on the Somme. The defenders had made use of the natural caves of the region to carve a network of defensive caverns. Even the element of surprise was lost, as Nivelle's plans were the talk of Paris, and soon the details of the offensive were passed to Berlin via Germany's active net of spies and saboteurs inside France.

Instantly, the Germans took steps to counter the attack. They put into effect a long-drawn-up plan for a huge strategic withdrawal from the central sector of the Western Front. This plan, named Operation Alberich, after the mischievous destructive dwarf of the Nibelung sagas, went into effect on February 2 with typical Teutonic thoroughness: between Arras and Soissons, in a co-ordinated series of moves. The Germans pulled back their armies to the prepared positions of the 'Siegfried-Stellung'—known to the Allies as the Hindenburg Line. The towns of Bapaume and Péronne—towards which the Allies had struggled in vain on the Somme, were given up without a fight, though important buildings, bridges and road and rail junctions were blown up. Ham, Roye, Noyon, Chauny and La Fere were also abandoned. In the countryside, the Germans left a trail of total devastation—orchards were levelled, villages razed to the ground, wells poisoned, cattle rounded up and sent to the rear, and a string of booby-trap bombs left in the desolate landscape to greet the cautiously advancing Allies.

By March 19, the German withdrawal was complete, and a 50-mile-wide swathe of France was literally left as scorched earth. A newly-installed French Government was even more dubious about Nivelle's plans than its predecessor, and used the withdrawal as an excuse to beg him to postpone or cancel the great attack. But he refused to be moved. Waving aside the German withdrawal, he offered his resignation if the Government forced him to call off the offensive. Swayed by his supreme confidence, though with misgivings, the Government gave the final go-ahead. The troops were assembled and buoyed-up with hope, and there could be no going back now. Besides, Nivelle's plans were in the hands of the Germans, and no one wanted to disappoint them!

Before the British overture to the offensive opened at Arras, there occurred two world-shaking events: the Russian Revolution and the American entry into the war. At the time, they almost cancelled each other out: the overthrow of the Tsar meant that Russia was on the way out of the war—and the great numbers of German troops tied up in Russia would, by the end of the year, be on their way to the west. But the US declaration of war, on April 6, sealed the fate of the Central Powers. The New World, with her huge reserves of manpower and modern industrial muscle, would step in to save the old. But it would be months before her might would begin to be felt on this side of the Atlantic. For the moment, the European powers would continue to slug it out between them.

Both these events were evidence of the increasing privation of all the combatants—Russia had been brought to revolution by her military reverses and by sheer starvation. Germany's economic plight was no better; cut off by Britain's sea blockade from her imports of raw materials, she struck back with the blunt weapon of the U-boat, and her desperate policy of unrestricted submarine sinkings had, together with an inept attempt to involve Mexico in an invasion of the US, conspired to push Wilson from neutrality into the waiting arms of the Allies. France too, was feeling the economic pinch; a Paris jeweller displayed a lump of coal in his window as a symbolic sign that winter fuel was becoming as rare as gold dust. The Government knew that if Nivelle's offensive went awry, the consequences would be dire indeed.

On Easter Sunday, 1917, the overture opened: British and Canadian forces struck south and north of Arras. At Vimy Ridge, north of the city, 100,000 Canadians swept forward to rush the ridge, aided by a number of underground subways which brought them up to its foot. They cleared the Germans from this strategic height in four days, capturing over 4,000 prisoners, for the loss of nearly 10,000 of their own men.

Advancing in freezing snow across open ground, the British, south of Arras, made heavier weather of the attack than their Canadian cousins. Strongpoints like Railway Triangle, Telegraph Hill, and a trench cluster known as the Harp, created difficulties, but the advance persisted, and when it was called off a few weeks later, the British had gained 14,000 prisoners, 180 guns and three to six miles of land—at the cost of over 100,000 casualties. This was hailed as a success by the exacting standards of the Western Front.

On April 16, the same day that Lenin, transported by the Germans in a sealed train, arrived in Russia, the Nivelle offensive opened. Like Arras, the weather conditions were foul. Sleet and snow drove into the faces of the French troops, many of them Senegalese, cowering in the jumping-off trenches. Nivelle's hollow-sounding order of the day—'The hour has come! Courage and confidence!'—cut little ice with the men in that chill dawn. At 6 a.m., the leading companies went over the top. At once it was clear that the most gloomy pessimists had been right—the artillery preparation, massive though it had been, was still not enough to dent the mighty defences and in many places soldiers were faced with uncut wire. Nivelle's much-vaunted creeping barrage, which the soldiers were supposed to follow closely, crept on into the distance as the French struggled within yards of their own lines.

Reserves, coming into the trenches with clockwork precision, found their way forward jammed by the numbers already there and unable to move. By noon the weather had worsened and communications had collapsed.

The Senegalese, their white officers killed and their hands too frozen to hold their rifles, broke and ran, even commandeering hospital trains in desperate efforts to get to the rear and safety. In turn, the Medical Corps broke down under the strain of the enormous numbers of wounded.

By dusk, instead of Nivelle's hoped-for six miles, a bare 600 yards had been gained along the Aisne front. Mangin's Sixth Army, from which great things had been hoped, with its Commander boasting that he would have midday coffee in Laon, was pinned down by German machine-guns.

The next day, despite a bag of 20,000 prisoners, and a gain of a mile and a half, it was clear to all that Nivelle's offensive was done, and with it, its author. In vain Nivelle pleaded for more time. The politicians reminded him of his pledge to break off the battle if no breakthrough had been achieved within 48 hours.

Casualties had been enormous—between 120,000 and 200,000 men fell in the first fortnight of the battle, as they toiled up the deadly slopes towards the crest of the Chemin des Dames. The effect of this new disaster on French morale was immediate and catastrophic: by the end of the month, her armies were in open mutiny.

Fortunately for the French Government, the mutinies were not an armed uprising occurring in one sudden pent-up explosion; they were

The memorial crowning Vimy Ridge. The foreground is entirely composed of shell craters. Photograph taken in March 1982

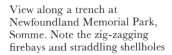

Artificially preserved trench at Vimy Ridge. Note concrete sandbags and duckboards

View along a trench at Newfoundland Memorial Park, Somme. Note the zig-zagging firebays and straddling shellholes

The great British retreat, Spring 1918. Soldiers squeezing sustenance from a captured cow

Manning a Lewis gun on the Lys canal, April 15, 1918

British troops crossing the Somme at Brie, March 1917, after the German retreat to the Hindenburg Line. A year later it was the British turn to retreat and Val Field was forced to burn his own tank here, minutes before the bridge was blown by the British

Modern bridge at Brie today

The unity of suffering: British and French troops with German prisoners pass a horse team struck by a shell. Battle of Tardenois, July 1918

The impartiality of death: German dead in trench struck by a shell

Man's humanity to man: padre succours wounded. Potize near Ypres, September 20, 1917

Some of the 15,000 graves outside the Douaumont Ossuary, Verdun

Rifleman Ernest Jones, the author's uncle, in the year of his death at the age of 18

His grave at Talana Farm cemetery, Boesinghe, Ypres. One of a million British Empire dead

Sgt.-Major Leslie
Ibbetson, Australian
Imperial Forces, killed in
action, September 29,
1918, aged 27

Will Holmes, 1st London
T. A., later Hampshire
Regiment, who lost his leg
in September 1918

A survivor: a Verdun veteran revisits the scene of his suffering

rather a chain of isolated incidents that continued throughout the spring and summer. Details of the mutinies are still shrouded in shame and official secrecy. But the general outlines are clear. Although the French refer to them as 'Outbreaks of collective indiscipline' and it is true that little violence was shown by the mutineers towards their officers, orders were simply ignored.

The mutinies were mainly confined to the Aisne area between Soissons and Reims. They began at the end of April when units ordered up into the Nivelle battle simply refused to move. Other regiments said they would defend their positions, but understandably declined to charge against undamaged wire and machine-gun nests. When official order was reimposed many men moved off making 'Baaing' noises, symbolic of sheep going to the slaughter.

By June the outbreaks were becoming more serious, and what was worse for the authorities they were taking on clear political overtones. Inspired by the previous month's Russian revolution, which also affected the two Russian brigades fighting in France, troops began to sing revolutionary songs, waved red flags, deserted *en masse* and even commandeered trains and attempted to drive them to Paris, where striking girl workers had allegedly been shot down by colonial troops.

Loyal cavalrymen, unbloodied by war, were brought in to stem the tide of revolution, and the Government began to carry out summary executions of ringleaders or representatives of mutinous regiments selected at random.

Nivelle had already been thrown to the wolves, and, with only an estimated two loyal divisions standing between the Germans and Paris, the Government appointed the hero of Verdun, Pétain, to be the new Commander.

At once things started to improve: Pétain proceeded with a mixture of ruthlessness and restraint. He shot at least 55 men as an example, but at the same time assured the rest that there would be no more senseless, Nivelle-style offensives. Knowing his reputation for caution, the men believed his promises that their lives would no longer be sacrificed for vain objectives, and the mutinies started to simmer down.

Pétain personally toured 90 divisions, meeting the men on the ground, giving pep talks, listening to their complaints and taking action to rectify the most outstanding grievances: the quality of food and wine was bettered, medical care was also reformed, above all, arrangements for leave was improved out of all recognition. Canteens and rest-rooms were established at railway stations, and Pétain cut down the time individual soldiers spent at the front, making sure that their rest areas were well to the rear, out of earshot of the guns.

Amazingly, unlike the offensive which preceded them, both the mutinies and their aftermath were kept a closely-guarded secret. The Germans did not act upon the vague rumours they heard, and even the British were kept in the dark about the true state of affairs in their ally's army.

But Pétain was in no position to cure the main cancer which lay at the root of the mutinies—the disaffection, political and industrial agitation and downright treason behind the lines in France. The nest of faint-hearts and traitors would have to wait until the advent of the 'Tiger', Clémenceau, for their day of reckoning.

For the time being, Pétain limited the French army to small, well-planned operations with strictly-limited goals. A model for such battles was his recapture of the Mort Homme, near Verdun in August 1917, which was preceded by an intense artillery blanket, bearing out the new chief's military motto: 'Firepower kills'. The British were told bluntly that no more could be expected from their ally for at least a year. The ball was now in Haig's court.

15. The Ladies' Way

Black smoke rolling across the mud,
Trenches plastered with flesh and blood—
The blue ranks lock with the ranks of grey,
Stab and stagger and sob and sway;
The living cringe from the shrapnel bursts,
The dying moan of their burning thirsts,
Moan and die in the gulping slough—
Where are the butterfly ladies now?

Crosbie Garstin, 'Chemin des Dames'

To walk along the Chemin des Dames road is to march along yet another of France's innumerable Via Dolorosa. Like the Voie Sacrée, it is a route with a tragic memory at every footstep.

The road itself is an oddity; the name, 'Ladies' Way', recalls its origins: it was built by order of Louis XV in the eighteenth century to ease the carriage of his daughters on their way from the Royal Palace of Compiègne to the country home of their friend, the Duchess of Narbonne, in the Château de la Bove. It is a straight road, wide and smooth, and makes for easy walking. The views, as I swung along from west to east, were spectacular. On my right, wooded slopes swept down to the Aisne from which Nivelle's armies launched their bloody and futile attacks.

Soon, on my left, a copse appeared, masking the main stronghold on the right flank of the Chemin des Dames ridge. This was the Fort de la Malmaison. In front of it is a vast German cemetery containing the dead of the Second World War, for this place was a battlefield in both conflicts.

The fort is hidden deep in trees, and access is impossible, except from the rear, because of the deep moat which still surrounds it. The inner courtyard, now just a clearing in the woods, is surrounded by the ruins of the fort's casement, which looked in such a parlous condition that I quailed at entering.

Back on the road again, I passed numerous monuments to individual units and single soldiers who fell here, before coming to the Cerny crossroads. This was a strategic village at the centre of the ridge, which was levelled during the course of the fighting but has been rebuilt nearby. The ruins are hidden in almost impenetrable thickets, which I forced my way through at the cost of severe scratches. The crossroads itself has a column commemorating the 1st Battalion of the Loyal North Lancashire Regiment who passed this way during the open warfare in 1914, and a memorial chapel commemorating the main Chemin des Dames battle. Large French and German cemeteries, containing many thousand graves, complete the melancholy sights.

Taking a right fork off the main road at Cerny, I walked down into the Aisne valley, looking for some of the fortified caves which had been the bane of the French attack. Just outside the village of Vendresse-Beaulne, I found them. They were hidden in the side of a steep hill, the Mont de Fleau, concealed behind bushes off a grassy track.

At first they did not look much, half cottage and half cave. But the second and third caves were more interesting—tunnels led out of vast chambers, and twisted and turned until the light of the entrance glimmered and died. Fortunately I had a pocket torch, but even with that, the pressing silence and the darkness beyond its feeble beam oppressed me. Odd things told of its wartime occupation—the remains of electric light installations along the chalk ceiling, old army boots flung in forgotten corners, abandoned metal equipment, unit numbers painted on the walls, '1915' and other dates in Teutonic numerals, and fortifications of wood and concrete which helped to strengthen the natural chalk walls.

The next village, Paissy, had caves a-plenty. These were utilized by the local people as barns and garages, and often had gates and doors across their mouths. This was the nearest thing to a troglodyte community that I had ever known, and the merest glance to the south where the Aisne disappeared in a misty haze showed how these fortifications could command the whole valley and everyone who showed their heads in it.

Three miles more of marching brought me to the Caverne du Dragon, a network of natural caves under the ridge that was extended and fortified by the German defenders. The monument is marked by an example of the French war-winning 75-mm field gun, and a French light tank for the Second World War. Descending some steps bounded by rusty barbed wire, I came to a tunnel entrance guarded by an extraordinary figure dressed in a ludicrous paramilitary ensemble, which looked vaguely of Great War vintage; lace-up boots, khaki socks rising above the knees, jodhpurs, military jacket and cap. This motley character turned out to be a member of M. Coilliot's 'Souvenir de France' outfit. It transpired that he livened up his week by doing a turn as guide for the Cavernes, which are maintained by the 'Souvenir'. A few francs admitted me to a flickering film show presenting an old movie of the fighting, with once again a glossing over of the essentially disastrous nature of the battle. This, together with the man's bombastic commentary as he showed his visitors around the caves, seemed to illustrate the slightly sinister, slightly comic nature of the whole organization. But the caves were impressive indeed; used by the Germans as a command post and store depot, the caves also housed large numbers of men and quantities of ammunition. One glass case, containing fragments of uniform and weaponry and a few shreds from a French newspaper, represented, our grisly guide informed us, the only worldly goods of a soldier whose skeleton had been discovered when the Caverne's car park was constructed a few years previously. The Cavernes also boasted a well, which was poisoned by the French when they attacked in an effort to root out the defenders.

Part of the cave was devoted to a military museum, containing a British corner distinguished by a Union-Jack, as well as a massive bronze head of General Mangin which had originally stood in Paris. The Germans destroyed the equestrian statue in the Second World War and threw the head into the Seine from where it was rescued by faithful patriots.

The General had incurred German wrath, not only by his sterling service against them in the war but also by his post-war attempts to weaken Germany by setting up a separatist Rhineland state. This had been frustrated by his mysterious early death—there were rumours that he had been poisoned by nationalists incensed by his comment, when told that his black troops had been molesting German women, that 'His' Senegalese were 'Too good for Boche bitches'.

Leaving the Caverne, I came in a few yards to a monument at Hurtebise Farm commemorating the two battles fought there a century apart—the first by the great Napoleon himself. The first Hurtebise battle was fought in 1814 during the Emperor's Campaign of France, the desperate winter when, with his adolescent army hastily raised to replace the legions lost in Russia, Napoleon beat a fighting retreat on Paris, harried by the armies of Russia, Prussia, Austria and Sweden, yet fighting—and winning—a battle every four days. Hurtebise had been one of these. The same ground was fought over again in 1914, 1917 and

1940, a fact brought home to me when I met a Frenchman and his wife. He told me he was searching for the spot where his father had fought as a private in 1917, and where he had led a futile bid to stop the German Panzers as a Chasseur Captain in 1940.

A left turn at the farm took me off the Chemin des Dames and away, for a moment, from World War memories. The road led to the ruins of Vauclair Abbey, a picturesque pile set in a Forêt Domaniale of the same name. The ruins are remarkable for a perfectly-preserved herb garden, grown originally by the monks, and now preserved by the curators. The Abbey is a curiously beautiful place of peace, a still centre in the whirlwind of ancient wars that surrounds it. Reminders of those wars are not far to seek, for the surrounding woods are full of the usual tell-tale trenches and shell craters, albeit used today by moto-cross bike riders.

A hike across the California Plateau, a key target for Nivelle and Mangin, brought me to a newly erected outsize statue of Napoleon, unveiled by the then French Minister of the Interior, Prince Poniatowski, a direct descendant of one of Napoleon's marshals, in the 1970s. The statue of the Emperor overlooking his battlefield almost seemed to be saying: 'I beat them—why the hell didn't you?'

I was making for Craonne, at the extreme right of the Chemin des Dames, and a sizeable town in 1917. I had forgotten that the place had been absolutely destroyed, and the new Craonne was a tiny farming village with barely a café—let alone a hotel. I was directed to the next village, Corbeny, past the remains of old Craonne, now a curious collection of mossy humps and bumps on the edge of the forest. Hurrying through the woods I felt considerable concern about my finding overnight accommodation in this rural fastness; 'La France profonde', as Giscard d'Estaing was wont to call it. However, a Hotel du Commerce in Corbeny proved able to put me up, though I was directed onto a nearby main road between Reims and Laon to find my supper at a Routier, or French transport café, where I had one of the most sustaining and satisfying cheap meals I could ever remember.

The next day I visited the only visible curiosity that Corbeny had to offer—a bee farm and museum entitled 'L'Abeille Vivante', (the living bee)—though, judging by the gloomy tone of some of the exhibits, it would be better entitled the 'Dying Bee', since, as the captions informed visitors, the pollution which is the curse of our age was destroying more and more of the region's wild flowers which are the bee's life support system. Consequently, the bee population grows smaller and smaller by the year. The place also specialized in producing 'Hydromel', a liqueur made from honey, but one taste of this noxious poison dispelled my illusion that it bore any relation to the English mead, to which I am very partial. Declining the hydromel I bought a jar of honey and hit the road north for Laon, resolving that I at least would make Mangin's interrupted journey from the Chemin des Dames to that city, once the Carolignian capital of France.

Laon rears out of a flat plain astride a ridge, with a nondescript new town at the foot of the hill, and the beautiful old town at the top, connected by winding hairpin roads and a deserted tramway. Laon is remarkable for its beautiful Gothic cathedral, whose gargoyles betray the bucolic region it serves—they depict cows, sheep and other farm-yard beasts.

I went inside to find a wedding in progress, with the mellifluous tones of the priest intoned through a microphone echoing through the place. This ceremony of new life and renewal seemed an appropriate way to wash the memories of the Ladies' Way out of my mind.

16. The Big Bang (The Messines mines— prelude to Passchendaele)

Gentlemen, I don't know whether we are going to make history tomorrow, but at any rate we shall change geography.

Maj.-Gen. 'Tim' Harington, Plumer's Chief of Staff

All we had said had come true. There was not the slightest doubt that the frontal attack without the mines would have been an absolute failure and would have cost 50,000 men. This stupendous artificial earthquake shook the ridge from end to end . . . and enabled the army, as we had promised, to walk to the top in comparative safety.

John Norton Griffiths, 'Father' of British mine warfare

The moral effect of the explosions was simply staggering. The 7th June cost us very dear.

Field Marshal Paul von Hindenburg

When Haig heard from Pétain that the French army, maimed by mutiny and defeat, would be a lame duck for the rest of the year, he was by no means downcast—now was the chance for him to assert Britain's role as the—temporarily—senior partner in the Alliance. The losses on the Somme ten months before were beginning to be made up by troops enlisted under the previous year's Derby Scheme—a preliminary form of conscription,—and Haig saw the opportunity to put into effect his long-cherished scheme for a decisive attack on the old battleground of Flanders.

His resolve was strengthened by fears expressed by Lord Jellicoe, Britain's Naval Supremo, that Germany's submarine warfare was slowly strangling Britain's food supplies. The main U-boat bases were around Ostend on the Belgian coast, and the obvious place to break through and clear that coast was the old Ypres salient.

Sadly, the salient was still dominated by German-held high ground, in particular the long Messines Ridge, south of Ypres. An obvious preliminary to a successful offensive would be the capture of this ridge. The job was entrusted to the Second Army, commanded by Sir Herbert Plumer. Plumer, a Boer War veteran, looked the very model of a blinkered blimp—small, pot-bellied, with white hair and a walrus moustache. But the unprepossessing appearance concealed a sharp mind and a quality that was in dire shortage among his colleagues—imagination.

Plumer knew exactly how he proposed to take the ridge, indeed he had been nurturing his plans for years. As long ago as 1915, tunnelling companies had won approval for four enormously long shafts to be dug towards the ridge around the village of Wytschaete ('Whitesheet'). As work went on throughout 1916, with heavy mechanical drills breaking down and being abandoned in favour of the sheer slog of human 'clay kicking', more tunnels were added to the scheme—two mines were laid to the north, at Hill 60 and Caterpillar, another at St. Eloi, another further south at Spanbroekmoelen, and several others near Messines village. At last, a total of 22 mines were being worked, all in an enormous ten-mile crescent running from Ypres to Ploegsteert ('Plugstreet'), pointing at the heart of the German positions on the ridge.

One of the mines, at Petit Douve Farm, was discovered and destroyed by the Germans, but work continued on the others at a furious rate. At last Plumer told Haig that he would be ready to go on June 7, 1917. The Western Front was to see a new style of warfare in action.

Of the 21 remaining mines, Plumer decided that the southernmost pair, near Ploegsteert Wood, were too wide of the ridge to be used, and so they were charged and held in reserve. They were never used. The British Government promised to dismantle them but their positions were lost during the 1918 fighting, and they disappeared from history until the night of June 17, 1955, when a thunderstorm set one of them off! No one was hurt by the 20,000 pounds blast, but the position of the twin mine—containing 40,000 pounds of ammonal—remains unknown to this day, and some Belgian cattle may yet be in for a rude shock!

The rest of the mines, 19 in all, were wired and 'tamped', ready to be blasted simultaneously at zero hour on June 7, prior to Plumer's infantry rushing the ridge. The northernmost top two mines, Hill 60 and Caterpillar, had 53,500 lbs and 70,000 lbs of ammonal respectively. Then came the largest mine, a single mighty charge of 95,600 lbs at St.

Eloi. Next, at Hollandschuur, came three mines, two more at Petit Bois, another at Peckham Farm, and another 'biggie' at Spanbroekmoelen. Another trio of mines were placed at Kruisstaat, another single large one at Ontario Farm, and finally near the hamlet of Warneton two more pairs, at Trench 127 and Factory Farm-Trench 122: a total of more than a million pounds of high explosive lodged a hundred feet below the earth in tunnels stretching, in some cases, over a thousand feet out from the British lines under the unsuspecting Germans above.

The High Command were still mistrustful of the mines, and just in case they did not do the required job, 2,400 guns and howitzers had been assembled to further blast this small section of the German lines. Seventy-two tanks were also to be brought into action.

The thunder of the artillery stopped in the early hours of June 7, just as the fingers of dawn began to light up the eastern sky and the dark mass of the ridge. Plumer knelt at his bed in prayer as his staff officers gnawed their knuckles and the waiting troops stumbled sleepily to their jump-off trenches in the dark.

At 3.10 a.m., the earth exploded. Great sheets of flame sprang skywards from the ridge. They seemed to Montague Tutt, watching from Ypres, 'like a lot of fairy lights'. The ground rocked and heaved as the greatest explosions in human history roared and rippled along the ridge. The blasts from the nineteen mines swept the plunger officers, half a mile away, off their feet, then rolled out over the channel to be heard as far away as Dublin!

Captain C. W. Ashton, 32nd Battalion, The Royal Fusiliers:

We were out of the line from the end of May. Every officer and man was put through the practice of knowing the speed and direction of the attack. I was nominated to lead the attack from east of Hill 60. It was difficult to get the troops into position in the dark, even with guidelines. Too many other units cut through my forces. Precisely at 3.10 a.m., every Second Army gun, 10th Corps artillery, heavy Naval guns and nineteen land mines let loose. It was the most terrifying experience. As leader, I jumped the parapet, looking at my men who in the light of explosives, were yellow. Only one followed me—my Sergeant Major. For over three hours, we were alone and in a stumbling mess. We encountered a body of about 50 German officers and men. Foolishly we two ran towards them and ordered them to retire in the direction of our advance. This, they did. Afterwards I wondered why we escaped as casualties. Shortly afterwards my men had caught up and by 8.10 a.m. I sent a message by runner to HQ stating that we had captured the Black Line (Gondezone Farm). It was a hot and sunny day and, thirsty, we ordered groundsheets to be put out when a short shower fell, then stuck our noses in the filthy moisture. Eventually, the 1st Battalion, Royal Fusiliers, came up through us and we retired. My losses were only a few light wounded.

Everywhere along the ridge the story was the same; the advancing British were met, not as so often before by volleys of machine-gun fire from invulnerable positions, but by huge numbers of Germans, totally confused and shocked by the earth-shattering blasts.

Weeping men stumbled about in shock. Others sank to their knees and embraced the legs of their British captors, sobbing in stunned disbelief. The dreaded concrete bunkers had been overturned like so many children's bricks, and mighty chasm-like craters gaped where wired trenches had been. Between 10–20,000 Germans had been entombed alive by the blasts and 7,300 prisoners were taken. The villages of Wytschaete and Messines were in British hands by seven a.m., and the whole of the ridge had fallen by midday, when the Germans to the rear began to recover from their shock and inflict the first serious casualties on the attackers.

The months of nail-biting tensions, and agonizing set-backs, as the mines advanced foot by painful foot, had proved worthwhile, and Plumer's patience and persistence had delivered to the British their first unqualified success on the Western Front. It was now up to Haig to exploit that success.

17. Mud—(Passchendaele)

The very name with its suggestion of splashiness and of passion, at once, was subtly appropriate. This nonsense could not have come to its full flower at any other place but at Passchendaele. It was pre-ordained. The moment I saw the name on the trench map, intuitively I knew what was going to happen.

Wyndham Lewis, 'Blasting and Bombardiering'

To my mind, nothing can compare with the utter desolation and despair of the Passchendaele Ridge.

L. C. Stewart, Royal Garrison Artillery

And the wind
Blowing over London from Flanders
Has a bitter taste.

Richard Aldington

If the slaughter of the Somme had been Britain's Verdun, the third Battle of Ypres—known to its participants and history by the one word 'Passchendaele'—was her Chemin des Dames. The battle was the straw which broke the camel's back, and war became, even in the words of that crusty old militarist Ludendorff, 'no longer life at all—it was mere unspeakable suffering'.

The quality of the battle that has so deeply etched the word 'Passchendaele' upon the nation's collective memory, can be summed up in one word: Mud. The very word 'battlefield' was a mockery of the reality—men, mules and munitions were sucked into an ocean of glutinous, oozing, stinking mud. It is not too much to say that in that noisome ocean of filthy slime humanity itself reached and surpassed a new height of horror.

Haig's illusion of a breakthrough in Flanders had been boosted by the success at Messines, and he used that battle as a weapon to beat down the voices of caution at home. Lloyd George was as sceptical of success as ever, wishing to move men from Flanders to Italy to shore up that sagging front and if possible beat a path into Germany's 'soft underbelly' of Austria.

At last, after lengthy cabinet debate, Haig's battle plans were approved by the War Cabinet in late July, and a fortnight's intensive preliminary bombardment began. This sustained barrage—four million shells fell in ten days—was to be a major factor in bringing about the Passchendaele death trap, for, as we have seen, Flanders was not really dry land at all, merely marshy ground reclaimed from the sea and dependent for drainage on a complicated network of ditches and streams. The bombardment put the finishing touches to destroying this irrigation system completely, and water which should have slid away to the sea was left lying in pools which became lakes and finally fatal quicksands of sucking mud.

Another mistake was to assign primary responsibility for the offensive not to cautious old Plumer and his experienced Second Army, but to the newly-formed and unbloodied Fifth Army under the youthful Sir Hubert Gough, at 47 by far the youngest Army Commander and an eager cavalryman,—a 'thruster' itching to prove his mettle and aggression. The Second Army would play a largely supporting role, and Rawlinson's Fourth was slotted in along the Belgian coast, ready to rush the U-boat bases when Gough had achieved the expected breakthrough at Ypres.

On July 31, Gough's men duly went into action and attacked Pilkem Ridge, north-east of Ypres. One of the officers who led his men over the top that morning was Montague Tutt:

> An officer called Glaister arranged for us to have a good time before going into battle, as he didn't expect to come back. So we had plenty to eat and drink before we went up the line. We practised our attack on replica trenches in the rear. Then, on July 31, 1917, we went up the line past Hellfire Corner along the Menin Road out of Ypres. When we arrived at the front they had left one officer to hand over the sector to us. This was Noel Chavasse VC, the son of the Bishop of Liverpool and a Royal Army Medical Corps officer; I had a few words with him and then he left us.
>
> The platoon was to go and lie in No Man's Land a few minutes before zero hour. I gave them their rum ration on orders about two hours before we were due to go out. I was feeling very nervous, and almost had a nervous collapse. Capt. Glaister probably saved my life; his coolness and courage were encouraging to everyone. I

poured out a large tot of rum into a tin mug and placed it on top of the parapet. Once I'd taken it I felt as if I could have walked straight to Berlin!

We took up our positions in front of the line under cover of darkness. At zero hour, pandemonium broke out. There were double lines of 18 pounder guns firing as well as howitzers, and trench mortars that fired a projectile that looked like an oil canister turning over in the air, before landing and bursting into flames. The Huns took to their heels, those that survived the bombardment—there was no opposition. I had a barrage map showing the supposed lines of the bombardment. I was dressed in a private's uniform and carried a rifle, because the Jerries picked off men in officer's uniforms.

When I got close to the Jerry trench, I found myself almost alone. A Jerry tossed a bomb over, and it wounded me. I lost the little finger of my right hand and had a leg wound and lesser wounds all over my body. I walked back to the dressing station and got my wounds treated along with other 'walking wounded'. It was here that Captain Chavasse won a bar to his VC. He treated many wounded under fire and was unfortunately killed, but his heroism was recognized.

I saw two German prisoners carrying one of our wounded on a stretcher. They were both blown over by the blast of a shell that landed nearby, but they promptly picked themselves up, got the stretcher and continued. They were very brave, the Germans.

I held onto the back of an ambulance, and despite a bumpy ride, got to the rear. I was pleased to be sent to Blighty. I got taken to Manchester and then to Cambridge. I was home for nine months, as my wounds took a long time to heal . . .

Slowly, the Fifth Army slogged forward: each painful dragging step and its inevitable counter-attack was dignified by the army's historians with the name of a battle. After Pilkem Ridge fell, Gheluvelt Plateau was next. Langemarck (August 10), where Edwin Campion Vaughan recorded his battle experiences so vividly, followed in the middle of the month.

The first day's casualties—an estimated 15,000 to 25,000—compared favourably with the 60,000 incurred on the first day of the Somme, but the Army Commanders were well aware that the worst was yet to come, while on the Somme casualty figures fell drastically after the disaster of July 1.

On the very first day of the attack, the vital factor that was to characterize Passchendaele forever came into play: it began to rain. Even earlier, the unseasonable wet weather had hampered air reconnaissance, and on July 31 the future military theorist J. F. C. 'Boney' Fuller noted from Tank Corps HQ that the Steenbeek brook was already a 'wide moat of liquid mud'. Fuller and his officers prepared 'swamp maps' which they despatched to HQ until the Higher Command, no doubt not wishing to see what they did not wish to exist, requested that the information be stopped.

But even Haig's notoriously over-optimistic Head of Intelligence, General Sir John Charteris, noted on August 4: 'the weather has killed this attack. I went up to the front line this morning. Every brook is swollen and the ground is a quagmire'. Naturally the wonder weapon—the tanks—immediately bogged down on the first day of the action, and every move in the landscape became a struggle to extricate a foot from one hole and plant it in the next.

Val Field, 'E' (5th) Battalion, Motor Transport Division, Tank Corps:

In 1917 we went into action in the battle of Passchendaele. We were due to support an infantry attack, but the ground was so soft that we never got to the front line. We just bogged down and stuck.

Gunner William 'Mac' Francis, 91686, 'E' (5th) Battalion, Tank Corps:

Our objective was some pillboxes near Zonnebeke and St. Julien villages. When we got to them there was not two bricks standing together. Total ruin: our tank *Enchantress*, got ditched in the soft mud. My pal and I got out of the tank (one on each side) to uncouple the unditching gear—a solid wood beam six feet long, two feet wide and square, but it was useless. The tank sank very slowly in the mire. When I was outside, a big shell landed a yard from me but did not explode because of the thick Flanders mud. But it covered me from head to foot with slime and mud. All our crew stayed inside the tank from about 7 a.m. to 5 p.m., and all the time shells were dropping all around us, and we were rocking like a small boat on a rough sea.

We made our way back on foot over many scores of dead men, British and Germans, and very many dead mules (or were they horses?) Some had been there for many weeks, and the stench was terrible. Many of the bodies were half in and half out of the ground. Our Tank Officer told us that when the Salvage Corps went two or three nights later to collect the tank, only a foot or two of it were above ground.

When we got back to a First Aid Post, they gave us a mug of 'Sergeant Major's' tea, thick brown stuff. I have been a tea specialist in my trade for 50 years, but I have never tasted tea which I appreciated so much.

Generally speaking the tanks were useless on the Flanders Front because of the thousands of shell-holes, all filled with water from the water courses and ditches broken by shelling.

Like an inane weatherman, Haig's chief military ally, Sir William Robertson, Chief of the Imperial General Staff, wrote to him on August 23: 'this rain is cruel luck, but it will get fine in time'. Unfortunately, the rain was not to get right, but was to get—steadily—ever more wrong.

After the reverses of Gheluvelt and Langemarck, Gough lost heart: he told Haig that success, if not impossible, would be too costly in the prevailing conditions.

Haig's only concession to this view was to alter his strategic goals. Abandoning hopes of a massive breakthrough to the coast, he now stated that the object of the battle was to wear down the Germans inch by inch, a regular battle of attrition. So the attacks went on—nibbling, nit-picking advances that wrested a hundred yards of sticky soil here, and a pillbox bunker there . . . and still the rain fell.

At the same time, the main role in the battle was transferred from the dispirited Gough back to Plumer. In keeping with his cautious character Sir Herbert called a halt to Gough's impetuous attacks, and devoted the first three weeks of September to meticulous preparation of another artillery barrage, to cover the limited infantry advances he was planning.

Back on the battlefield, conditions were going from bad to worse: British and Empire casualties were 74,000 by the end of August—to the Germans' 50,000—and morale on both sides had slumped. The fighting was duplicating that at Verdun, with small but savage struggles for isolated strongpoints. (One small copse, known as Inverness Wood, changed hands 19 times!) On, or rather, in, the ground, everyone, even the officers, were wondering what all the suffering was for.

Alas the rain flooded the whole area, which was pockmarked with artillery fire—at one time the water was up around my waist. The First Schleswig's attacked my line. All were either killed, wounded or taken prisoner. I had about fifty of the enemy lying in my base, an old dug-out previously used by the German High Command. The entrance was of course facing the enemy, and by day I could not evacuate my prisoners. Only first aid was available, no other treatment. The continual cry 'Wasser!', was pitiful—but the only water at hand was in the water bottles and the dirty puddles all around.

(Ashton)

On September 20, Plumer was ready and his first attack went in along the infamous Menin Road Ridge. After a minutely plotted creeping barrage, the British were able to advance at 5.20 a.m. and by midday the day's objectives were successfully secured and a German counter-attack in the afternoon was repulsed. Ludendorff gloomily admitted that the 'terrible onslaught' had been successful. Thanks in large part to the valour of Australian contingents, the front had been pushed forward a further 900 yards and 3,000 prisoners were taken. But casualties had been high: around 22,000 on either side.

Five days later, Plumer took another step, at Polygon Wood on September 26. Another 1,000 yards was bitten off on a five-mile front. The wood itself was partly cleared and most of the shattered skeleton which had once been the village of Zonnebeke was occupied. Cost: 17,000 casualties on each side.

Archie F. Gale, Pte., 11th Royal Sussex Regiment 39th Division, Second Army:

On Sunday afternoon, we marched to a place with plenty of cover until it was deemed we were ready to go into the line. This was at a place called 'Tower Hamlets' near Polygon Wood. We were in the support trenches that night and took over the next evening from the Black Watch who were in the front line. Next morning we were ordered over the top to take trenches with a pillbox at one end. Although successful, and taking several prisoners, we ourselves suffered heavy casualties. We went over behind a barrage put up by our artillery and so the Jerries were made to keep their heads down, otherwise we should have suffered more.

By the end of September, which had been reasonably dry, the British had made a total advance in two months of three miles. But in October, the rain began again. Encouraged by the small successes in capturing terrain, Haig ordered Plumer to press on with more attacks, even though the worsening weather made it impossible for the guns to move forward and provide sufficient artillery cover for the 'poor bloody infantry'.

On October 4, Plumer struck again, at Broodseinde, the next village on after Zonnebeke. Gough was allowed back in the sticky arena to attack Poelcapelle in the north of the salient. As the depressing drizzle fell, the British fought their way onto the lower slopes of the Passchendaele ridge—an advance of 700 yards—and took Poelcapelle and Gravenstafel and the rest of Polygon Wood, but to the troops enduring the misery of the mud, these were merely paper gains. They were still facing an apparently endless sea of grey bog, marked here and there by a deadly machine-gun nest or a hidden wire fence. Mules and men on their way to the front slipped from the 'Corduroy' roads made of logs, and drowned in the unforgiving swamps. This success, trumpeted by HQ as a decisive victory, tasted of ashes—and 26,000 more men were dead, wounded or taken prisoner.

By October 7, when Haig's commanders gathered at his château for a conference, the drizzle had changed to a full-blown downpour and both Plumer and Gough advised that the battle be broken off. Haig resolutely declined to do so. His reasons for not calling the hopeless campaign to a close must remain a mystery but, overriding all opposition from Whitehall and his subordinates, he flogged his sodden soldiers once more into the dripping jaws of death. 'Just one more push', sceptics and critics were assured, 'and we will be through'. Plumer was ordered to attack again on October 9. His initial target was to be securing the ground beyond Poelcapelle, followed by a push to the top of Passchendaele Ridge and the village itself.

Early in the morning 9,000 men waded rather than walked into battle. This time the artillery barrage was less than adequate, as the guns had mostly bogged down on their way up the line. Troops once again were faced with the nightmare of uncut wire and intact machine-guns spitting death behind it. There was no escape. Those who took shelter in shell-holes found themselves being sucked down to an even more ghastly end in the greasy mud. Stretcher-bearers were unable to operate normally: it took between six and nine men to carry a single casualty through the mud. Even Haig's chief contemporary apologist, who has written a whole book striving to show that Passchendaele was 'inevitable', has admitted that October was, for the troops, 'a month of dire misery and absolute frustration'.

At home, Haig's reputation reached its nadir, and the Cabinet even called his predecessor, French, out of retirement and asked his advice. French counselled a defensive waiting policy until the Americans arrived in strength. (There were already 100,000 in France, but they were still in training.)

Meanwhile, the Commander-in-Chief himself was limbering up for the final operation: the capture of Passchendaele. Australian and New Zealand troops were brought up for the attack, only to find themselves facing masses of wire some 30 yards in depth. Gough asked for the attack to be aborted but Haig and Plumer both refused to be diverted: the men would go in as planned on October 12.

The story of Poelcapelle was repeated on a bloodier scale: the Anzacs struggled into the wire only to be cut down by the chattering guns. Allied artillery could not negotiate the flooded Steenbeek—now 100 yards wide. The result was an infinitesimal 100-yard strip of mud taken, but 'victory', whatever that hollow word meant, was as far away as ever. In their down-to-earth way, the Antipodeans voiced their view of Sir Douglas Haig, both then and thereafter. It was not complimentary.

Then, far away, fate intervened to halt the catastrophe: on the morning of October 24 the Austrians, bolstered by six German divisions, struck at the Italians near the village of Caporetto. Within a few hours the Italian line was broken and their troops were being chased south in a helter-skelter retreat. Frantically, Italy signalled to her allies for help. Lloyd George seized his chance. Brushing aside Haig's protests he snatched away five divisions from the BEF and sent them through the Alps to prop up the crumbling Italian front. Even if he wanted to, Haig would not have the reserves necessary to pour into the Passchendaele bloodbath.

Archie Gale remembers a typical experience of the front at this time:

> We were transported up by lorries to as near the line as the transport could get. Thereafter it was foot-slogging in the dark to our appointed destination. This was halfway up the Ridge, and on our way in pouring rain we had to cross what was once a small stream, bridged by the Royal Engineers. We were in single file on duckboards and these stretched across the mud of the stream.
>
> We had some reinforcements and I was somewhere in the middle of the crocodile of men, fully equipped with the trappings of the infantry soldier. On arrival at the bridge we encountered Jerry shell-fire which knocked out several men and left many floundering in the mud as the bridge broke down.
>
> The young officer who was leading us in hurried forward with those on the further side, leaving us to sort out the mess. There

were one or two fresh arrivals in front of me and I heard a call from behind, possibly from a sergeant, to get a move on.

I pushed on, got down off the duckboard and waded up to my knees in mud to get to the other side. To make matters worse, among the high explosives Jerry had put in one or two gas shells which just exploded in the mud with a dull plop.

These were cunning devices which smelled like sweet pineapple and tempted the unwary to have a sniff or two. Having had the experience before I called out 'Gas!' and hoped that everybody put their gas masks on. This was all in pitch darkness and I couldn't see what was going on except in my close vicinity. We got under way once more and a little further on I heard muffled voices—we were not far from the enemy lines. But the voices were English, and I no sooner called out 'Any Sussex here?', than what turned out to be a Staff officer called to me and said: 'Any more noise and I'll blow your bloody brains out!'

Being of a somewhat retiring nature, I took him at his word and made myself scarce to drop into a shell-hole where there were three of my mates. We spent that night and all next day huddled up under groundsheets until we were relieved in the evening.

But irritatingly, Passchendaele still remained out of Haig's reach, on its little ridge. It must be taken, and Plumer was told to make a final fling: October 26 was the chosen date. Once again, Gough, unnerved by yet more freezing rain on the eve of the assault, begged for the operation to be called off, to no avail. This time the Canadian Corps were to bear the brunt.

Yet again the familiar story unrolled: a dawn attack, no progress on most fronts, a few pathetic yards gained elsewhere: casualties: 12,000 men.

On October 30, the Canadians tried again . . . They were now within 500 yards of Passchendaele. On November 6 they attacked again . . . and in a chill rain, took the sad huddle of pillboxes and shell-holes that had been the village of Passchendaele.

The next day, Haig's Chief of Staff, Sir Lancelot Kiggell, was driven up near the front for the first time. As the staff car neared the porridge bowl that had been the salient, Sir Lancelot began to exhibit an un-Arthurian agitation. Finally, he burst into tears: 'Good God', he asked his companion, 'did we really send men to fight in that?'

18. Tanks—(Cambrai)

I'd like to see a Tank come down those stalls,
Lurching to ragtime tunes, or 'Home Sweet Home',
And there'd be no more jokes in Music Halls,
To mock the riddled corpses round Bapaume.

Siegfried Sassoon, 'Blighters'

After the poisonous shambles of Passchendaele, imagination once again briefly gained the upper hand in the counsels of the British Army, with the first mass use of tanks as a primary offensive weapon in the Battle of Cambrai.

The British were still in the hot seat on the Western Front as the French remained deep in the toils of political turmoil—the row following the mutinies had bubbled throughout the summer, and come to the boil following a bitter Press campaign by the aged patriotic politician, Georges Clémenceau. Relentlessly, the man whose fierce antagonisms had won him the nickname 'Tiger', assailed those who he considered really responsible for the mutinies—the corrupt and lazy politicians, and left-wing union leaders and pacifists who openly consorted with outright traitors in the pay of Germany.

His first target was the Interior Minister, Louis Malvy, who had refused to arrest the traitors or suppress the pacifist Press, which was more or less openly funded by German gold. Having succeeded in discrediting Malvy with a withering speech in the Chamber of Deputies, Clémenceau turned on the men behind the most notorious of the pacifist sheets, *Le Bonnet Rouge*, and very soon they were facing a firing squad in the fortress of Vincennes.

By November, the exhausted and demoralized deputies were prepared to put Clémenceau in the post of Premier, with virtually unlimited power, and soon the 'dauntless, aged beast of prey' in Churchill's phrase, was sharpening his claws on his enemies at home and abroad. He had only one policy, he informed his mesmerized fellow politicians—'to make war'—and this he proposed to do with a ferocious pride and the speed of an old man in a hurry. France girded her loins for the final confrontation, and thanks to her ancient dictator, there would be no more talk of peace until the last German was expelled from the sacred soil of the Republic.

While France was licking her wounds and beefing up for the final fray, Britain again turned to the attack: hardly had Passchendaele petered out in the mud than men were sent streaming south to attack the formidable Hindenburg Line itself near the small town of Cambrai.

This time the attack would not follow the usual pattern of prolonged artillery bombardment followed by unprotected infantry going over the top. Fortunately, the Generals had at last learned the lesson of the tanks' individual failure on the Somme, at Arras and at Passchendaele, and were prepared to use the new machines not just as support for the infantry but as a weapon in their own right. It was, as one of the tank's prophets, Basil Liddell Hart, declared, 'the dawn of a new epoch' in warfare and ultimately was to sound the knell of the static stalemate on the Western Front.

The idea of Cambrai had germinated in the fertile mind of Tank Corps General 'Boney' Fuller in August 1917 as he saw his beloved machines floundering like dinosaurs in the Passchendaele mud. He drew up a memorandum condemning the use of tanks in this futile struggle and suggesting a raid in strength on a German-held town like St. Quentin or Cambrai. Fuller took his idea to Sir Julian Byng, Commander of the Third Army, in whose sector Cambrai lay. Byng approved the scheme but expanded the plan into a full blown tank offensive. In turn he took the idea to Haig who also approved it in principle, but postponed its execution until the dreary duel at Passchendaele was done.

Byng earmarked two Infantry Corps (six divisions) and a Cavalry Corps, 1,000 guns—and no fewer than 381 tanks for the operation. Unfortunately there were no reserves, so when the longed-for break-through came, and on the first day, it could not be exploited.

Crossing the wide trenches of the Hindenburg Line might prove a problem, so each tank carried a 'fascine', or giant bundle of brushwood, which, when dumped in a trench, proved an admirable bridge for the tank to roll over.

Next, the British organized a series of feints and minor raids up and down the lines around the area targeted for the breakthrough, and this, together with the deliberate lack of a preliminary artillery barrage, served to confuse and disorientate the Germans who, methodical themselves, were by now used to the familiar British pre-attack tactics.

By November 20 all was ready, and just after 6.20 a.m. the tanks clanked forward out of the early morning mist. What was it like for the men in those machines, as almost blind, they lumbered across the uneven ground in their hot and noisy steel cans, cut off from the world outside their metal skins?

The tanks were Mark IIIs and Mark IVs. They had a crew of eight—a driver and the officer up front. The C.O. was always a commissioned 1st or 2nd Lieutenant. There was a man on each side manning the machine-gun, or the six pounder gun if the tank was equipped with those. In the middle were the two 'Gearsmen'—that was the lousiest job of all. You could veer the tank a few degrees to right or left but it was very hard work to swing it. You couldn't speak inside the tank because the engine made a hell of a row, and what with the guns and shells going off all around you, nothing could be heard—so you communicated with hand signals. You'd hold fingers up to indicate the speed wanted.

The top speed of the tank was 4 mph on good level ground, but we never were on good ground so we crept along at 1–2 mph. We couldn't use our top gear.

In June 1917 we went into action in the Battle of Passchendaele. We were due to support an infantry attack, but the ground was so soft that we never got to the front line. We just bogged down and stuck. The Germans were still scared of us at that time, as they had no anti-tank weapons.

I've never been able to fathom out how I felt about going into action. People may think I'm boasting, but I wasn't afraid of being killed, but I was afraid of being maimed and becoming a cripple.

Visibility in the tanks was of course terribly restricted. You couldn't keep the front flap open as you would be shot through the head straight away. So they left a slit with two glass prisms in it reflecting, a sort of primitive periscope. But the glass kept chipping, so they invented a silver plated copper thing, but the trouble with that was that it distorted the vision so that you thought a shell crater was a deep valley—so they had to get rid of it. I found the best thing was a row of small holes with a padded armour plate behind it to protect the driver, you rested your head on the pad and squinted through the holes. We didn't wear steel helmets inside the tanks. I wore a leather and steel mask, with a chain mail veil to protect my face from splinters.

Our tank was big enough to go across all normal sized trenches except at Cambrai where the Hindenburg Line was. Some of the trenches there were 20 feet wide and they had dug-outs 25 feet deep. I went down one, and there were passages and rooms. The camp bunks were luxurious—planks, wire netting and canvas. I had heard German trenches were better than ours but that was extreme.

Barbed wire in some parts of the Hindenburg Line was 100 yards deep. It was absolutely impossible for the infantry to get through that, although 'Butcher' Haig didn't seem to think so. Oh, yes, we called him 'Butcher'. His one idea was to send enough men and some would get through. He was cavalry-minded, and much disliked, I can tell you.

In August or September 1917 we gradually moved down to the Somme near Albert to get ready for the Cambrai attack. We had to take all the badges identifying us as tankmen off, so that word wouldn't get through to the Germans that we were there. On top of the tank we piled our 'fascines'. They were ten foot long and five foot across. When we got to a trench we would drop a 'fascine' in and roll straight over it, sticking a flag there to mark it so that other tanks could follow us over and not waste their 'fascines'. A tank carried 75 gallons of petrol in three separate containers, so that if one was punctured you still had some fuel. It was enough to do 50–75 miles, far more than we could manage in a day.

The tank I was in at Cambrai was named *Eldorado*; being 'E' company, all our tanks began with that letter—the next was called *Enchantress*. But when a shell went over us at Cambrai and took our silencer off, I didn't think it was much of an Eldorado!

In the Battle of Cambrai our battalion went in at Flesquieres which had been held by the French. Our battalion lost sixteen tanks out of 36 on the first day, but my tank was in it three days in all—the first, second and fourth days of battle and we didn't have a scratch.

Cambrai was a fiasco. 'Butcher Haig' had his cavalry assembled all ready to go through into open country after we'd made the breakthrough, but with all his wonderful knowledge, he hadn't any infantry reserve. The Cavalry just galloped here and there and got caught on the wire. Our men were battered after Cambrai and exhausted, and they got no reserves, so when Jerry counter-attacked they pushed us right back and regained two-thirds of the ground that we had taken.

(Field)

Amazingly, I was able to trace one of the men in the next tank to Val Field's *Eldorado* at Cambrai, William 'Mac' Francis, who was in the tank *Enchantress*:

> Tanks were of both sexes, male and female. The female was 'manned' by four and sometimes five Lewis guns, the male by two heavy six-inch guns.
>
> One thing that plagued all tank crews were tiny hot thin flakes that came off the inside of the armour, caused by the impact of machine-gun bullets on the outside. The sores on hands and arms often became septic and did not heal for weeks.
>
> The German soldiers were a very brave lot. I witnessed from our tank a German climb on top of another when it was travelling fairly slowly—perhaps one mile an hour. He was trying to open a peep hole on top of the tank; no doubt he intended to throw a bomb inside, but when closed with a metal catch from inside, these hatches could not be opened, from the outside. This Jerry must have been an acrobat in civil life! I've never seen anything like it—how he managed to stay on and keep his balance is beyond me. However he was spotted by another tank coming up behind and was 'popped off'. He certainly deserved the Iron Cross, First Class!
>
> At the Battle of Cambrai the ground was excellent for tank warfare. We made our way under cover of darkness from Havrin-court Wood. Every tank was able to follow the route because miles of white ribbon, about one and a half inches wide, were run out over fields, through woods, sunken roads, lanes, trenches, up over many chalk quarries and we got to our 'jumping off' places without any trouble.
>
> As it was just getting light we went 'over the top'. We had not gone more than 100 yards when I saw a sight I will ever remember: a German soldier and a British one had bayoneted each other at the same time and there they were, dead—but in a standing position, just locked together with each other's bayonets.
>
> About half an hour later, our crew got out for a short break and a breath of fresh air, and our battalion C.O., Captain Cave Brown, who became a Major-General in the last war, saw me shivering from head to foot. I heard him tell my tank officer that I was badly shell-shocked. I told him I wasn't. 'Anyhow, this will soon put you right', the Captain said and gave me about half a pint of whisky. 'Drink the lot', he said, and I did! In a couple of minutes, I was perfectly fit and felt ready to face the whole German army. I

have always been pretty well TT, and I cannot understand why it did not make me drunk: but it did not make me unsteady in the least, and I did not shiver afterwards. (It was neat, the real stuff).

Later that day, our tank received a direct hit; we abandoned tank, and I took my Lewis gun with me. My tank driver, Barney Gallacher of Ayr, with my help, dragged into our shallow trench two British wounded soldiers who were still exposed to enemy fire. We had made them fairly comfortable when a German plane came over. I could see the German cross very plainly, and I raised my Lewis gun to my shoulder. My officer shouted to me: 'Put that bloody gun down—it's one of ours'. I obeyed him, but told him I was certain it was a Jerry, but he wouldn't have it. It came over a second time, I repeated my action with the gun, and once again he told me to put the gun down, and I obeyed him for the second time. The plane went round in a circle and for the third time came right over us. I raised the Lewis gun to my shoulder and my officer, Lt. Nightingale from Chester, again shouted: 'Put that bloody gun DOWN!' But this time I fired. Hardly were the officer's last words out of his mouth when he said: 'Bloody good shot, Francis'. And that is how I won the Military Medal for disobeying orders.

A couple of months later I was called to my C.O.'s office and, expecting trouble, I was surprised when he left his desk, saluted me and said: 'Congratulations, Francis, you have been awarded the M.M. and the Brigadier has asked me to tell you that the plane you shot down was commanded by the officer in charge of the whole German area on the Cambrai front, and many maps of airstrips and other intelligence fell into our hands?

At the beginning of the battle, one of the Divisional Commanders, Gen. Sir Hugh Elles, told his men in an Order of the Day: 'England expects every tank this day to do its damnedest!'—and they did. At first, surprise was complete. Except for the northern sector of the six-mile front, at Flesquieres, where the tanks were allegedly held up by the single German gunner, a massive breakthrough was achieved: the tanks swept forward, even crossing the St. Quentin canal, making a five-mile advance in a single day (10,000 prisoners and 2,000 guns were taken). Three defence lines had been penetrated, and only one more lay between the British and the open country beyond Cambrai. But the Germans, unlike the attackers, had reserves ready to plug the gap that the tanks had punched: a division freshly arrived from Russia was rushed in to cover the hole. By nightfall on the 20th, five more German divisions were on their way to Cambrai.

On November 21, the British made some further progress. Flesquieres was cleared and captured, but by night on this second day, the tank crews were tired and the lack of reserves—apart from the cavalry, who as usual were hamstrung by machine-gun fire—was beginning to be felt. Meanwhile German resistance was stiffening, as their reserves arrived in the line.

Haig had ordered that the battle be concluded in 48 hours, but, typically, now that hopes of a breakthrough were fading fast, he changed his mind and ordered the attacks to continue—belatedly ordering fresh divisions to join the battle. For the next few days, ding-dong fighting went on, with villages and woods changing hands in bitter battles. But the Germans were preparing a strong counter-attack, and on November 30 they struck back.

Using newly-developed infiltration tactics, they filtered through the British in the southern sector. The British doggedly fought back, but were forced to evacuate most of the areas won so swiftly on the 20th.

On December 7 the battle ended in a stalemate, with the British hanging on to some of their gains in the north and the Germans newly established on previously British-held ground in the south. British casualties totalled 45,000; the Germans lost 42,000.

Cambrai had been a brilliant opportunity, perfectly executed, although subsequently botched by bungling carelessness. But it had demonstrated what the tank could do if tactics and terrain were right, and thus was an important portent for the future. Ironically the Germans, so technically minded, were slow to appreciate the value of 'those terrible tanks', but in May 1940 they turned the tables on their opponents with a vengeance. The Blitzkrieg was born at Cambrai.

While the battle was going on, momentous events had been in progress on the east. The Bolsheviks, who had come to power in a coup in October, had lost no time in carrying out their promise to withdraw Russia from the war. So eager were they for peace, and so hopeless was Russia's economic and military position, that the Germans were able to dictate what terms they liked.

The result was the vindictive treaty of Brest-Litovsk, which forced Russia to cede Poland, and huge tracts of Russia itself, to the Germans as the price of peace. Germay could now at last dispense with her war on two fronts and rush the vast bulk of her Eastern Armies to the west to strike one final and, they hoped, crippling blow at the Allies before the

Americans arrived in sufficient numbers to tip the scales finally against the Central Powers.

As the old year ended, both sides wearily braced themselves for the coming final showdown, which all knew would be decisive. It was a race against time.

The Cambrai battlefield yields little to the modern pilgrim, particularly if the explorer, as I was, is on foot. And as desperately tired as the soldiers of the Great War must often have felt as they tramped along France's cobbled pavé roads. After fifteen miles of marching along the round stones, said one veteran, they began to feel exactly like hot nails sticking up into the soft flesh of the feet.

I took the road to Cambrai from Arras. This road, the D.939, is Roman and as straight as a die. It crosses a series of rises and dips which gradually had a soporific effect as I walked. Slowly my body went onto automatic pilot, and I was hardly conscious of my boots squelching down into the tarmac melting under the sun. (The cobbles have long since been covered up by progress, as presumably they covered up medieval mud, which in turn covered up Roman stones).

The road passes many places which hold poignant memories of the war: Monchy and Bourlon Wood being the most notable. In his novel *It was the Nightingale*, Henry Williamson, who fought at Bourlon, returns to the wood in the 1920s by motorbike with his young bride Barley. Lying under the trees together, he tries to convey to her the hellish place it was, but cooing birds and the innocence of her body get in the way of his memories. All he has is the already rusting detritus of war. But when I visited the wood, even these were gone.

Indeed, the only relic I found, apart from the many monuments and cemeteries lining the road, was a single cartridge case. I entered Cambrai and refreshed myself in a peculiarly depressing café with a concrete floor and space invader machines winking and shuddering in the corner. I lingered long over my coffee and the fleeting cold comfort it gave, before forcing my tired limbs to take the road south, toward St. Quentin and the climactic battlegrounds of 1918.

Part Six
Germany's Last Gasp –
The Ludendorff Offensives

19. 'Michael' in March

We must beat the British. It will be an immense struggle that will begin at one point, continue at another and take a long time. It is difficult, but it will be successful.

General Ludendorff

After forty-four months of hard fighting they [the German officers and men] threw themselves on the enemy with all the enthusiasm of August 1914. No wonder it needed a world in arms to bring such a storm-flood to a standstill. In the course of time . . . history will recognize that we fought as no people ever fought before.

Ernst Jünger, 'Storm of Steel'

For the Germans, the winter of 1917–18 was the worst of the war. They called it the 'turnip time', because that coarse animal fodder was about all there was left to eat: supplies of oil, rubber, and basic foodstuffs were being slowly throttled by the increasingly effective British blockade. Sailors of the German fleet, bottled up in harbour since the indecisive Battle of Jutland in 1916, mutinied in frustration. A wave of strikes ran through the factories. The military oligarchy who ran the country knew they must act—now or never.

Ludendorff laid his plans: on November 11, 1917, a year to the day before the war ended, he called a conference of the German generals at Mons. They concluded that the strike must be made against the British in the west, and left Ludendorff to work out the details. He prepared a number of different contingency plans under codenames, calculating that if one attack did not pay swift dividends, another could be tried. In this indecisiveness lay one of the fatal flaws of his plan, for the Germans, though temporarily boosted in numbers by the end of the war in Russia, did not have enough men or *matériel* to support a wide range of operations. Ludendorff might have done better to stake all on a single mighty stroke, indeed, his first attack, named 'St Michael', very nearly proved decisive. He inflicted a signal defeat on the British which

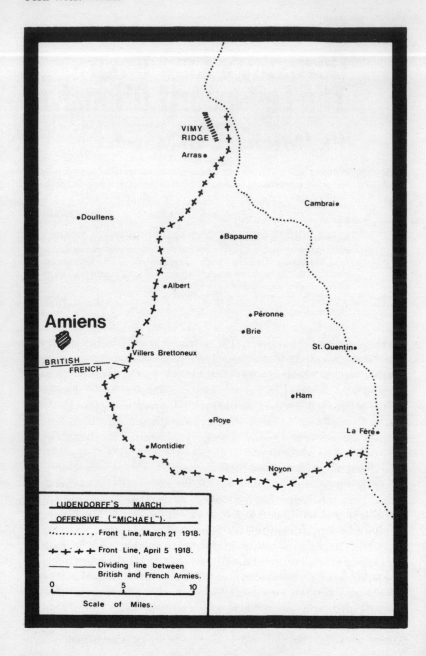

VIMY
RIDGE

Arras ●

Cambrai ●

● Doullens

● Bapaume

Amiens

● Albert

● Péronne

● Brie

St. Quentin ●

● Villers Brettoneux

BRITISH

FRENCH

● Ham

● Roye

La Fère ●

● Montidier

Noyon

LUDENDORFF'S MARCH
OFFENSIVE ("MICHAEL").

· · · · · · · · · · Front Line, March 21 1918.

+ + + + Front Line, April 5 1918.

————— Dividing line between
British and French Armies.

0   5   10

Scale of Miles.

almost—but not quite—succeeded in severing the French from the British armies.

'St. Michael' was launched from the prepared positions of the Hindenburg Line at the central sector of the Allies around St. Quentin. This was a weak link in the allied chain of command as it was the spot where the French and British armies met. In addition, this originally French sector had just been occupied by Gough's Fifth Army, smallest and newest of the British armies, a force composed mainly of raw reservists and exhausted veterans.

The area covered the region devastated by the Germans during their retreat in spring 1917, and proper defensive trenches were non-existent.

> I was in the Fifth Army under Gough. He was made the scapegoat for the initial defeat during the big German advance, but he was outnumbered 4–1 and his 'Green' reserve trenches were just cuts in the turf.
>
> *(Lamb)*

Ludendorff divided 'Michael' into three sectors: Von Below's Seventeenth Army was to attack Byng's Third Army north of Cambrai (over the Arras-Cambrai road which I traversed in the last chapter) and break through to Bapaume; Von der Marwitz's Second Army was to hit Gough just north of St. Quentin, and reach Péronne; and Von Hutier's Eighteenth Army was to drive in on him south of the city, across the Crozat canal, and head for the town of Ham. The eventual strategic goal of all three armies was to turn north, split the French and British and force the BEF back to the coast.

The British had plenty of warning of the coming storm: the number of intelligence-gathering and harassing German trench raids increased and intensified through January and February:

> We knew that there was a big German offensive coming, but we didn't know exactly when it was to be launched.
>
> *(Lamb)*

Quickly but methodically, Ludendorff assembled his forces for this massive battle, which the Germans were to dub 'The Kaiser's Battle' or, simply, *der Grosse Schlacht in Frankreich* (the Great Battle in France). They would attack along a front fully 50 miles wide—the largest battle area yet fought over in France. Ludendorff collected 6,000 guns, 3,532 trench mortars, and 82 squadrons of planes to support the three armies—all in all a force totalling nearly a million men. The spearhead of the attack was to be the *Jäger* ('Hunter') or *Sturm* battalions, hand-picked élites consisting of the youngest, fittest and most battle-hungry men in the Army.

These men, in their distinctive green uniforms, were to head the attack in small, mobile units. Their goal was quick penetration. If they came up against organized opposition they were to skirt round it and leave the mopping-up to the regulars bringing up the rear. They were to create confusion behind the British lines and do the maximum damage in the swiftest time possible.

The weight of numbers bearing down on the British was vast: Ludendorff would throw 43 of his 63 divisions into the attack against Gough's 13. The short artillery bombardment which would precede the attack was to be the heaviest ever seen on even that battered front: orchestrated by a certain Lt.-Col. Georg Bruchmüller, known as *Durchbruchmüller* (Breakthrough Müller), some 6,000 guns would spend five hours knocking hell out of the British. Concentrating first on the enemy guns, the fire would switch methodically to signals stations, communications lines, ammunition dumps and finally to the trenches themselves. The bombardment would dwarf not only all the barrages of the war to date—it even exceeded any launched in the Second World War.

March 21 came in cold and chill for the men of Gough's army. A heavy mist, originating in the Oise valley, rolled out over the lines, making the eerie silence heavy with menace. Just before 5 a.m. the guns spoke: almost simultaneously, along the 40-mile section of front between the Sensee and Oise rivers, the artillery let loose, jolting awake even officers behind the lines. Like some great conductor, Bruchmüller directed the orchestra of fire, the bass of the big guns joining the rattling percussion of the smaller cannons. Into his evil brew of high explosive, Bruchmüller stirred in plenty of mustard and lachrymatory gas shells which, mixed with the mist, added to the confusion in the British lines as the British strove to respond to the hurricane which had hit them. Under the weight of steel, the earth heaved and jolted, the laboriously-laid phone lines parted, and whole headquarters disappeared into the ground.

Herbert Sulzbach was one of the German artillerymen who were laying down the carpet of fire.

Herbert Sulzbach, 2nd Lt., 63rd (Frankfurt) Field Artillery Regiment:

The artillery fire begins at 4.40 a.m., and at 9.40, that is after a five-hour barrage, came the infantry assault and the creeping barrage. Meanwhile the evening has come on, and I'm sitting on a limber and can hardly collect my impressions of today. I'd like to write volumes about this day; it really must be the greatest in the history of the world. So the impossible thing has been achieved; the breakthrough has succeeded! The last night of the four years of static warfare passed, as I have said above, in the greatest possible excitement after the starting time had been fixed for 4.40 a.m. The exact time, down to the last second, was given through three times. 4 o'clock. The darkness begins to lift, very, very slowly; we stand at the guns with our gas-masks round our necks, and the time until 4.40 crawls round at a dreadfully slow pace. At last we're there, and with a crash our barrage begins from thousands and thousands, it must be from tens of thousands, of gun-barrels and mortars, a barrage that sounds as if the world were coming to an end. For the first hour we only strafe the enemy artillery with alternate shrapnel, Green Cross and Blue Cross. The booming is getting more and more dreadful, especially as we are in a town between the walls of houses. Meanwhile an order arrives: H. M. the Kaiser and Field Marshal von Hindenburg have arrived at the Western theatre in order to command the Battle of St. Quentin in person.

So we are stationed right at the most decisive place, and the hottest.

In the middle of this booming I often have to make a break in my fire control duties, since I just can't carry on with all the gas and smoke. The gunners stand in their shirt-sleeves, with the sweat running down and dripping off them. Shell after shell is rammed into the breach, salvo after salvo is fired, and you don't need to give fire orders any more, they're in such good spirits, and put up such a rate of rapid fire, that not a single word of command is needed. In any case, you can now only communicate with the gun-teams by using a whistle. At 9.40 the creeping barrage begins, and under its cover the thousands, and thousands more, and tens of thousands of soldiers climb out of the trenches, and the infantry assault begins.

At 9.40 a.m., the first wave of infantry climbed out of the trenches and moved forward. Confidently, they had their rifles slung on their shoulders. The familiar 'potato masher' grenades swung on their belts, ready to wipe out any pockets of resistance that had survived the earthquake.

One of the first to lead his squad of stormtroopers over the top was Captain Ernst Jünger:

> The officer patrols who were to cover our advance left the trench at 9.10. As our front line and the enemy's were here 800 metres apart, we had to move forward even during the artillery preparation and to take up our position in No Man's Land in readiness to jump into the enemy's front line at 9.40. Sprenger and I climbed out on to the top after a few minutes, followed by the men.
>
> 'Now we'll show what the 7th Company can do!'
>
> 'I don't care for anything now.'
>
> 'Vengeance for the 7th Company.'
>
> 'Vengeance for Captain von Brixen.'
>
> We drew our revolvers and crossed our wire, through which the first casualties were already trailing back.
>
> I looked to the left and right. The distribution of the host presented a strange spectacle. In shell-holes in front of the enemy lines, churned and churned again by the utmost pitch of shell-fire, the attacking battalions were waiting massed in companies, as far as the eye could see. When I saw this massed might piled up, the breakthrough seemed to me a certainty. But was there strength in us to smash the enemy's reserves and hurl them to destruction? I was confident of it. The decisive battle, the final advance, had begun. The destiny of the nations drew to its iron conclusion, and the stake was the possession of the world. I was conscious, if only in feeling, of the significance of that hour; and I believe that on this occasion every man felt his personality fall away in the face of a crisis in which he had his part to play and by which history would be made. No one who has lived through moments like these can doubt that the course of nations in the last resort rises and falls with the destiny of war.
>
> The atmosphere of intense excitement was amazing. Officers stood upright and shouted chaff nervously to each other. Often a heavy trench-mortar fired short and scattered us with its fountains of earth; and no one even bent his head. The roar of the battle had become so terrific that we were scarcely in our right senses. The nerves could register fear no longer. Every one was mad and beyond reckoning; we had gone over the edge of the world into superhuman perspectives. Death had lost its meaning and the will to live was made over to our country; and hence every one was blind and regardless of his personal fate.

Three minutes before the attack my batman, the faithful Vinke, beckoned to me, pointing to a full bottle. He recognized, in his own way, the need of the hour. I took a long pull. It was as though I drank water. There was only the cigar wanting, the usual one for such occasions. Three times the match was blown out by the commotion of the air . . .

The great moment had come. The fire lifted over the first trenches. We advanced . . .

The turmoil of our feelings was called forth by rage, alcohol, and the thirst for blood as we stepped out, heavily and yet irresistibly, for the enemy's lines. And therewith beat the pulse of heroism— the godlike and the bestial inextricably mingled. I was far in front of the company, followed by my batman and a man of one year's service called Haake. In my right hand I gripped my revolver, in my left a bamboo riding-cane. I was boiling with a fury now utterly inconceivable to me. The overpowering desire to kill winged my feet. Rage squeezed bitter tears from my eyes.

The tremendous force of destruction that bent over the field of battle was concentrated in our brains. So may men of the Renaissance have been locked in their passions, so may a Cellini have raged or werewolves have howled and hunted through the night on the track of blood. We crossed a battered tangle of wire without difficulty and at a jump were over the front line, scarcely recognizable any longer. The attacking waves of infantry bobbed up and down in ghostly lines in the white rolling smoke.

Against all expectation a machine-gun rattled at us from the second line. I and the men with me jumped for a shell-hole. A second later there was a frightful crack and I sank forward in a heap. Vinke caught me round the neck and turned me on my back: 'Are you hit, sir?' There was nothing to be seen. The one-year's service fellow had a hole through his arm, and assured us, groaning, that he had a bullet in his back. We pulled off his uniform and bound him up. The churned-up earth showed that a shrapnel shell had burst at the level of our faces on the edge of the shell-hole. It was a wonder we were still alive.

Meanwhile the others were on beyond us. We scrambled after them, leaving the wounded man to his fate, after we had stuck a bit of wood in the ground near him with a strip of white muslin as a mark for the wave of stretcher-bearers that were following the fighting troops. Half-left of us the great railway embankment in the line Ecoust-Croisilles, which we had to cross, rose out of the mist.

From loopholes and dug-out windows built into the side of it rifles and machine-guns were rattling merrily.

Even Vinke had disappeared. I followed a sunken road, with its smashed-in shelters yawning in its banks. I strode on in a fury over the black and torn-up ground, from which rose the suffocating gas of our shells. I was entirely alone.

Meanwhile, behind the British lines, all was confusion: battalion, battery and brigade headquarters attempted—often in vain—to make contact with their men in the forward and battle zones. From the front there came an ominous silence: runners did not return, telephones had gone dead, messages were not received.

From Jünger's and other accounts, the story can be partially reconstructed—in the main, the men of the Fifth Army who had survived the artillery storm, fought and died at their posts. A handful were taken prisoner, others were killed in cold blood by the enraged enemy.

In some places the resistance was bitter and prolonged: at Manchester Hill, directly in front of St. Quentin, Lt.-Col. 'Big Ben' Elstob, a former schoolmaster, told his men of the 16th Manchesters: 'There is only one degree of resistance, and that is to the last round and the last man', and proceeded to carry out his own advice, defending his redoubt with stubborn tenacity throughout the day. Twice wounded, he personally led sortie after sortie to drive the surrounding hordes of Germans off his hill. Finally, the enemy brought up field guns to point blank range and blasted the last survivors. Elstob himself was shot through the head—and won a posthumous VC for his sacrifice. In the extreme south, at Fort Vendeuil, an old French position of 1870 war vintage, Captain 'Flossie' Fine of the Buffs, commanding a motley garrison, held out until the evening of the 22nd, when the tide of battle had long passed, before surrendering.

The chaos caused by the overwhelming offensive is still remembered by the survivors of that day:

On March 21, all hell broke loose at last, so there was no question for me of home leave—which I had been expecting as it was my 21st birthday. We didn't know what was happening at first, it was very misty that day, and no runners were getting through to HQ.

Towards evening we went up to the front line. Norman Edge was C.O., but he put his head over the parapet, got a bullet in the neck, and had to go back. I took over. We were in a re-entrant valley, and I put a machine-gun on each side to cover me while I went forward. I heard the sound of voices coming through the mist. As the people came closer, I realized they were Germans, so I went back, told the machine-guns to open fire, and checked them. We stayed static for a while, and then got a message saying we had to go back and join what was left of the Army at Péronne.

(Lamb)

On March 21, the day of the big German offensive, we made our way up towards the line. The fog was so thick that you couldn't distinguish anything. We saw a large group of people coming back through the fog, and someone said they were Jerries. It was lucky we didn't open fire for we could have killed the lot, because when they came up we found they were our own people. It was still foggy the next day—had it been clear weather we would have lost half-a-million men, it would have been an absolute slaughter. As it was, they had us on the run. It was like pushing a boulder—all you have to do is start it with a shove, and it moves itself.

(Field)

The Germans made the most progress that first day in the southern sector, where von Hutier pushed right up to the line of the Crozat canal. On the 22nd the rout continued, with the Germans pushing forward and threatening to split the remnants of Gough's Fifth Army from Byng's Third, north of St. Quentin. Harry Greig was near Arras at the extreme northern edge of the battle zone:

I lost my two younger brothers in the March battles. One was a Lewis gunner, and a shell dropped directly on his group. The other was wounded and died in hospital at Etaples, where he is buried. From where we were at Arras, we could tell the progress the Germans were making as each evening the flares receded further and further behind our backs as they advanced. On our right the City of London Fusiliers were overrun in one attack, and I had to bomb my way along a trench to clear the Germans out.

As the days of late March wore on, the Germans continued to press relentlessly ahead, driving the British before them, never giving them time to draw breath or construct new defences; Gough had given orders to pull back west of the Somme, and this sensible, life-saving decision was made the excuse to sacrifice him as a scapegoat for the defeat. Haig relieved him of his command on March 28, and General Sir Henry Rawlinson took over.

By that time the Fifth Army was in ruins—desperately, men were scraped together to form makeshift lines in an all-out bid to stem the tide. Artillery men, cooks, military police, engineers, and tank men without tanks, all were given guns and pushed into battle:

> We got back to the river Somme at a village with a small bridge, called Brie. The bridge was mined with a plunger 100 yards down the road all set to go off and a sentry guarding it. I was with our new tank and the officer gave me two minutes to destroy it and get over the bridge. I loosened the caps to let the petrol flow out all over the engine. Then I reached in and fired my revolver and it blew up—it's lucky I didn't stand too close; as it was I felt a blast of hot air singe me as it burst into flames. I went over the bridge, but they didn't blow it for another hour, when a man came along and said a big party was coming up. They blew it then because they thought the new people were Jerries, but when they arrived they were another batch of our men, and they had to wade over the river. On the other bank were old trenches from battles in the previous year.
>
> The men in the retreat were being organized any old how into new units by General Carey. All the stragglers from disorganized regiments were lumped together and known as 'General Carey's Forces'. We gave them our Lewis gun and ammunition—they were very pleased to have them, and we went back on foot.
>
> Eventually, on March 25 or 26, we found our own battalion. They took away the gunners for emergency service and left us drivers, but it got so bad that we too were sent off in a lorry, to fight, with more Lewis guns. We were supposed to assist the infantry in holding back the German advance which was still continuing.
>
> The lorry dropped men off here and there in pairs. I was left with a man named Andrews. We were completely lost and didn't know where we were, so we set off across the fields looking for our own men. Shells were passing overhead. Andrews was carrying the gun and I had two boxes of ammo. We set up the Lewis on a ridge that gave us a good view. There were three circular plantations of trees about 200 yards ahead of us. Scattered on the ground around us were infantrymen with rifles—I think they were Devons. Their lieutenant was very pleased that we had arrived with the machine-gun.
>
> Suddenly someone said: 'Look over there—there's thousands of

the bastards!' We saw the Germans 4–500 yards away. They were well spaced out, with the old coal-scuttle helmets and carrying their rifles. There really must have been thousands of them. They would run a short burst then flop down on the ground for cover, then get up and run a bit further—getting closer all the time. We opened our ammo boxes. Each box held eight pans of bullets. We pressed the trigger and opened fire and saw some of them go down. But there were too many of them, and they just kept coming on. Our officer was just wandering around, as unconcerned as if he was watching a football match, although there were bullets whistling around. He came and told us that he would retreat with his men, and wanted us to cover them as they went back. By this time we had about two pans of ammunition left. He said: 'Give us three minutes then run yourselves, don't be bloody silly and try to stay on—remember, "He who fights and runs away, lives to fight another day". I'll always remember how cool that officer was, even though I never saw him again.

By this time the Germans had disappeared into the plantations in front and we couldn't see anyone. But we fired at the woods anyway and they were packed in there so densely that we must have got a few. We blasted off our remaining pans, then sat on the wooden ammunition boxes and tobogganed down the grass of the steep slope behind us. At the bottom the ground was low and not visible to the Germans. There was a sort of hollow leading out of it and Andrews decided to run down there and that was the last I saw of him. I heard later that he was wounded in the leg and taken prisoner. I went through the valley and up to the top on the other side where I joined one or two others. An officer saw me without a rifle and said: 'Bloody Tank Corps—never have any weapons.' I saw his point— I was useless to him with only a revolver, but that was our standard equipment and a Lewis gun was useless without ammo.

(Field)

We got back to Péronne on the 25th. We had no food for four days because the organization had broken down in the chaos of retreat. At the Somme bridge in Péronne we took up position on the west side of the river. The Jerries were coming up on the east, though by then they weren't pressing too hard. I believe they were slowing down to eat the provisions we had left behind. I had booby-trapped a small supply of food with a Mills bomb, in the hope that they would find it and be blown up.

At Péronne, Major Hurlbat was in command and Lt. Roston was acting as his adjutant. Foolishly they went back across the bridge to reconnoitre and they were both caught by snipers and killed. I was left in acting command of the British remnants: I checked the ammunition and found that we only had an average of three rounds each, which wasn't enough to stop Jerry. I told them we had a choice of staying where we were and putting our hands up or making a dash for it. Most decided to go, and most got away.

(Lamb)

Even the artillerymen were caught up in the chaos of retreat:

Things became hectic . . . We were lodged in an empty house a mile or so back and were engaged in culinary experiment. We had a dixie lid full of real bacon fat and fried rounds of soaked bread in it. The taste was sublime . . . Outside could be heard the continuous rumble of gunfire, and when we saw ambulances full of men, and the colour of their bandages, we realized that all was not well.

Abandoning our feast, we made our way to our battery, to find the gunners playing cards on the gun trail. The real seriousness of our situation came to our notice when staff officers arrived and commandeered our lorries, which were required to move machinery from the town where a huge repair depot was maintained.

Having received instructions to retreat, we hand-hauled our guns rearward to temporary safety. I really don't know where we got to for the next three days: sinister signs marked our route, cases of bully beef were dumped in a sort of do-it-yourself ration dump for the unattached stragglers who knew only that they were going the wrong way. There were chilling sights on the way. We came across a barbed wire former enemy-prisoner enclosure, but there were no enemy prisoners. Instead the entrance was guarded by military police, and any unattached passing that way were sent in, later to be formed into combatant units, irrespective of regiment.

The roads were jammed with anything that previously had been an army, and progress was slow. Luckily the air arm hadn't been developed sufficiently to take advantage of the situation. A few aircraft flew over the columns and let go with their machine-guns but I didn't see anyone hit.

Further on was the railhead, where you started your leave and where you returned. Those returning from leave during this period must have reached the depths, because on alighting from the trucks they were formed into units again irrespective of regiment or technical ability. Cooks, clerks, pioneers, gunners, infantrymen all joined the same unit, were given arms and became the new line—a dismaying experience. We still had our guns and were included in the temporary defence effort.

The enemy also had problems, chiefly of maintaining supplies over a considerable distance. This gave us a breather, and gradually we were able to renew communications and thus get some order from unimaginable chaos.

(Hancox)

Mr Lamb's comment about the German advance being slowed by the British booty they found was proving accurate: Ludendorff was discovering that success brought its own problems. Firstly, the ground which his armies were winning was in the wrong place—success was being achieved in the south, which was leading the Germans towards the French, whereas Ludendorff's aim had been to break the British and push them up to the Channel.

His northern attacks near Arras had met stubborn resistance, and little ground had been gained. Secondly, the starved German armies fell upon the plentiful British supplies like hungry wolves. The discovery of these ample hoards of food, new boots and equipment had a depressing effect on the Germans, who had been told that their U-boats had brought the British to the brink of economic ruin. The temptation was too great and many of them turned aside from the pursuit to gorge themselves on the goodies.

Finally, the British lines had been bent back, but they had not entirely broken. Everywhere, there were men still prepared to offer resistance. 'Michael' had driven a great, breast-shaped wedge into the Allied front which was vulnerable to being pinched off by attacks on its flanks.

Nevertheless a vast victory had been won—80,000 prisoners and 1,000 guns had been taken; the Germans had driven forward 40 miles; Péronne, Albert, Ham, Bapaume, Roye, Noyon and Montdidier had fallen and the morale of the Allies had been shaken almost to breaking point.

So much so that the top Allied brass, meeting at the tiny town of Doullens just behind the front on March 26, made a momentous decision that they had put off taking throughout the war: they unified the Allied Command, and General Ferdinand Foch, the old fire-eater of 1914, was appointed supreme Generalissimo of all Allied armies.

The hour of crisis had called forth the man of destiny; the cautious pessimist Pétain and the unimaginative Haig were passed over in favour of the redoubtable Gascon. Foch appreciated the paradox, telling Lloyd George and Clémenceau: 'It is a hard job you now offer me. A compromised situation, a dissolving front, a battle in full progress turning against us. Nevertheless, I accept.'

By the beginning of April the grand retreat was over. The vital rail junction of Amiens was saved, and the vanguard of the German attack was halted at the village of Villers Brettoneux, on high ground just east of Amiens. Foch brought French forces into the battle to shore up the southern front, and the remnants of the Fifth Army, bolstered by tough new Australian and Canadian Corps, gave Rawlinson enough leeway to hold on and prepare for a counter stroke.

> We were collected together and got back as far as Villers Brettoneux. We still had got no rations and were almost starving. We had to pick up root vegetables. We would have been too weak to resist, so we just kept retreating. The Germans could have won the war then if they'd had the logistics, but they couldn't keep supplies up with their own advancing troops. At Villers we were able to block them and the French came up to help us stop them.
>
> *(Lamb)*

We retired to Villers Brettoneux and nobody seemed to want us. Being a village lad I was always on the scrounge. The town had been evacuated a couple of days before as the Germans moved up, so I found a food store and went in. It was a store for a big food shop—there was all sorts of stuff there: frogs' legs, tins of beef and salmon, even some cases of champagne, and I took some of that too. I piled it all on a sort of bricklayer's barrow and was wheeling it out when a Frenchman came along waving his arms. I suppose he must have been the owner, I dropped the barrow and told him there were other people in the store and he rushed inside. As soon as he had gone, I picked up the barrow, took it back to the lads and we had a good feed.

Later I found a couple of chickens—well, actually, I went into a coop at night and grabbed them. I got back to the billet and cooked them when someone thumped at the door and said: 'Jerry's at the other end of town.' (This must have been March 30). I stowed the chickens in my haversack with some bottles of champagne. We marched out of town, but the Germans never did take it. It was the furthest they got.

Seven or eight kilometres out of town we stopped for a rest and made tea. I got our officer on one side and we had chicken and champagne for breakfast—I bet we were the only people in the whole British army who had such a good meal that day.

(Field)

For Ludendorff, the first throw of the dice had yielded a major tactical victory, but strategically he was no nearer to ending the war and by April 5, when the battle closed, his casualties had climbed to 250,000 compared to 240,000 of the enemy. It was time to look for another site for the next thrust.

20. Backs to the Wall

There is no other course open to us but to fight it out. Every position must be held to the last man. There must be no retirement. With our backs to the wall and believing in the justness of our cause, each one of us must fight on to the end.

Sir Douglas Haig

By the end of March, Ludendorff's roving eyes were already moving away from Michael and looking further north. He was preparing to revert to his original plan of attacking the British on the old Flanders battlegrounds. He had shied away from this in the winter, but March had proved dry and he was now willing to risk his troops becoming bogged down in the unforgiving Flanders mud—besides the speed of events left him little choice: 'Michael' had, despite its great gains, been a disappointment to its author. The British, though bloodied, remained unbowed and in the field. To hit them hard, he thought he must strike much nearer home—a successful attack in Flanders would leave the British no room to manoeuvre or carry out the sort of retreat they had just managed with 'Michael', they would be forced back to the coast immediately, and face the choice of flight or annihilation.

Unfortunately for Ludendorff, 'Michael' had cost him so many men, and he still needed to leave many more to hold the huge salient he had carved out, that the numbers available for the new operation, eleven divisions, were hardly adequate. So much so, that one of his more sarcastic staff officers rechristened the plan, which had been code-named 'St George', 'Georgette'.

Another factor which worried Ludendorff was that the American armies—there were now more than 325,000 of them in France—were completing their training and were almost ready for battle. Time was not on the German side.

Early in April, Bruchmüller took his artillery north and prepared for the attack. The chosen ground was, once again, a weak spot in the

British armour: the sector between Ypres and the La Bassee canal to the south held by Plumer's Second Army and Horne's First. The southern-most part of the sector, around the village of Neuve-Chapelle, where the British had attacked in 1915, was thinly held by two Portuguese divisions. These men, far from home, were infected by both venereal disease and revolutionary ardour (a political upheaval was currently in progress in Portugal).

At 4.15 a.m. on April 9,—Ludendorff's 53rd birthday—with the Kaiser once again in attendance, Bruchmüller's barrage opened. Along a twelve-mile front around the River Lys, the usual storm of gas and high explosive shells tore into the defenders. The Portuguese did not wait for the Germans to come—they took to their heels, even com-mandeering the bicycles of the British Cycle Corps to hasten their escape. The men of the German Fourth Army moved forward six miles, while Horne's staff at Ranchicourt (with my father among them) fever-ishly rushed reserves up to fill the gap—including the battle-hardened 51st Highland Division, who had taken Beaumont-Hamel on the Somme the previous year.

The next day, Ludendorff shifted the weight of the attack onto the north sector, with the German Fourth Army striking at Plumer's Second along the infamous Messines Ridge. Messines and Wytschaete villages fell once more into German hands, as Plumer sensibly took the decision to shorten his line by abandoning the precious positions which had cost so much blood and pain to take the previous year. But he held grimly onto the high ground at Mount Kemmel, south of Ypres, until on April 16, the new Generalissimo, Foch, released a French Corps to relieve the bruised British.

Antoine Godde was one of the men transferred to the sector:

We relieved the English on Mount Kemmel; there were no trenches in this sector, so the troops had to dig foxholes in the ground for shelter. We didn't have a lot to eat, but some soldiers were designated to bring food up from the rear. Conditions were so bad that the men sometimes arrived with just one or two loaves for the whole unit, having lost the rest *en route*. It was rarely possible to see the Germans—I was designated as an observer and went to a forward position. I spent eight days in this sector in hellish con-ditions, with severed arms and legs scattered everywhere. Then the whole company was incapacitated by a gas attack. I had to be hospitalized in Nantes and was discharged from the army on May 18. I still suffer from the effects of the gas.

Although 'Georgette' was carried out with so few men, the British did not notice the difference—the Germans were fighting with a grim fury, and for a few days something akin to panic gripped the Allied High Command. The towns of Armentières and Bailleul fell as the Germans pressed the British backwards.

As this supreme crisis approached, even the stoical Haig—temporarily—lost his customary coolness. On April 11 he issued his famous 'Backs to the wall' order of the day. After exhorting his men to fight and die where they stood the order concluded: 'The safety of our homes and the freedom of mankind alike depend on the conduct of each one of us at this critical moment.'

Still the Germans pressed on. By April 26 they had prised the French off Mount Kemmel, threatening the vital railhead at Hazebrouck which in turn commanded the approaches to the Channel port of Dunkirk. But the attack had run out of steam: the assault troops were too exhausted to move a single step further forward, their guns were running short of ammunition and the resistance ahead was hardening. The most critical moment for the British had passed, and Ludendorff shifted his focus once again, this time to the French.

Meanwhile, von der Marwitz's Second Army had made one more effort to seize Amiens: on April 24, nine divisions supported by artillery and a small force of thirteen tanks surged forward at Villers Brettoneux. Here, for the first time, tank met tank:

> The German tanks were solidly built and cumbersome, and were much bigger than ours. They looked like ships with a pointed prow, so that shells fired at them from the front would just hit at an angle and ricochet off. They had a field gun sticking out of the front and eight machine-guns—four on either side. They could do a lot of damage if they got amongst you. Once I saw a test with one of the captured tanks. They fired the famous French 75 field gun at it at 200 yards range, but it only dented and cracked the side. It had 3–4-inch thick armour plate at the side and one and a half inch thick armour at the front.
>
> *(Field)*

By a supreme effort the Germans managed to seize Villers Brettoneux, but the next night the 13th and 15th Australian Brigades counter-attacked and drove them out.

April ended, and the first weeks of May brought a lull all along the front as both sides took stock: the Germans had lost 50,000 of their best men killed, and a further quarter of a million were wounded. The British had lost nearly 30,000 dead and their other casualties totalled nearly 240,000. Both sides were exhausted, but the Allies could afford to wait—every day now more Americans were streaming into France on the Atlantic troopships, while Ludendorff was increasingly aware that time, men and money were running out.

However he still had enough up his sleeve for further blows, and, considering where to strike next he hit upon yet another old battle-ground: the Chemin des Dames, gained by the French with such frightful losses exactly a year before.

This front on the Aisne was now held largely by four British divisions who had been severely mauled in the March fighting and then again in April on the Lys. They had been sent to the Aisne in exchange for the French reinforcements who had held Mount Kemmel. It was regarded as a rest area, trenches were rudimentary, and the tired men relaxed in the balmy spring sunshine.

The French were certain that the Chemin des Dames would remain a quiet front, but Ludendorff had other ideas: his plan now was to make a diversionary attack here, on the hinge of the Western Front, at the point where the line passed close to Paris. He calculated that the French would panic at the prospective loss of their capital, and under the cover of their disarray he would be able to deliver another blow—codenamed 'Hagen'—at the British around Ypres.

Preparations for the stroke, named 'Blücher', were put in train. Bruchmüller's guns and 44 divisions of infantry, including Storm-troopers were assembled north of the Chemin des Dames along the Aillette river. On May 27, out of a clear sky, a withering bombardment hit the unsuspecting British with the force of a tornado. The guns, delivering a high proportion of gas shells, mixed with high explosive and smaller mortar rounds, never gave the defenders a chance. By 5.30 a.m., the French had been driven off the Chemin des Dames ridge, and by 9 a.m. the German tide was lapping the Aisne itself. To the east the British were pushed back towards the cathedral city of Reims.

The Germans threw pontoons across the Aisne and flooded south, and in Paris the rumble of guns on the eastern horizon stirred uneasy memories of August 1914. The Kaiser and Crown Prince Wilhelm were near the front, cock-a-hoop over the victory. By nightfall, 10,000 prisoners had been taken and the Germans were on the River Vesle, halfway between the Chemin des Dames and the Marne. On a 25-mile front a twelve-mile deep wedge had been driven into the front. The unexpectedly easy breakthrough prompted yet another change of plan in the mercurial mind of the German commander. Junking the planned 'Hagen' assault in Flanders, Ludendorff resolved to convert 'Blücher' from a sideshow to a genuine breakthrough. He decided to thrust westwards out of the salient his men had made, and take the shortest route to Paris—the prize which had eluded Kluck and Moltke four long years before.

One of the German soldiers who distinguished himself in these days was Corporal Adolf Hitler, who won his second Iron Cross for capturing four French soldiers single-handed.

By dark on the second day of the attack, the garrison town of Soissons had fallen; 50,000 prisoners and 800 guns were captured and the forward German units were only eight miles from the Marne. But the more Ludendorff's bullet head butted into the bulge he had created, the more vulnerable his flanks became to side attacks: to the east was Reims, still untaken, with the French Fifth Army around it, while to the west loomed the forest of Villers-Cotterets, whose woods concealed more French troops. Even in the hour of triumph, all was not as well as it seemed for Ludendorff's armies.

But for the moment, the initiative was theirs: on the last day of May the Germans reached the north bank of the Marne near Château-Thierry. By that evening they had secured bridgeheads on the south bank between Château-Thierry and Dormans. It seemed as though nothing could stop them, and even the indomitable 'Tiger' Clémenceau talked gloomily of evacuating Paris.

But another miracle of the Marne was in the making; two divisions of American troops, the 1st and 3rd, had been rushed to the battlefront and the 3rd was already deploying around Château-Thierry. The French Commander, Pétain, was preparing to nip in the German salient from the flanks, and meanwhile the eager, young and un-bloodied Doughboys had staunched the fatal haemorrhage of men and morale along the Marne.

It was time for Ludendorff's second fist to swing: he ordered von Hutier to break out of the salient south-west between Noyon and Montdidier. Their target was Compiègne, HQ of the whole French army, and from there—Paris, less than 40 miles distant. As Hutier moved his men up, the US marines, striking north-west from Château-Thierry, drove the Germans out of a strategic position in Belleau Wood. This hot little encounter was the first real blooding the young 'Leather-necks' had had, and they acquitted themselves well, striking fear into their German opponents with their energy and aggressive fighting spirit.

On June 9, Hutier attacked with fifteen divisions; the battle was codenamed 'Gneisenau'. Bruchmüller did his usual stuff with the artillery and the French gave way—though it was noticed that their retirement was an orderly retreat, not a rout as it had been on the Aisne the month before. The first day the Germans pushed forward six miles, crossing the Matz river. By dusk, Hutier's 18th Army had broken the three French divisions opposing them and had taken 8,000 prisoners. The next day they continued to advance.

At this dire moment in French fortunes, it was clear that exceptional men were needed—luckily one was to hand, . . . none other than our old friend Charles 'The Butcher' Mangin, who dropped out of sight in 1917 after 60 per cent of his men were slaughtered in the Nivelle offensive. Now restored to favour, the Reserve Army plus an additional Corps, were placed in the hands of the grim Colonial Commander and he was told to do his best—or his worst.

Calmly, watched by Foch and Clémenceau, the man who now held the fate of France in his hands issued orders for a counter-offensive the very next day, June 11. His subordinate officers squealed that this was impossible. Stolidly Mangin replied: 'You will do exactly what I have ordered'. He decreed that the counter-attack should be without benefit of artillery support, so as to ensure surprise. Sure enough, Mangin's men swept out of the blue the next morning. Initially masked by mist they caught the Germans in the open, and threw them back, stopping 'Gneisenau' at half cock.

With his right flank stymied by Mangin and his centre stalled by the Americans on the Marne, Ludendorff decided to take out Reims, the big city which bulged on the left flank of his newest salient. He still hoped to effect some sort of break in the south which would enable him to strike effectively against the British in the north.

But he had asked too much of his troops—they were weary of continued offensives which seemed only to gain more ground to march over, and took so many lives. Victory seemed no nearer now than it had been when the fighting opened in March. Unaware of how near the Allies had come to total collapse they faced the future with diminishing enthusiasm.

Ludendorff's latest—and as it proved, last—offensive was codenamed *Friedensturm* (Peace Storm) and for the Germans it was indeed the last offensive of the war. Ludendorff planned to drive in a two-pronged attack east and west of Reims on July 15. But this time his prolonged preparations and assembly of artillery had been observed by the Allies and they moved back out of range. Besides, Foch had his own plans for a counter-attack on July 18. It was time to strike back.

Just after midnight on July 15, Bruchmüller's guns opened up yet again—but this time they did not have it all their own way. French batteries barked back, and many of the assembled German ammunition dumps went up in flames. Forty-eight German divisions surged forward, to be awaited by an almost equal number—43—of French and US divisions.

East of Dormans, the Germans crossed the Marne by boat and pontoon, but east of Reims they were met by heavy American artillery fire and could not establish a finger hold on the chalk hills.

Although the Marne bridgehead was being extended and was opening a dangerous bulge in the Allied lines, the impetus of the offensive was running out of steam before it had begun.

Despondently, Herbert Sulzbach noted in his diary that first night:

> The attack is coming to a halt; enemy resistance seems to be insurmountable. We haven't got the same morale we had on 21 March or 27 May. 15 July passes without our being moved forward. We are very depressed indeed, because if a giant attack like this does not succeed straight off, it is all over.

It was.

Even Ludendorff saw the inevitable. Enraged at the lack of progress east of Reims, he telephoned the Third Army's Chief of Staff to demand that the attack be pressed forward. He was told that the French had known all about the coming offensives and had simply withdrawn out of range of the artillery. Ludendorff's anger and his confidence collapsed at once like a pricked balloon; 'I quite agree that the attack be discontinued', he said meekly. 'I am the last man to order an attack that merely costs blood'.

21. Back to the Marne

See that little stream—we could walk to it in two minutes. It took the British a whole month to walk to it—a whole empire walking very slowly, dying in front and pushing forward behind. And another empire walked very slowly backward a few inches a day, leaving the dead like a million bloody rags. No European will ever do that again in this generation.

F. Scott Fitzgerald

I—or my feet—were about to discover what the Allied soldiers found in the spring and summer of 1918, that the static frozen nightmare of the trenches had cracked at last like the shell of some monstrous egg, and armies were sent spilling across the landscape like yolk.

Generals began to think again in terms of miles and outflanking movements, instead of yards and frontal attacks. The war had opened up, and the battlefields of that final year of the struggle reflect the change. Instead of the compressed hell-holes of the Somme, Verdun, Ypres and the Chemin des Dames, I was now walking across whole regions, moving down from Artois and Picardy through the forests of Compiègne and Villers Cotterets before finally emerging along the Marne into the rolling countryside of Champagne. I would then take a final stroll in the Argonne Forest and the St. Mihiel Salient—where the last battles of the Western Front were fought out.

I started by walking along the course of the German front as it was on the eve of 'Michael'. This can be conveniently done by dropping down the N.44 road, north to south, from Cambrai via St. Quentin. The landscape is unexciting; flattish and well watered by the St. Quentin and Sambre-Oise canals, as well as the River Somme itself, which meanders through a large and marshy valley, encompassing many wooded islands and peninsulas—ideal country for angling and duck shooting. Bothered by the heavy traffic I turned off the road to the right just after it fords the St. Quentin canal at the village of Masnières. I took the D.56 in order to explore the villages where the British assembled their tanks in the strictest secrecy before the attack on Cambrai.

The road, the D.56, took me through Villers-Plouich and Gouzeau-court:

> The tanks were hidden in woods at Villers-Plouich and Gouzeau-court before the battle. Sometimes they wanted to use them as stationary artillery and then they would just drive them straight into the village houses which were only made of wattle and lath. The people had all been evacuated. In fact the last I saw of my tank *Eldorado* after the retreat from Cambrai, it was being prepared for use as an ordinary stationary field gun by the Royal Engineers.
>
> *(Field)*

Hoping that the traffic had lessened, I made my way back to the main road, recrossing the canal at Bantouzelle. I was trying to trace the course of the Hindenburg Line, the fortifications from which the Germans launched their 1918 offensive. I had some trench maps with me which originally belonged to Arthur Lamb, and they showed the line clearly, with its menacing belts of barbed wire, at least 40 yards across, which protected the front line trenches. Behind the two deep front trenches of the Hindenburg Line came a support line, and further back two more subsidiary lines, the Catelet-Nauroy line and the Masnières-Beaurevoir line, each protected by its own field of wire. It could easily be seen how formidable were the defences behind which the Germans sheltered for a year, and what a mighty barrier the British had to break before final victory. Little can be seen today of the line; the wire and works have long been ploughed back into the soil. But by carefully following the contours of the hills I was able to detect the occasional ruined 'abris' or strand of barbed wire which showed me where the lines had been—and how carefully the German engineers had utilized the lie of the land to take advantage of every small slope and hillock.

The road soon brought me to the village of Le Catelet, which marks the northern end of the St. Quentin canal tunnel. This fortuitous fortress, built in Napoleon's reign, was swiftly seen by the Germans to be a natural defensive position, and so was incorporated as an integral and vital part of the Hindenburg Line. The entrance to the tunnel, where the canal passes underground, is on the D.57 road just to the right of Le Catelet. The tunnel takes the canal on a subterranean journey for some seven kilometres, emerging at the hamlet of Riqueval.

The tunnel lies fifteen yards underground and was proof to even the heaviest shelling. The Germans built many sub-shafts to connect it to the lines overhead and used the tunnel for a variety of purposes—depots, repair workshops, ammunition and food stores, hospitals, stables and dormitories for the troops. The upper ground was protected by concrete machine-gun nests, skilfully placed to sweep with fire all approaches.

The job of breaking the line at this point was allotted to green American troops of the 2nd Corps, acting under the orders of the Australian General Sir John Monash, one of the war's more imaginative and successful commanders. The attack on the canal was fixed for September 29, 1918. Despite heavy losses, the Americans and Australians carried the line in bitter fighting, and that very day Hindenburg and Ludendorff advised the Kaiser to sue for peace 'to avert catastrophe'—setting in process the chain of events that was to lead to the armistice just a month and a half later. A big American cemetery at Bony and a huge monument overlooking the old lines mark the sacrifices made by the Tennessee mountain boys in this decisive action.

Just after the canal emerges into the daylight at Riqueval a bridge spans it carrying a minor road: this is the very same structure that was seized by the British 46th Division under Gen. J. V. Campbell VC after they captured this section of the canal.

Soon afterwards the road levelled and entered the northern suburbs of St. Quentin, a bleak area of high-rise tower blocks. Only when I got to the city centre did the place begin to resemble the descriptions of the men who were here in 1914–18. Two buildings especially give the city appeal—its fifteenth-century town hall and its huge cathedral, begun in the thirteenth century and finished in the fifteenth. St. Quentin himself was a Romanized Gaul and one of the earliest Christians in France. He was martyred in 287 on the site of the cathedral. If you look carefully near the base of the tall columns of the cathedral, you can see the holes drilled by the Germans just before they evacuated the city in 1918. These bore-holes were filled with dynamite, but fortunately the French troops entering the town cut the wires before they could detonate, and the remarkable basilica was saved.

After spending the night in St. Quentin, and sampling a local speciality, 'andouillette', a sort of sausage that tasted of nothing so much as boiled india rubber, I set off for the south, still following the N.44. After some twelve miles I turned right at Vendeuil, and just beyond the village came to the old fort where the British stragglers held out on March 21. The fort has now been turned into a zoo, and there is little reminder of the battles here in 1918, beyond an exhibition of photographs of French troops in action.

By back 'D' roads I made my winding way to Ham, target of Hutier's successful southern thrust on the 21st. Ham's main claim to fame is an old fortress, now almost a ruin, where Napoleon III spent several years in captivity after an abortive *coup d'état* in the 1830s. After several years of enforced idleness during which he wrote several books on social reform and (inevitably) took a local girl as his mistress, the young Bonaparte made his escape by the simple expedient of deliberately damaging his rooms and then disguising himself as one of the workmen sent in to repair them. He strolled out with a plank over his shoulder and made his way to English exile. But ever after, his opponents derisively called him 'Badinguet'—the name of the workman he had impersonated.

The next day I pushed north to Péronne on the D.937, roughly following the route of the great British retreat of March, passing the village with the shortest name in France, 'Y'. Péronne is an ancient town on the Somme which has seen more than its fair share of wars, ancient and modern. It was reduced to a shambles in the Great War, first by persistent shelling, and then, as a matter of deliberate policy by the Germans when they evacuated it during their retreat to the Hindenburg Line in the spring of 1917.

I decided to spend the night in a new campsite on a spit of land marking the point where the Somme river divides into northern and southern canals. A bridge nearby stands on the site where Arthur Lamb realized that he did not have enough ammunition to hold out against the advancing enemy.

The town today is a bustling market centre, with its main market square dominated by a charming Renaissance Hôtel de Ville. A small citadel off the square is open to the public, and a group of surly youths sold me a ticket and then followed me round the few ill-lit subterranean caverns to make sure that I did not pick up the handful of rusty helmets and few other relics on display. The next day I headed south again until I reached the village of Brie, where Val Field scuppered his tank. There was not much in the modern concrete bridge to remind one of the war, and just as I was exploring a towpath along the Somme the rain began. It was a persistent, skirmishing drizzle, and it followed me westwards as I made my way along the St. Quentin-Amiens road, the N.29 they call it today—though it originated as a Roman road and runs straight as an arrow towards Amiens. And an arrow it must have seemed to the advancing Germans as they plodded down it in 1918, hard on the heels of the remnants of the Fifth Army, leading them on, as they hoped, to victory.

That victory was prevented at the village of Villers Brettoneux by the gallantry of the British stragglers and the Australian Corps. Villers was also the scene of the British counter-thrust on August 8, that Ludendorff termed 'The black day of the German army', and which sent them reeling back down the Roman highway at the start of the long march home. The village has street names recalling its connection with Australia and recently opened an Australian war museum.

Just north of Villers, on the road to Corbie, is the hill on which stands the tower of the Australian National War Memorial and a large grave-yard containing the tombs of many of the 10,000 men who fell here between April and August 1918. As I was contemplating the German-held ground to the east and the spire of Amiens Cathedral, so temptingly close, to the west, a Mercedes drew up with West German number-plates and a middle-aged couple from Hamburg took pity on my bedraggled state and invited me into the back seat to share a hot flask of coffee. They told me they were returning from a rain-dogged holiday in Normandy and were visiting the Western Front out of curiosity. They were both doctors and regaled me with horror stories of life on the Eastern Front, where he had been wounded, and she had been a nurse in Poland. They exhibited that gentle, bruised, slightly guilty courtesy of their generation: expressing horror of war and all its works, yet underneath, a sort of dreadful fascination. I accepted a lift back to Amiens where I found a bed for the night.

The next day, I moved south-east on the D.934. The rain had eased into fitful showers, and I made good progress, taking time out to visit Hangard Wood, just south of Villers Brettoneux, the scene of some of the most vicious fighting during the August 8 breakout. The wood crowns a little hill and in its lee stands a small cemetery, notable for the grave of Private J. B. Croak of the 13th Royal Highlanders who lost his life and won a posthumous VC in taking out seven machine-guns and three howitzers which were holding up the progress of the attack.

Returning to the main road I walked steadily south, turning on to the D.935 which winds through the attractive wooded valley of the Avre through Moreuil to Montdidier. I was virtually following the line of the farthest German advance in 1918, but as this was only briefly part of the firing line, the war has left little trace of where it passed; so this part of the walk can be quickly summarized. The road continued from Mont-didier across the line of the River Matz, where Mangin stopped the *Gneisenau* offensive, and finally I was in the town of Compiègne.

This historic town, beneath whose walls—still standing in places—Joan of Arc was captured by the Burgundians, is most notable for its château, built in austere style by Louis XV as if to compensate for the flamboyant extravagances of his great-grandfather, Louis XIV at Versailles. The château has been the scene of many historical events, not least the marriage of Napoleon I to Marie Louise of Austria, and the splendid Bonapartist court of Napoleon III who loved the nearby forest of Compiègne. General Nivelle moved the HQ of the French army from Chantilly to Compiègne just before launching his disastrous offensive, and from here Pétain directed the suppression of the subsequent mutinies. The château, with its First and Second Empire furniture, is open to visitors, and I joined the throng, gazing out of the magnificent windows at the weeping trees in the park, and feeling the stark contrast between my rain drenched self and the elegant environment.

I stayed the night in Compiègne, and took the opportunity to clean up before venturing into the huge forest which lies south-east of the town.

There are an estimated 300 crossroads in the forest, which is divided into segments by the neat and narrow roads bearing traffic to and from Paris. It is signposted and too tame for my taste. I like forests to be wildernesses where there is at least a faint chance of getting completely lost—as the dauphin Phillippe Auguste is reputed to have done for two days in Compiègne.

Compiègne Forest is, of course, most famed for being the scene of the signing of the Armistice which ended the Great War, on November 11, 1918. Marshal Foch's mobile HQ in a *wagon lits* railway coach was shunted onto a spur of the Compiègne railway in a clearing in the forest near the village of Rethondes, to await the arrival of the German envoys who had crossed the front lines two days previously to seek peace terms.

Foch's terms were hard—though not hard enough for some—and while the plenipotentiaries procrastinated the news came through from Germany that the Kaiser had been forced to abdicate and Germany was a republic. Hastily the Germans signed. But the small clearing in the woods was to have another moment of fame; with a fine sense of irony, Hitler decreed in June 1940 that the armistice ending hostilities between his Wehrmacht and the beaten French should be signed on this very place, and in the self-same railway wagon. After this deed of humiliation, the carriage was sent to Berlin for exhibition, where it was eventually destroyed in an Allied bombing raid. A replica coach, faithful in every detail to the original, now stands in a shed on the site, together with the inevitable exhibition of stereoscopic war pictures and statue of Foch, and a large memorial proclaiming that this was the site where the 'criminal might of the German empire' was humbled.

A surprisingly large crowd of people were visiting the site—including several Germans, who must have had mixed feelings. I moved on out of the forest via the town of Pierrefonds, a favourite resting place of Napoleon III. It was he who instructed the architect Viollet le Duc to restore the ruins of a huge castle here, originally built in 1400. The rebuilding, with fanciful embellishments, continued for much of the rest of the nineteenth century, and the end result is a veritable fairy-tale 'castle in the air' replete with huge walls, towers, battlements, draw-bridge, moat and courtyards.

From Compiègne a brief stretch of clear country was soon swallowed up in another forest, the Cot-de-Retz, surrounding the town of Villers Cotterets, birthplace of the creator of the *Three Musketeers* and the *Count of Monte Cristo*, Alexandre Dumas père. It was in these glades that Mangin concealed his army before leaping out like a leopard on the unsuspecting Germans on July 18, 1918, assisted by swarms of newly-built French tanks. After visiting the town, whose streets are stacked with timber planks from the surrounding woods, I located the site of Mangin's battle headquarters, off a small forest road north of the town. As usual the old fire-eater was in the heat of the action. He had constructed an observation tower, 60 feet high, from which eyrie he commanded the surprise attack which marked the final recovery of France from the disasters of 1917, and the beginning of the road to victory. The hill on which Mangin overlooked the battlefield is marked with a stone representation of his tower. I had a late picnic lunch here, before making my way south through the forest to Ferte Milon where I spent the night.

This tiny town was the birthplace of the French dramatist Racine. It boasts a fifteenth-century château and was besieged, unsuccessfully, by the English in the Hundred Years' War. A relic of those days is the church of St. Nicholas which, like many farms in the area, has a battlemented belfry and watch tower to guard against the bands of brigands and unemployed soldiers who marauded abroad in the Middle Ages.

I was now in the pleasant country of the Marne, an area of small villages which, despite their close proximity to Paris, seem wrapped in timeless sleep. A few miles' march brought me to the village of Belleau. Belleau Wood, where the Americans won their first glory in the war, lies just south of the village. A chapel with an adjoining American cemetery commemorates the action, and nearby there is also a huge German cemetery with over 8,000 graves. The wood itself contains several memorials to the men of the US 2nd Division who stormed it on June 25, 1918, and the more tangible reminders of the day—in the shape of field guns, mortars, trenches and craters—still lie preserved among the trees.

Château-Thierry, which stands on the Marne itself, is a few kilometres below Belleau. It is dominated by the wide river and by a massively impressive American War Memorial which resembles a Greek temple, on Côte 204 above the town. I spent the night in Château-Thierry, and the following day decided to slow my pace as I walked along the Marne following its course upstream to the east. The wooded hills on either side of the valley, and the occasional vineyard becoming more numerous the closer I got to Champagne provided an ever changing and beautiful backdrop.

Around lunchtime I idled away an hour in sunbathing at one of the innumerable locks that punctuate the river. The lock-keeper was an amiable cove; an ex-army officer, clad in swimming trunks with a huge moustache, he would venture out of his cottage whenever a coal barge or a dinghy hove into view and energetically turn the handles which operated the lock gates, graciously allowing me to assist him at his work. By the day's end I had only progressed up the river as far as Dormans, where there was a convenient campsite on the edge of the river. Dormans, was one of the bridgeheads which the Germans threw over the Marne during operation 'Blucher' and looking up at the brooding hills of the valley to the north of the campsite it was easy to envisage the men in *Feldgrau* breasting the rise and swinging down to dip their coal-scuttle helmets in the placid waters of the Marne.

The next day I moved further up the valley, continuing to follow the river east, until I reached Epernay, with Reims one of the twin capitals of the Champagne region. The Champagne vineyards are everywhere here, their neatly trimmed rows riding up hill and down dale. Each village has its string of small producers, but the big Champagne names—Laurent-Perrier, Bollinger, Taittinger and Moët et Chandon—are based in Reims and Epernay. I elected to tour the Moët cellars. Incredibly, these run for more than 20 kilometres below the ground, and there are an estimated 50 million bottles of Champagne, stored, necks down, in racks all round, with chalk-marks denoting the various stages of fermentation. The bottles are slowly tipped upside down in a gradual process that allows the excess sediment to gather at the neck. The necks are then frozen, the ice-pellet of sediment expelled, et voilà!—your Champagne. The Moët men made no secret of their worries about the future of the industry; three bad harvests in succession had proved ruinous to the major houses which control the bulk of the Champagne trade. It seems that the British are the major mainstays of the wine these days, still importing vast quantities of the stuff to celebrate the least occasion with the pop of a cork. After the tour of the cellars, we were led aloft to sample a (free) glass of bubbly on the expectation that most people would then feel obliged to buy a bottle, or even a case. Most did.

From Epernay I headed north over the hills to Reims, the ancient city where the Kings of France used to be crowned in the magnificent cathedral, reduced to a shell during the Great War but splendidly restored. However, fatigue was taking its toll and I was more than slightly glassy-eyed as I ended my tour here.

Part Seven
The Peace of Exhaustion

22. Recovery

The building is beginning to crack. Everyone to battle.

Marshal Foch

As Ludendorff's last offensive faltered and died around Reims, Foch gave the order to hit back. The first Allied blow was struck at Villers Cotterets where Mangin had secretly assembled his Tenth Army, in the forest of Retz. Under cover of the trees and a torrential thunderstorm, the 'Butcher' had collected some half a million men—Frenchmen, Africans and Americans. At 2 a.m. on July 18, he took his place at his forward observation tower. The troops were to be supported by a huge force of 4,000 new French tanks of the *St. Chamond* model, fast, light and each mounting one of the famous 75mm guns and four Hotchkiss machine-guns. Over 2,000 guns were due to bring down a lightning barrage on the enemy just half an hour before the infantry went in.

The attack was spearheaded by the battle-hardened Moroccan Division—including the legendary Foreign Legion—flanked by the 1st and 2nd US Divisions, veterans of the Battle of Belleau Wood. The barrage and the attack came as a complete surprise to the Germans, many of whom were caught in the open fields foraging for food. The attacking waves broke straight through the first and second lines of defence, taking thousands of prisoners and sustaining few casualties from the bewildered defenders.

By midday, as the tide of battle threatened to sweep across the Soissons–Château-Thierry road, the only channel of communications and supply for the whole salient that Ludendorff had carved out south of the Aisne, Crown Prince Wilhelm gave orders to evacuate the bridgeheads his men had won at such cost across the Marne. The long retreat had begun.

Thoroughly alarmed by the collapse at the front, Ludendorff called off a renewed attack he was planning on Reims, and recalled reserve divisions that he had already despatched to Flanders, thereby post-poning his cherished 'Hagen' offensive, as it turned out, for ever.

Meanwhile the cautious Pétain had made his way to Mangin's tower along forest tracks clogged by broken-down tanks and columns of marching men. Frightened by his own success, the pessimistic peasant told Mangin to leave his unorthodox HQ and scale down the attack, and refused the 'Butcher's' request for more troops to throw into the battle.

By nightfall, the front had been pushed forward a full six miles, but casualties had worsened and in the heat of high summer the men were parched with thirst. The next day the offensive continued against mounting opposition and smothering shell and machine-gun fire. The Americans fought their way onto the Soissons–Château-Thierry road, but at a fearful cost—their two divisions had taken a total of 11,000 casualties.

Meanwhile, Pétain had ordered the French armies all around the Aisne-Marne bulge to join in the attack: one army drove up from the Marne, another smashed westward from Reims. All along the front it was remarked that the Germans were not fighting as hard as they once had, and thousands were simply surrendering without a battle.

This realization had a depressing effect at German Supreme HQ. The Kaiser described himself as 'a defeated warlord' and Ludendorff, swinging from over-optimism to a fit of black depression, began to quarrel both with his monarch and with his superior, von Hindenburg. Sunk into gloom by the failure of his five mighty offensives, Ludendorff suffered a collapse of morale that brought him close to the brink of insanity. All might yet have been well had the Allies paused and given the Germans time to regroup, but there was now no chance of that: on August 8, it was the British turn to attack.

The late spring and early summer had seen a great British recovery which had more than made good the fearful losses of March. This was largely the work of Sir Henry Rawlinson, Commander of the Fourth Army in the Amiens sector, who now conceived the great blow to be struck at Villers-Brettoneux which was to lead to Ludendorff's final discomfiture—the famous 'Black day of the German army'. Fresh troops, including many Australians, were buttressed by plentiful supplies of two new types of tank, the heavy Mark Vs and the light Whippets. Haig, too, was a new man. His staff had been purged of the two evil geniuses most responsible for the carnage of Passchendaele—the Intelligence Head, Charteris, and the Chief of Staff, Kiggell—and now at last Haig's bulldog, offensive spirit and his unquenchable optimism that victory was to be found in the west in 1918 came into their own.

The plan for attack was a surprise frontal assault on a broad front in front of Amiens. Utilizing the straight Roman roads and the open countryside, the Fourth Army, spearheaded by the Australian and Canadian Corps, were to strike out, aided by the tanks and the newly-formed Royal Air Force, and kick the Germans back the way they had come.

Meanwhile, Ludendorff had successfully extricated his men from the untenable bulge south of the Aisne, at the cost of 25,000 casualties, and French troops were brought in to support the southern wing of the attack. Preparations went on in the strictest secrecy, and roads were muffled with sand and straw to deaden the noise as 100,000 men, with 430 tanks in support, moved up to their positions.

Zero hour was fixed for 4.20 a.m. on August 8, which came in with mist as thick as it had been on March 21. At the appointed hour, more than one thousand guns opened up. They were followed by the infantry, who attacked along a twelve-mile front with reckless bravery. Almost everywhere, the assaults were successful, the troops broke through the defence wall like jets of water breaching a crumbling dam. Although a quarter of the tanks were knocked out, the majority gained their objectives and even roamed far ahead, strafing the fleeing Germans down the ruler-straight Roman roads. Even the cavalry were brought into play to pursue the broken enemy. The official German report on the day's action is aptly titled *The Catastrophe of August 8th* and Ludendorff remarked that it put the moral decline of his forces beyond doubt.

Von der Marwitz's Second Army lost 27,000 men as casualties and 15,000 as prisoners, besides hundreds of guns and other war materials. After the first day the usual pattern reasserted itself: the German resistance stiffened, Allied casualty rolls lengthened and the amount of ground gained decreased. But despite the loss of nearly 300 tanks, the attack gained a further three miles and 12,000 more prisoners were put in the bag for 22,000 British casualties.

By the morning of the 10th, the attack had reached the broken-up old battlefield of the Somme and progress slowed even further. Wisely, and in defiance of Foch and Haig, Rawlinson decided to close the operation down. The battle had achieved its tactical objectives, but it was clearly running out of steam and 'Rawly' refused to be drawn into a repetition of the Somme or Passchendaele.

What none of the Allies knew was the devastating effect the action had had on German morale. The news of the breakthrough, coming hard on the heels of his failure at Reims and Mangin's audacious attack at Villers-Cotterets, almost drove the frantic Ludendorff into a frenzy. What made an already grave situation even more ominous from the viewpoint of Germany's leaders were the mounting reports of indiscipline among their own men, previously almost mechanically obedient. 'I was told of glorious valour', wrote Ludendorff later, 'but also of behaviour which, I openly confess, I should not have thought possible in the German army; whole bodies of men had surrendered to a single trooper, or isolated squadrons. Retiring troops, meeting with a fresh division going bravely into action, had shouted out things like 'Blacklegs' and 'You're prolonging the war'. 'Even officers', Ludendorff complained, 'had been swept along in the prevailing tide of pacifism and war weariness'. He concluded: 'August 8 marked the decline of our military power and took from me the hope . . . of discovering some strategic expedient that should restore the situation in our favour . . . The war had to be ended.'

At last the inescapable truth had entered even Ludendorff's bullet head. The war, no matter how it was prolonged, could have only one outcome, and the longer it was prolonged, the worse the situation became inside Germany. Already strikes were escalating into food riots, left-wing parties and politicians were becoming increasingly bold in their calls for the overthrow of the ruling military caste. New conscripts, the old, the unfit and the very young, carried with them to the front the germs of Bolshevism and defeatism. From an exhausted, hungry, miserable populace one cry went up . . . peace, peace at any price.

But the war was not over yet. The German military leadership, although moribund, still held the reins of power with the twitching fingers of death. And the armies still had their leavening of determined, obedient veterans—men like Adolf Hitler—who would go on fighting for the Fatherland until the bitter end—and beyond. The dying beast of German militarism was still able to administer some savage kicks as it expired:

Private Walter Smith, King's Own Scottish Borderers:

In July 1918, I came back to the front and was hit by a sniper during an attack. I crawled into a shellhole and my mates said they would come and pick me up in the evening—but they never returned. In the afternoon, there was a hell of a bombardment and they may have died in that. The British lines were too far away to shout; once I heard someone going past and when I put my head over the side of the hole someone took a pot-shot at me so I stayed where I was and waited.

It rained like hell and I was able to fill my water bottle. I was also able to eat the rations of the corpses that were in the shellhole with me. After six days stuck there I decided to try and get back to our lines. I crawled on my hands and knees and went some way, but then I felt done in and dropped flat on my face. As I lay there I was hit by bullets twice more in the hips. I continued to make my way towards a wood, shouted, and got an answer. I called again and the voice answered in broad Scottish. I reached a hedge and a hand came out and pulled me through. They were Gordon Highlanders. I was taken back to a cornfield and interrogated as to who I was. When I said I came from Croydon, they asked me detailed questions about the town—they obviously thought I was a German dressed in a British uniform.

But eventually I was released and carried to an ambulance. The doctor in the field dressing station said the only thing that had stopped my wounds from festering was the fact that the wounds were crawling with maggots which had eaten the pus and so stopped poison from forming. The maggots had kept me clean. I have got them to thank for being alive today.

Mr Smith, a Chelsea Pensioner, was crippled by his wounds and has always walked heavily on a pair of canes. The war also left its mark on other men:

Will Holmes, 15th Battalion, Hampshire Regiment:

On September 4, 1918, we marched to our front line trenches near the villages of Meteren and Wytschaete by Messines Ridge. After liberal rum rations we went 'over the top' at dawn. We shortly found ourselves facing fierce machine-gun fire from the enemy. Between the two lines in No Man's Land, my knee cap was shattered by a machine-gun bullet, and many other Hampshires were killed and wounded. The cries of the wounded for stretcher bearers were pitiful. I was fast losing blood from my wound which eventually turned to gangrene. I had fallen into a shallow shell-hole—lying there was an uninjured lance corporal whose name I was to learn was Walter Grubb. He tended me for 30 hours in No Man's Land, bandaging my knee, giving me sips of water, while in the meantime crawling along the ground to do what he could for the other wounded, although many were beyond help. But he always returned to me in my shellhole to rebandage my knee and give me a little more water. In point of fact I was dying and beyond caring.

Eventually, as hostile firing ceased, L/Cpl. Grubb managed to get me on his back, and took me back the best part of a kilometre to where the survivors of the battalion had gathered. I was handed over to stretcher bearers, taken to a First Aid post and thence to an Australian Casualty clearing station. All stretcher cases were lined up outside the marquee operating theatre. While awaiting surgery, a Roman Catholic padre bent over me and asked about my wound. As best as I was able I told him how Walter Grubb had tended me and eventually carried me back to the Hampshire lines. The padre remarked that Grubb was a brave man and stated he would write to let Battalion Headquarters know and recommend him for a bravery award.

In the meantime my condition grew worse and at the end of eight days the Australian surgeon suggested that my left leg be amputated at knee joint level. I was in such a low state that I told him I did not mind if he took off my head—but the amputation took place.

Despite hanging between life and death for several more weeks, Will Holmes eventually recovered and by chance met Walter Grubb after the war on the London Underground. He learned that his message to the Padre had been passed on and Grubb had been awarded the Military Medal. By an ironic twist of fate, Will was one of the chief mourners at his saviour's funeral when Grubb died of tuberculosis in 1925. The fighting in September also took the life of the Australian signaller Leslie Ibbetson whose diary I have previously quoted.

On August 11, the day the Battle of Amiens was concluded, the French Army of General Debeney, detached from Rawlinson's right flank where they had performed sluggishly, redeemed their reputation by seizing Montdidier. The next day, his neighbour to the south, General Humbert, struck towards Noyon and took Lassigny, and on August 18, a month after his victory at Villers-Cotterets, Mangin pounced again, sweeping past Soissons and seizing the strategic and blood-stained heights above the Aisne.

The drumming pattern of these new-style attacks was now established—a blow on one front, a breakthrough, and then the attack would be broken off as resistance stiffened. The action would move to another sector—another blow, another breakthrough; never letting the

Germans pause for breath, harrying them with ever-increasing superiority in numbers, equipment and morale. Spurred on by Foch, the French began to belabour their ancient enemy with the stored-up enmity of centuries of conflict.

For their part the British, with the help of the Australians and Canadians, matched the French battle for battle. On August 21, it was the turn of Byng's Third Army: with 200 tanks surviving from the tank graveyard at Amiens, Byng struck out over the old Somme battlefield north of Albert, and on the following day Rawlinson chimed in south of the town, capturing Albert itself on August 23.

The victorious troops noticed that the golden statue of the Virgin, which had hung over Albert after being dislodged by shellfire from her position on top of the basilica, had finally been destroyed. It was the most widespread superstition in the British Army that when the Virgin fell the war would end; now reality looked like bearing out the myth.

Between them, the Third and Fourth Armies took some 10,000 prisoners, and by August 25, the Fourth Army was nearing Péronne and the Third was approaching Bapaume. On August 26, Horne's First Army, spearheaded by the Canadian Corps and the 51st Highland Division struck out of its base near Arras towards Queant and Monchy, and Ludendorff, almost in a panic, gave orders for a withdrawal.

On August 31, not to be outdone, the Australians took Péronne. (Bapaume had fallen the previous day.) All along the line the Germans were in retreat, and by September 9, they were back to the Hindenburg Line, having lost virtually all the ground they had gained in their spring attacks and suffered a terminal haemorrhage of men (100,000 prisoners—even more killed and wounded), material and morale. The end could not be far off.

23. America Advances (St. Mihiel and the Argonne)

If you will assign me a sector I will take it at once.

General John Pershing to Marshal Foch

O German mother dreaming by the fire
While you are knitting socks to send your son
His face is trodden deeper in the mud.

Siegfried Sassoon

Exhilarated by his string of victories, Haig, on August 27, let his habitual reserve slip a little and wrote offering a humble piece of advice to his superior, Marshal Foch. He proposed a pincer movement to finally break the fast-crumbling walls of the German defence. He himself would go all out for the north and breach the Hindenburg Line, and he suggested that the American armies—now totalling almost a million and a half men—should be thrown into battle in the south.

The same idea was already forming in the Marshal's mind: on August 30, he gave the US Commander, General John 'Black Jack' Pershing, control of the St. Mihiel sector of the line; this area, on the Meuse just south of Verdun, was at the extreme south of the active part of the Western Front. The Germans had swept across the river at the small town of St. Mihiel in September 1914 and ever since had sat comfortably ensconced in a salient that jutted into the French lines like a nagging thorn.

Under pressure from Pershing, Foch reluctantly agreed to give the untried Americans a free hand in planning and mounting a full-scale attack on the salient. Pershing's plan was to pinch out the bulge from all sides and roll it up by overwhelming numbers of men assisted by artillery, gas and tanks. Foch authorized the attack for September 12.

At 1 a.m. on the appointed day, in the middle of a drenching storm, nearly 3,000 guns roared out in a massive barrage around the salient.

Two American officers who were to win fame in a later war, were present during the battle: Lt.-Col. George Patton—'Ole Blood and Guts' as he was later known—was commanding 180 US and French tanks, and Brigadier General Douglas MacArthur was leading an infantry brigade. True to later form, on the way into battle, Patton spotted a G.I. apparently skulking in a dug-out. He dived in to bully the man into battle, only to find the doughboy had a bullet through his brain and would never fight in any battle again.

The shells and a gas barrage did their work, and the demoralized Germans either fled or gave up virtually without a struggle. By noon, facing an assault by 400,000 men, the German General Fuchs ordered the complete evacuation of the whole salient. Ludendorff, when told the news, was said to be 'a completely broken man'.

As they counted their gains the following day, the Americans estimated they had advanced thirteen miles, captured 16,000 prisoners and over 440 guns. Pershing had proved the worth of his men, and Foch was happy to let him proceed with the next objective: the German stronghold in the Argonne Forest between Verdun and the Champagne plains.

To accomplish his assignment, Pershing now had to swing half a million men to the north, along with 4,000 guns and 40,000 tons of ammunition, within a fortnight. The objective would not be the walkover that St. Mihiel had been. The Argonne was considered by some to be the hardest objective on the whole front—an enormous area of thick forest in which the Germans had spent four years of almost uninterrupted labour in strengthening their defences. The forest was studded with heights giving the Germans all-round observation points, and the woods themselves were sown with concrete machine-gun nests and thickets of barbed wire to a depth of ten miles.

The detailed planning for the attack was the responsibility of another American officer who would later win worldwide fame: General George Marshall. To make things worse for the Americans, the autumn rains had arrived in earnest, and the approach roads to the Meuse-Argonne sector swiftly became almost impassable streams of thick mud.

But the Yanks doggedly persisted with their preparations. The plan was for an attack on a front of 24 miles. To outflank the worst of the forest, Marshall planned to drive down the valleys of the Meuse and Aire rivers, isolating the heights of Montfauçon, and turning the left flank of the Argonne. One advantage that the Americans did have was that of numbers, the second that of surprise.

Around 600,000 green Doughboys, some of whom did not even know how to fire a gun, were to join the battle, against only five German divisions—a numerical superiority of eight to one. Again there would be heavy support from guns and tanks. The secret of the coming assault was kept until the last minute: the Americans disguised themselves in the uniforms of the French troops they were replacing to make their reconnaissance, and the troops moved into the forward positions on the very eve of battle.

At 2.30 a.m. on the 26th, the guns opened up. At 5.30 a.m., the infantry surged forward behind the barrage. Once again in that year of misty battle dawns, the fog closed in. For some time it obscured news of progress, but it gradually became clear that, despite initial confusion, the attack had gone well all along the front except below the heights of Montfauçon which remained in German hands as night fell.

Patton, once again leading a column of tanks, took the village of Varennes—where Louis XVI and his family had been arrested during their abortive flight from revolutionary Paris. But Patton was hit and temporarily put out of action. Casualties were high among the raw Doughboys, but one future American President was spared—Harry Truman, then a private in the 129th Field Regiment.

The following day, determined attacks at last carried the formidable Montfauçon heights, but the element of surprise was gone and German resistance hardened all along the front. Six reserve divisions were brought up to bolster the defences. Nevertheless, by the end of the month, the Americans had slogged their way forward by ten miles, although it would take them another month of heavy fighting to finally clear the Argonne of Germans.

The Americans left over 26,000 dead and nearly 100,000 wounded on the field of battle, and the exuberant Yanks began to realize by painful experience, something of the agony that the soldiers of Europe had endured for four long years. That agony was finally now approaching its climax and its surcease.

All this time, as the Americans were tempered in the forge of war, the British had been by no means idle; on September 27, in a joint operation, the Third and First Armies struck at the Hindenburg Line itself. The First Army chewed its way three miles into the Line near Cambrai. To the south, the Third Army reached the line of the St. Quentin canal.

Haig was transfigured—with his new staff he had abandoned his HQ near the coast and was now running the war from a mobile train near the front. At last his hour had come, and with every day that passed, he could sense that all the suffering was finally paying a dividend. Whether that dividend could ever cancel out the debt represented by the mountains of dead remains an open question.

At the end of the month, in a final brilliant flourish, the British, Australians and Americans, vaulted the St. Quentin canal. The Hindenburg Line was breached.

Val Field gives the flavour of the fighting in that last month of the war:

At the beginning of October, when the Germans were really on the way out I was sent up to near St. Quentin. Jerry was falling back and no longer digging trenches. They were carefully selecting defensive positions where they had the field of fire in their favour and they really chose some strong places.

One day we got an S.O.S that some infantry were in trouble— they had got stuck in front of a German strongpoint. We started the tanks and went to help. But by the time we arrived some stupid bastard had ordered the cavalry to attack the German position.

We were just in time to see the charge. They were mowed down just like a machine cutting corn. The machine-guns just wiped them out. We went in and opened up from 500 yards. We got close and ran over some of the forward machine-gun posts. We used to mangle them by putting one track on top and slewing the tank round. Once at Cambrai, I saw something fly past my field of vision and realized that it was a human arm that we had crushed. I didn't stop to shake hands with it!

The cavalry had charged with their sabres and it was absolutely terrible. Injured horses were charging about screaming; the whole thing was totally unnecessary, and we only hoped that the bugger who ordered the charge had gone in with it. They didn't have a cat-in-hell's chance. As we went forward the machine-gun bullets on the tank sounded just like rain on a tin roof.

When we got close the Germans surrendered; they were a mixed bunch—young and old—but they certainly weren't the cream of the German army.

On October 11, we had orders to take the tank to a battery of 18-pounders. We took two guns with us and set off. The battery had been bombarding a château and there were machine-guns down in the cellars at low level. The guns had reduced the château to a heap of rubble, but the Germans carried on firing with seven or eight machine-guns.

They opened fire on us as we went in, but we held our fire, until we got up to about 200 yards from them. The driver veered to the left, so our right hand gun could fire forwards. We put a couple of rounds in and zig-zagged while the infantry came up behind us.

The Germans had buried some of their five-nine shells with their nose caps pointing upwards—a sort of primitive land mine. We must have hit one just as we opened fire again on the Jerry-held building. The next thing I knew was waking up on the floor. Everything was dark, so our little electric lighting system must have been destroyed. I was feeling very 'muzzy' but I tried to get up, only to find that my feet were trapped and I could not move. Something had tangled them. What worried me was seeing a flicker of flame at the front. I thought to myself 'Christ, if you don't get out of here, you're going to be burned alive'. I had seen men burned to death in tanks and it was absolutely awful; I didn't want to end up reduced to a blackened piece of charcoal about three feet long.

I called out, but got no reply. I discovered later that the officer and gunner had been wounded by the blast and had already got out. I suppose they thought I was dead, as most of the rest of the crew were. Then I heard something move, and it was another crew man, called Parker. As he got up, it released whatever was trapping my leg. I asked if he was O.K. and he replied: 'Don't know'. I suppose he was feeling as muzzy as me. He was snorting and grunting.

I put out the fire and pushed open one of the side doors. It shows how muzzy I was, because that was the door facing the Germans. If they had waited a moment more they would have got me—a machine-gun blast came along the side of the tank, and I shut the door. Parker could see through our periscope and he put two shells into the building, and then we escaped. We got out of the blind side of the tank and ran down the hill into hollow ground where we eventually rejoined our own men—that was the end of the war for me, because I was due to go back to Blighty the next day, and a month later the Armistice came.

24. Armistice and After

In November came the Armistice. I heard at the same time of the deaths of
Frank Jones-Bateman, who had gone back again just before the end, and
Wilfred Owen who often used to send me poems from France . . . The news
sent me out walking alone along the dyke above the marshes of Rhuddlan
[an ancient battlefield, the Flodden of Wales], cursing and sobbing and
thinking of the dead.

Robert Graves

The writing was on the wall for the German military caste . . . and the
wall was crumbling on their heads. The breaking of the Hindenburg
Line was the last straw to be added to the insupportable weight of defeat
beneath which the Central Powers were buckling to their knees.

Everywhere their forces were falling back—in the Middle East,
General Allenby, Colonel T. E. Lawrence and the Arabs chased the
Turks out of Jerusalem and Damascus . . . In Italy, the Italians,
boosted by French and British contingents, took revenge for Caporetto
at Vittorio Veneto and hounded the Austrians up into the Alps . . . In
Macedonia, the French, British and Greeks broke the Bulgarians and
advanced towards the heart of the Balkans . . . On the Western Front,
the overwhelming weight of Allied might pushed the Germans ever
backwards out of France and into Belgium. It was the end.

But it was not only from the outside that Nemesis pressed in upon the
warlords—in October, the Hungarian, Czech and South Slav elements
of the Austrian Imperial Armies mutinied and refused to fight on—
presaging the nationalism that was about to rip apart the ancient, faded
and multi-national patchwork quilt of the empire.

The spirit of mutiny spread to the sailors on the German High Seas
fleet cooped up in the Baltic ports. Ordered out on a last death cruise
against the British, the sailors doused their ships' boilers and raised the
red flag of revolution. The uprising spread from Kiel to the inland cities
and embittered workers joined in.

Like wildfire the rage of revolution raced to the front itself—sailors' and soldiers' councils were set up along the lines of the Bolshevik Soviets. Officers were initially ignored and later physically assaulted.

When the Kaiser, isolated from reality at the small Belgian town of Spa offered to lead his armies on a last-ditch attack, his staff had to gently tell him that hardly a man would follow him; 'Treason, Gentlemen! Barefaced treason!', Wilhelm spluttered, but it was the anger of impotence.

The last Imperial Chancellor had fallen, and his successor, the liberal pacifist Prince Max of Baden, had despatched an armistice delegation through the lines near Sedan.

Ludendorff was gone; only Hindenburg, the wooden Titan, stood beside the discredited monarch. While the haggling over armistice terms went on in the clearing near Compiègne, news came through that the Wittelsbach dynasty had been overthrown by revolutionaries in Bavaria, and the German Communist leader, Karl Liebknecht was planning to do the same for the Hohenzollerns in Berlin.

He was forestalled by the impeccably moderate and respectable Socialists of the German Social Democratic Party who, bowing to the pressure of the crowd, proclaimed the German Republic from the steps of the Reichstag.

After further spluttering, the Kaiser and his son bowed to the inevitable and took a train for the nearby neutral Netherlands. The Kaiser arrived at a convenient château and demanded a cup of 'good strong English tea' as his nation collapsed behind him.

Early in the morning of November 11, the Armistice was signed at Compiègne and the message was flashed to all fronts that hostilities were to cease at 11 a.m. that day. All along the lines, the guns, as if tired to death, fell uncannily silent. The war to end war was over.

I had put in for a transfer to the RAF and got sent home. There, I got a dose of the Spanish flu that was around at the time and I was in bed when I heard about the Armistice.

(Lamb)

I ended the war at Malplaquet in Belgium, where Marlborough fought a battle. I didn't know the Armistice was coming—I didn't even know where we were at the time. We were camped in ruined cellars and out on burial parties for dead horses, all blown up and bloated. The French troops nearby were celebrating like hell and when we went to find what all the fuss was about they told us: 'Guerre finie!'

(Thacker)

We ended the war at Mons—where we had begun it. What futility.

(Haddock)

After losing his finger at Passchendaele, Montague Tutt had returned to France and was blown up by a shell and wounded again within a week. When convalescent, he was pronounced fit for active service again and moved to London ready for a third tour of duty in France . . .

One day at ten to eleven an officer said to me in the street: 'They are going to sign the Armistice in ten minutes'. I was outside Charing Cross and there was pandemonium. Typists were hanging out of windows, banging their typewriter cases, Australian officers had taken over taxis and were careering through the streets, riding on top. Everyone was gloriously happy. People went completely mad with joy.

(Tutt)

Just round the corner in Whitehall, Geoffrey Muir was also out for a stroll in the streets:

When we were about halfway down, about where the Cenotaph stands today, the maroons exploded . . . and we knew the Armistice had been signed. The effect was unimaginable—every piece of waste paper came down from the office windows, and within minutes everyone came into the streets.

(Muir)

On the night of November 10, we pulled into a small town and some of us found a place to sleep on the floor of a bakery. All sorts of rumours were in the air, but after 1550 days of uncertainty, despair, gloom, filth and sorrow, only something definite would satisfy. This came soon after breakfast when the Sergeant Major pinned to the wall an Army Form on which was written: 'Hostilities will cease at 11 a.m.'

I don't think there is one adjective in any language to interpret fully the emotions engendered by this laconic statement. There was no euphoria, perhaps we were dazed. There might have been an extra tot of rum or perhaps a little more exotic food from the resources available, but that night, we went to sleep with the security of a few more sure tomorrows.

(Hancox)

But for between eight and ten million men—more than a million of them citizens of the British Empire, there would be no more tomorrows.

I don't know what the war was all about, or what we fought for, but any future war will be worse.

(Godde)

When the war ended, I was elated, naturally. But I felt sad for my friends who had been killed. I still do, I still do. There was no point in the war at all—it was all totally futile. Will there be another war? Oh, yes, as sure as God made apples.

(Foster)

The war still lives with me—I can never get the noise out of my head, the shells, and then the cry 'Stretcher bearers . . . Stretcher bearers!'

(Blaber)

Some were left with philosophical reflections:

The horror of the war, and the suffering I witnessed, the grief and devastation, shook me out of my well-grounded belief in the creed and dogma of Christianity. I had to reject the concept of an omniscient and omnipotent Being. I was just left with faith in Christ and his ethical and moral example of life to man.

(Lamb)

There can never be a war as bad as World War One—particularly for the infantry. It was a tragic waste of life, but it was necessary to fight, although the politicians could have avoided it all earlier. Today we are materially better off, but spiritually less so. The young are inclined to vandalism and values have been lost—though this does not apply to everyone. I had thought the nation was decadent but the response to the Falklands war has shown that we still have some fibre left. War is terrible, but national feeling is very strong, you know . . . but one must think of the effect on future generations.

(Greig)

I bloody well think that the world is a worse place than it was then. Important things have been lost—like respect for others. A spirit of egotism rules today, and in England, the class divisions still do so much harm, while they have all but disappeared in Germany.

(Sulzbach)

For a few, the memories were humorous:

There was in the Battery a Sergeant whose outstanding feature was a very large and unsightly nose, so that behind his back everyone called him 'Nosey'. Because it was due to be re-barrelled, one of our guns burst while being fired and a fragment of steel, flying through the air, cut off the Sergeant's nose. He was sent down the line to hospital and that was the last we thought we would see of him. But several weeks later, he unexpectedly arrived back in the Battery with a nice-looking dainty nose that had been grafted on to make him quite a good looking fellow . . . Join the Army for free beauty treatment!

(Stewart)

For others, time does not take away the enduring bitterness:

Believe me, 'Bull' reigned supreme, in and out of the line. I personally served 21 days Field Punishment for just missing a roll call behind the lines (tied to a wheel two hours daily—now abolished). Blancoing our webbing equipment, cleaning our brasses, boots and so on within ten or twelve hours of leaving the trenches for a rest! Yes, Nigel, Bull! Bull! Bull! I bear no malice, but one cannot but have memories of a dreadful war filled with unforgettable SLAUGHTER.

(Holmes)

Arthur Lamb achieves a balanced view:

The balance sheet, for me, shows a definite gain. On the debit side there was the horror, the distress, the mental and physical agony, the repressed fear, the terror of bombardment and the lice that would never leave you. On the credit side, there was the physical fitness, the strength of constitution brought on by the constant outdoor life, the activity—and above all the comradeship that a peacetime life could never equal.

L. C. Stewart's words probably sum up the feeling of the majority of men:

> A veteran, talking to us before we left England said: 'There will be times when things seem good and you'll hardly know there is a war on, but there will be times when you will lose your pals, when you will be fed-up and cold and hungry and with very little sleep—and still you will have to cary on'. It is this determination to carry on regardless that wins wars.
>
> And we did carry on, for four months, making the return journey over the old Somme battlefields, forcing the Germans back and back, until on November 11, it was all over. The chase after the enemy had been just as exhausting as the retreat before him, and when the order came to cease fire, near Mons, where the first encounter had taken place in 1914, we pulled off the road and all went to sleep.
>
> The motto on my cap badge was 'Quo Fas et Gloria Ducunt'— 'Where Duty and Glory Leads'. There had been very little glory but satisfaction, that in some small measure, my pals and I had done our duty.

And I, nearly seventy years after, had reached the final stage of my long march. I left Reims and faced the seemingly endless plains of Champagne, that stretch all around to the horizons. The road runs like a ribbon to the east, until it disappears—on hot days—into a shimmering wall of water.

This is a historic route—Attila, Caesar and Charlemagne walked this way, invaders have rolled over these plains into the heart of France from the huge plains of Asia. And the liberators have rolled them back—the Americans used it in the autumn of 1944.

After the gloomy garrison town of Châlons, from which the sick Napoleon III led his last army to defeat at Sedan, the next landmark to loom up on the left of the road, is the mill of Valmy, another fulcrum on which the history of France once tipped.

A reconstructed mill still exists, marking the spot where General Kellermann supervised the cannonade that turned back the Austrian armies of the Duke of Brunswick and ensured the survival of the egalitarian ideas of the French Revolution.

Shortly afterwards, the glades of the Argonne Forest closed in on the road at the beautiful eighteenth-century town of St Menehould. This woodland is one of the wildest in all France, and it teems with game. If you have time, you can hire a horse to search out the more remote tracks which often lead to little lakes stuffed with fish, to delight the heart of an angler.

The woods are also replete with reminders of the war almost rivalling Verdun. Near the village of Varennes, for example, is a crumbling concrete structure, known as the 'Crown Prince's Abris'. The bunker was indeed once the headquarters of the vainglorious yet shrewd 'Little Willy'. The bunker was specially built for him in 1915, and is unusual in the large windows with which it is provided—obviously it was not intended for front line action, though the woods around are covered with trenches and barbed wire and are still said to be dangerous owing to the amount of live ammunition left lying around.

Varennes itself is full of mementoes of its historic past. There is a bridge over the River Aire, where Louis XVI's coach was ambushed, before his return to Paris.

Then there is the impressive Pennsylvania Memorial, built by that state to commemorate her sons who fell in the Argonne, and another for the boys from Missouri. The memorial surmounts a hillside which is still honeycombed with bunkers and entrances to tunnels.

For those interested in French culture, the village also boasts a Musée d'Argonne which has imaginative displays of the life, art and history of the region—including a special section devoted to mine warfare.

Ten miles to the north is the American Meuse-Argonne memorial and cemetery, containing 14,000 US graves and a memorial chapel. Turning south-east in the familiar direction of Verdun, I came to the *Butte* of Montfauçon itself, the height which cost the Americans so many men in their opening attack on the Argonne; the ridge is crowned by a column curiously similar to the Monument in London which commemorates the Great Fire.

From the height of the hill which is 336 metres high, the visitor can overlook the whole battlefield on a clear day. The green woods nestling at your feet give way in the distance to a hazy blue, a similar colour to the *Horizon Bleu* of First War French army uniforms.

Originally a monastery stood on top of the hill. The Germans took it in 1914, and it remained in their hands throughout the war until the

Americans captured it in September 1918. The fortified ruins of the monastery still stand, the sturdy stone columns pitted and scarred with shell and shrapnel marks.

From here I made my way to Verdun via the Mort Homme. On the next day I set out from my favourite French town to the south, to reach the town of St. Mihiel. The road runs along the valley of the Meuse, parallel to the river on the right, where an occasional placid barge wallows through the turgid stream.

The road runs towards the Lorraine Regional Park, with high ground rising and falling on the left, in a series of deep valleys. These conceal a number of villages, typical of Lorraine and of nowhere else in France—the hamlets are strung out along a single road, with all the houses, most of them originally farms, set back from the street behind wide pavements. The farmhouse dung-heaps used to be dumped on these sidewalks, and the heaps, by their size and the richness of their odour, were a status symbol by which snobbish Lorrainers would score points off their less-well-endowed neighbours.

St. Mihiel, sixteen miles south of Verdun, bears few marks of war, but on the hills overlooking it there are some particularly well-preserved remains.

One of these, the 'Thirsty Trench' (*tranchée de la soif*) contains an intricate system of bunkers and dug-outs so vivid that, peering down one flight of steps into the woody earth I almost expected a fierce grey or blue figure to emerge, festooned with grenades.

Another height, the Mont Sec, is crowned with a huge circular American battle memorial to the taking of the St. Mihiel salient. Built between the wars, it was the site of a desperate fight in the closing days of the Second World War, when an SS unit with a machine-gun held out for several hours before being overwhelmed.

The area contains several deserted French forts, stubbornly holding out against the surrounding ploughland with aged, useless defiance.

On a back road behind St. Mihiel, I came across two decrepit looking memorials which had been built by the Germans during the Great War to commemorate their camp here. Sadly neglected, the inscriptions on the monuments had been laboriously chipped away by a chisel-wielding French patriot. Each stroke of the chisel a little revenge.

Footsore from the sharp stones of the hills, I returned slowly to St. Mihiel to sip a solitary Pernod. At the café, I reflected on the end of that war, which was now ending also for me.

When Foch heard the terms of the Versailles Treaty he gloomily predicted that it was an armistice for 20 years—which proved an accurate prophecy. The Second World War was spawned by the First. The Germans were allowed to march their armies home in good order to quell the stirrings of revolution, and foster the myth that Germany had not been defeated but stabbed in the back by Jewish profiteers and pacifists.

Humiliated and economically crippled by the Treaty, a vengeful nation rose up again in 1940 and once more rolled into France. The consequences of the Second World War live with us all—they were only too apparent to me even in that peaceful provincial café as a French super Etendard jet screeched malevolently overhead towards the ever-ominous east.

The First World War is history now, yet it is also part of us all. It lives, not only in the memories of old men, but in the dangerous divided world of two armed camps, piling up arms, waiting for a shot to fire on some distant frontier.

I had come full circle and my journey was over. I turned, in this unremarkable little town, and headed for the Channel ports and home for Blighty.

My thoughts were mixed; I remembered Ypres, where that evening the faithful trio of firemen would again unsheath their silver bugles and send those crystal notes into the darkening air; I thought of the tower of the Verdun Ossuary sending its spinning light across the acres of graves and the rigid deserted woodlands with their forest of dark memories, and I thought of the Somme, and how Siegfried Sassoon wrote a poem called 'Before the battle' on June 25, 1916, just as the 'Big Push' began. It ended with the line: 'O river of stars and shadows, lead me through the night'. He knew that even that river of blood after many meanderings, wound with its memories somewhere safe to the sea.

The bones of the millions of dead of the Great War are mingled now with the earth, become one more layer for archaeologists to uncover, on top of Europe's myriads of dead. The scarred soil of the Somme is ploughed and smoothed over in the unchanging rhythm of the seasons.

We, the heirs, still live with the consequences of that conflict, and whether our species pulls through the coming night or not, who can doubt that tomorrow, on the Somme, a skylark will skid from the earth and stream, singing, upwards, until it merges with the infinite sky.

Appendix: More about the War

For readers whose interest in the First World War and the Western Front may have been stimulated but not satisfied by this book, here are a few notes on organizations and institutions catering for those who wish to study the subject more deeply, and some tips for those who may also want to visit the Western Front.

The primary and pre-eminent place for those who wish to find out not only about the First World War but all other major conflicts of the twentieth century, is the Imperial War Museum, situated in: Lambeth Road, London, SE1 6HZ. Tel: 01-735 8922. (Nearest Tube stations: Lambeth North, Waterloo, Elephant and Castle).

The Museum has a lively and well-informed staff only too pleased to communicate their enthusiasm to visitors and historians—amateur and professional. It houses an ever-changing permanent collection of weapons, equipment, uniforms, documents, paintings, posters and photographs (it has around 200,000 pictures relating to the Western Front).

Entry is free, and the public may make use of the library and photographic collection for private study. Photographs and documents may be copied and purchased at reasonable rates. The Museum also houses a cinema in which films from the First World War are regularly shown, and its sound archives hold more than 3,000 hours of historic recordings, including interviews with First World War veterans.

The library houses specialized documents on the Western Front, including original trench maps, regimental histories, and unpublished memoirs. Books, posters, postcards and leaflets are available from the Museum's modern shop.

The Museum is open from Monday to Saturday from 10 a.m. to 5.50 p.m. and on Sundays from 2 p.m. to 5.50 p.m. Entry to the reference departments, which close at 5 p.m., is by prior appointment only.

Another interesting museum, for those in the London area, is the National Army Museum in Chelsea, hard by the Royal Chelsea Hospital, where many war veterans still live.

For those in Scotland and the North of England who are unable to travel to London, the best material on the war is probably Mr Peter Liddle's 1914–18

Personal Experience Archive at Sunderland Polytechnic. The aim of the archive is 'to preserve permanently evidence of personal experience in the 1914–1918 war in order that this important aspect of British Commonwealth and European Heritage shall never be lost'.

To that end Mr Liddle has assembled many hundreds of letters, diaries, photographs and other documents from over 3,500 Great War veterans. The archive covers all aspects of the war, including the Air, the Home Front, the Navy, and campaigns outside the European theatre.

Mr Liddle, a Senior Lecturer in History, is pleased to welcome visitors and inquiries and may be contacted at: St Mary's Buildings, Sunderland Polytechnic, Chester Road, Sunderland, Tyne and Wear. Tel: 0783–76191.

A specialized society, the Western Front Association, was inaugurated on November 11, 1980 with the aim of 'furthering interest in the period 1914–1918. Its principal objective is 'to perpetuate the memory of those, on both sides, who served their country in France and Flanders during that era'.

The Society publishes a well-produced journal *Stand To!* devoted to all aspects of the Western Front, and organizes regular meetings in London and the regions, as well as talks, film shows, reproductions of trench maps, and frequent tours of the battlefields.

The current (1983) membership subscription is £7 per annum (£3 for veterans), which covers the cost of *Stand To!* and other bulletins. The Society's chairman, to whom enquiries should be addressed, is Mr John Giles, Guilton Mill, Ash, near Canterbury, Kent. Tel: Ash 812724.

Commercial tours of the Western Front are also organized by Major and Mrs Holt's Battlefield Tours. Prices range from £100 to £200 and visits are of three days' to a week's duration with accommodation in good hotels, and luxury coach travel. Brochures giving current prices and tour locations are available from: Oak House, Woodnesborough, Sandwich, Kent. Tel: 0304–612248.

The Royal British Legion, 48 Pall Mall, London, SW1Y 5JY. (Tel: 01–930 8131) looks after the interests of the veterans of the First, Second and subsequent wars in which Britain has been involved. As well as a chain of social clubs in virtually every town in Britain, the RBL publishes a magazine *The Legion*, and runs a village near Maidstone, Kent, where the poppies worn on Remembrance Day are made and where several veterans live in sheltered accommodation.

The Commonwealth War Graves Commission, 2, Marlow Road, Maidenhead, Berks SL6 7DX. (Tel: 0628–34221) was set up in 1917 to mark and maintain the graves of the Commonwealth Forces who fell in the First—and later the Second—World Wars, and to keep records and registers of the dead. This duty it fulfils meticulously to this day, as anyone who has visited the beautifully-kept cemeteries on the Western Front can testify.

The white headstones on the graves in the Commission's 1,400 cemeteries around the world are marked with the name, rank and unit of the fallen. Most cemeteries also have a tall Cross of Sacrifice in stone bearing a bronze sword, and the larger ones have a big stone of Remembrance with the inscription from the book of Ecclesiastes: 'Their Name liveth for Evermore'. Unidentified First War tombs have the classical inscription suggested by Rudyard Kipling: 'A soldier of the Great War: known unto God'.

The Commission, which has overseas offices in most of the larger towns on the Western Front, also maintains the major memorials like the Thiepval Arch on the Somme and the Menin Gate in Ypres. Records of individual graves are available on request, as are photographs of the graves, at a nominal charge of 75p.

For those who wish to emulate me and tour the Front by themselves, a few hints . . . Costs are not high, and a good meal can be had for 30 to 50 francs (£3 to £5). Restaurants are fairly plentiful in towns like Amiens, Lille, Arras, Ypres, Laon, Soissons, Cambrai, St. Quentin and Verdun. Between towns, keep a weather eye open for the famous 'Relais Routiers'—these are French transport restaurants, patronized by lorry drivers and other travellers. But forget visions of the greasy English 'transport caff'. The Routiers are renowned for their good, plentiful food, sympathetic ambience, and above all, reasonable prices. They are marked by a distinctive red and blue circular symbol.

Overnight accommodation is harder to find, as the battlefields, except in Champagne and near Paris, are off the usual tourist tracks (for me this was an advantage). The French National Tourist Office at: 178, Piccadilly, London. SW1. can provide relevant brochures and up-to-date hotel information, as can the local 'Syndicat d'Initiative' (Tourist Information) in the individual towns.

Hotels and restaurants are most thick on the ground around railway stations.

On foot, in the field, it can be a good idea to take a picnic meal. French loaves, 'Baguette', are almost universally available (except at lunchtime and on Mondays, the French shopkeepers' Sabbath). Supplementary food and wine can be bought in cheap supermarkets like Monoprix or Prisunic. But wine is not thirst-quenching—however ethnic you may feel drinking it!—and it is a wise plan to carry a flask or water bottle containing a soft drink, tea or coffee.

Under no circumstances touch any of the live shells or grenades you will certainly see ploughed up on the battlefields. The French Army still makes regular collections of this 'Iron Harvest' and several lives are claimed annually when unexploded ammunition goes off.

The best general guides to Flanders, Picardy, Artois and Lorraine are the green guides published by Michelin in French and English. Michelin also publish lists of the Routiers and the 'Logis'—a kind of provincial hotel.

Michelin too make the best general maps of France, the red maps being adequate to see the general lie of the roads.

More detailed maps—indispensable to the walker—are the 1:25,000 scale series, published by the Institut Géographique National, and available from: I. G. N., 107, rue de la Boétie, 75 008 Paris. (price around 20 francs—£2). A lot of fun can be had comparing these to trench maps and tracing original trench lines.

Trench maps themselves are available in reprints from the Western Front Association's own cartographer, Mr Norman Bing, 7 Charlton Close, Willesborough, Ashford, Kent, who can give full details of maps currently available. (But please enclose an SAE for reply).

The cheapest way of crossing the Channel is by night ferry, and a 72-hour return ticket—quite handy for a flying visit to the northern parts of the Front—is really very economical (currently £20). But this night-time travelling has its drawbacks. No cabins are provided, and sleep is out of the question. This may give the authentic 'insomnia' feel of the trenches, but is only to be recommended to the young, the fit, and the tolerant (and the patient! Long delays are inevitable, usually in freezing or infuriatingly overheated waiting-rooms or trains).

The best time to travel for the pilgrim is in spring or September, when the ground is seen to best advantage because of the winter ploughing, and the outlines of trenches can often be spotted; it is also the time when interesting war artifacts are most likely to find their way to the surface.

Real nostalgia is provided for in the evocative anniversary visits run by the Western Front Association (Armistice Day in Ypres, July 1 on the Somme), and by Goodwin European Battlefield Tours, 194, Domonic Drive, New Eltham, London, SE9 3LE. Tel. 01–851–9540, who also have available colour videos of the front.

Bibliography

Of the making of books on the Great War there seems to be no end, and several libraries could be filled with literature stemming from the conflict—studies, histories, memoirs, apologias, biographies, autobiographies, military treatises, recollections, reminiscences, novels, songs, poems and plays; they still, even seventy years later, pour from the presses in a never-ending stream that testifies to the enduring importance and fascination of the subject for our world.

Any bibliography in a book such as this has, therefore, to be strongly selective, and I have decided to confine my list to those works I have read or consulted during the preparation of the book, and which are fairly accessible to readers in the United Kingdom.

All the books mentioned here I have found interesting to a greater or lesser degree. Having in mind the interests of the general reader, I have omitted official and regimental histories, which though indispensable to the historian, tend to make dry reading. I believe a more vivid picture of the war can often be found in the words of those who were actually there, 'on the ground'. Although their picture of battle may be partial, fractured and incomplete as far as the academic historian is concerned, they are more 'real' and therefore, to me, more 'true'.

I have given most recent dates of publication:

Guidebooks
Immediately after the war, Michelin issued a series of guides to the battlefields, which are now only rarely available. Two English writers also wrote books of their own about the battlefields; these are also now rare.

MASEFIELD, JOHN. *The Old Front Line* (Heinemann).
WILLIAMSON, HENRY. *The Wet Flanders Plain* (Faber & Faber, 1929).

But the best, and only, modern guides are:

COOMBS, ROSE. *Before Endeavours Fade* (After the Battle, 1976).
GILES, JOHN. *Ypres, Then and Now* (1979). *The Somme, Then and Now* (1977).

Also useful is:

BANKS, ARTHUR. *A Military Atlas of the First World War* (Heinemann Educational Books 1975).

General histories

CRUTTWELL, C. R. M. F. *History of the Great War 1914–1918* (Paladin, 1982). A good general study which has stood the test of time.

FALLS, CAPTAIN CYRIL. *The Great War* (Longmans, 1959). Useful short study.

FERRO, MARC. *The Great War 1914–18.* (Routledge & Kegan Paul, 1973). An introduction concentrating on social aspects.

LIDDELL-HART, BASIL. *History of the First World War* (Cassell 1972, Pan). Masterly study not sparing the mistakes of the military commanders.

TAYLOR, A. J. P. *The First World War: An Illustrated History.* (Hamish Hamilton, 1963; also in paperback).

VANSITTART, PETER. *Voices From The Great War* (Penguin, 1983). Useful anthology.

History, Battles

BLOND, GEORGES. *The Marne* (Macdonald, 1965). Melodramatic account.

CAREW, TIM. *The Vanished Army* (Corgi, 1971). Good study of original BEF and Mons and Marne campaigns.

ASCOLI, DAVID. *The Mons Star* (Harrap, 1981). Covers similar ground.

WARNER, PHILIP. *Loos* (1976). Best available account of this neglected battle; relies heavily on eye witnesses.

MIDDLEBROOK, MARTIN. *The First Day on the Somme* (Allen Lane, 1971). Minutely detailed, brilliantly organized study of this catastrophic day from ordinary front-line soldier's viewpoint.

FARRER-HOCKLEY, A. H. *The Somme* (Batsford, 1964; Pan, 1983). Readable and sympathetic study of battle by serving soldier.

BLOND, GEORGES. *Verdun* (Andre Deutsch, 1965).

HORNE, ALISTAIR. *The Price of Glory: Verdun 1916* (Penguin, 1983). Best single book on war known to me. Poignant, Hawthornden prizewinning study of modern Europe's most profound tragedy.

HORNE, ALISTAIR. *Death of a Generation* (Macdonald, 1967). Short, well-illustrated popular study of Somme and Verdun.

WATT, RICHARD. *Dare Call it Treason* (Chatto & Windus, 1964). Well-researched in-depth study of Nivelle's offensive and French army mutinies.

MACDONALD, LYN. *They called it Passchendaele* (Michael Joseph, 1973). Riveting account of battle written from memories of survivors.

TERRAINE, JOHN. *The Road to Passchendaele: A Study in Inevitability* (Leo Cooper, 1977). Attempt to prove that mudbath was necessary and inevitable, using vast quantities of generals' correspondence.

WOLFF, LEON. *In Flanders Fields* (Penguin, 1979). Excellent account of Battle of Passchendaele.

COOPER, BRYAN. *Tank Battles of World War One* (Ian Allen, 1974).

WOOLCOMBE, ROBERT. *The First Tank Battle—Cambrai 1917* (Arthur Barker, 1967).

MIDDLEBROOK, MARTIN. *The Kaiser's Battle* (Allen Lane, 1978, Penguin, 1983). Splendid study of first day of 'Michael' offensive.

BLAXLAND, GREGORY. *Amiens 1918* (Frederick Muller, 1968, Star, 1981). Detailed, exhaustive study of Ludendorff attacks and British reply.

ESSAME, H. *The Battle for Europe* (Batsford, 1971). Military history of 1918, brisk, orthodox military viewpoint.

TOLAND, JOHN. *No Man's Land: the Story of 1918* (Eyre Methuen, 1981). Massive, readable study of the year, from front line soldiers to machinations of statesmen.

BROOK-SHEPHERD, GORDON. *November 1918* (Collins, 1982). Similar study of final weeks of war.

TERRAINE, JOHN. *To win a War* (Sidgwick & Jackson, 1978). Sweeping study of neglected Allied victories of 1918. See also His *Haig* (Hutchinson, 1963.)

SMYTH, SIR JOHN, VC. *Leadership in Battle 1914–1918* (David & Charles, 1975). Valuable study by a participant.

History, Specialized Studies

ASHWORTH, TONY. *Trench Warfare 1914–1918* (Macmillan, 1980). A sociological study.

BARNETT, CORELLI. *The Swordbearers* (Eyre and Spottiswoode, 1964). Fascinating study of psychology of military High Command in the war.

BARRIE, ALEXANDER. *War Underground* (Muller, 1962, Star, 1981). Enthralling study of subterranean war.

BROWN, MICHAEL. *Tommy goes to War* (Dent, 1978). Good survey of Western Front.

CLARK, ALAN. *The Donkeys* (Hutchinson, 1961). Biting attack on British Generals of 1914–15; inaugurated sixties fashion for debunking World War One 'Blimps'.

ELLIS, JOHN. *Eye Deep in Hell* (Croom Helm, 1976). Detailed study of trench warfare.

FUSSELL, PAUL. *The Great War and Modern Memory* (Oxford University Press, 1975). Unique account of the cultural atmosphere of the war and the place it still holds in our consciousness. A marvellous book.

LLOYD, ALAN *The War in the Trenches* (Hart-Davis McGibbon, 1976). Good, short popular study.

KEEGAN, JOHN. *The Face of Battle* (Cape, 1976). Interesting study of fighting man's view of war. Contains section on Somme.

MASTERS, JOHN. *Fourteen–Eighteen* (Michael Joseph, 1965). Copiously illustrated study by famous novelist.

MOYNIHAN, MICHAEL. *A Place Called Armageddon* (David & Charles, 1975). *Greater Love* (W. H. Allen, 1980). Letters from the Western Front. Moving.

LEED, ERIC. *No Man's Land* (Cambridge University Press, 1979). Psychological view of trench warfare.

TERRAINE, JOHN. *The Western Front 1914–18* (Hutchinson, 1964). Good set of essays. *White Heat: The New Warfare 1914–18* (Sidgwick & Jackson, 1982). Excellent account of the technology of war.

TUCHMAN, BARBARA. *August 1914* (Macmillan 1962; reissued in paperback 1980). Magisterial and masterly study of opening weeks of the war.

WINTER, DENIS. *Death's men: Soldiers of the Great War* (Penguin, 1979). Detailed, workmanlike study of how it felt to be a soldier in the Great War.

Personal accounts and memoirs

BEHREND, ARTHUR. *As from Kemmel Hill* (Eyre & Spottiswoode, 1963). An artillery man's view of the war.

BLUNDEN, EDMUND. *Undertones of War* (1930, reissued repeatedly, most recently Penguin, 1982). Quiet, almost ironic view of war from a pastoral poet rudely transferred to Western Front.

CAMPBELL, P. J. *The Ebb and Flow of Battle* (Hamish Hamilton, 1977). Charming account of a quiet gunner's experience of 1918 battles. *In the Cannon's Mouth* (Hamish Hamilton, 1978). Green gunner encounters war's terrifying reality at Passchendaele.

CARRINGTON, CHARLES. *Soldier from the Wars returning*. Horror of war as seen by simple young soldier.

CHAPMAN, GUY. *A Passionate Prodigality* (MacGibbon & Kee, 1981). A scholar's war: achieves the level of literature.

COPPARD, GEORGE. *With a Machine Gun to Cambrai* (HMSO, 1969). Straightforward account of war on the Western Front.

CRUTCHLEY, C. F. *Machinegunner 1914–1918* (Bailey Bros. & Swinfen, 1975).

DESAIGNEAUX, HENRI. *A French Soldier's War Diary 1914–1918* (Elmfield Press, 1975). Terse. Horrific.

DOLDEN, A. STUART. *Cannon Fodder* (Blandford, 1980). No frills account of an infantryman's life.

EDMONDS, CHARLES. *A Subaltern's War* (1929). Horror of war as seen by simple young officer.

GLUBB, JOHN. *Into Battle—A Soldier's Diary of the Great War* (Cassell, 1978). War Diary of the famous 'Glubb Pasha'.

GRAVES, ROBERT. *Goodbye to All That* (Cape, 1929, Penguin 1960 and thereafter). Deservedly famous; a quirky, individualist poet's view of war and warriors.

GREENWELL, G. *An Infant in Arms* (Allen Lane, 1972). Naïve young man grows up fast on Western Front.

HISCOCK, ERIC. *The Bells of Hell go Ting-a-Ling-a-Ling* (Arlington, 1976). Unpleasant boastful book about brief encounter with war.

eastcoast.co.uk/why

Why buy your East Coast ticket anywhere else?

• only we sell our **lowest fares** • $\frac{1}{3}$ off groups of 3+ • **no booking** fee • no credit card fee • **Points** for every pound you spend • gift vouchers • a new **mobile site** • **lowest fare** finder • Print@home • **choose** your own seat with our interactive seat map • online **discount** on lowest Advance fares • Advance ticket **alerts** • tickets to **mobile** • **discounted** catering vouchers • business **carnet** •

EAST COAST

EC/3502

EAST COAST

Reserved
Class | Coach | Seat

B   10

FACE

| To direction
| of travel

YORK.   -
Between NEWCASTLE.

NEWCASTLE.   -
   EDINBURGH.

1400 KGX - ABD
GR6420 : 22112012

JÜNGER, ERNST. *Storm of Steel* (Chatto & Windus, 1929). Noted German writer's brutally vivid account of life as highly-decorated war hero, notable for its mystic exaltation and glorying in act of war. A violent antidote to *All Quiet on the Western Front*.

MELLERSH, H. E. L. *Schoolboy Into War* (Wm. Kimber, 1978). Stoic account of a young officer's blooding on the Somme and at Passchendaele.

MURRAY, JOSEPH. *Call to Arms* (Wm. Kimber, 1980). Durham miner's progress from Gallipoli to Western Front.

SASSOON, SIEGFRIED. *Memoirs of an Infantry Officer. Sherston's Progress* (Faber & Faber, 1930 and many subsequent reprints). Semi-fictional autobiography of poet-hero turned pacifist.

SULZBACH, HERBERT. *With the German Guns* (Warne, 1981). Rare view of a German gunner's life. Soldierly spirit of duty and patriotism, tempered with common humanity.

TALBOT KELLY, R. B. *A Subaltern's Odyssey* (William Kimber 1980). Art master's war—Excellent illustrations.

VAUGHAN, EDWIN CAMPION. *Some Desperate Glory* (Warne, 1981). A gem of a book. Horrific account of hellish Passchendaele conditions that reaches the level of literature. Its factual tone heightens the horror.

The War in Literature

BARBUSSE, HENRI. *Under Fire* (Dent, 1916, 1926, 1975). Seminal novel based on author's war experience. First in field of realistic war-horror books. Rarely surpassed.

ALDINGTON, RICHARD. *Death of a Hero* (1929, Penguin, 1930s). Bitter, cynical, satirical war novel.

CLOETE, STUART. *How Young they Died* (Collins, 1969, Fontana, 1971). Convincing novel of trench warfare and life and love on home front.

HARRIS, JOHN. *Covenant With Death* (Hutchinson, 1961, Arrow, 1980). Novel based on destruction of new armies on Somme.

MANNING, FREDERIC. *The Middle Parts of Fortune* (Re-issue of classic *Her Privates We*) (Mayflower, 1972). Excellent and realistic, a masterpiece.

MOTTRAM, R. H. *The Spanish Farm* (Chatto & Windus, 1924, Penguin, 1936). Quiet, human story of Flanders.

WILLIAMSON, HENRY. *A Chronicle of Ancient Sunlight* (Macdonald/ Pan paperbacks, 1950s and 1960s). Fifteen novel sequence by a writer obsessed with the war, which permeates every page of a strange, tormented genius. See also *Patriot's Progress* by same author (Macdonald, 1968).

REMARQUE, ERICH MARIA. *All Quiet on the Western Front* (Mayflower Books, 1963 and later reprints). Pacifist textbook novel. Still powerful despite its familiarity.

Poetry

PARSONS, I. M. (ed.). *Men Who March Away: Poems of the First World War* (Chatto & Windus, 1965). Splendid anthology of best verse of the war.

GARDNER, BRIAN (ed.). *Up the Line to Death: the War Poets 1914–1918* (Methuen, 1964). Another excellent collection.

SILKIN, JON (ed.). *Penguin Book of First World War Poetry* (1979). Widens frontiers to include verse in other tongues.

LEHMANN, JOHN. *The English Poets of the First World War* (Thames & Hudson, 1981). Concise, well-written survey of the field. Good illustrations.

OWEN, WILFRED. *Collected Poems* (Chatto & Windus, 1967, and after reprinted). Generally considered greatest war poet-victim.

SASSOON, SIEGFRIED. *Selected Poems* (Faber & Faber, 1968 and after). Brilliant, biting and bitter poems of war from another master.

THOMAS, EDWARD. *Collected Poems* (Oxford University Press, 1978). Quietly resigned verse from patriotic countryman poet.

Index

229